PENGUIN
BRAHMINS AND

Raised in Mysore in the 1970s, Kavita Watsa is now based in Chennai. Her writing has appeared in *Outlook Traveller*, the *Economic Times*, the *Deccan Herald*, *Business Line*, the *Indian Review of Books*, *Reader's Digest* and *Fodor's India*. Following her wanderlust to new places every year, she has so far travelled to Myanmar, Singapore, Australia, the Persian Gulf, Scotland and the United States. *Brahmins and Bungalows*, her first book, is a tribute to her own backyard.

Brahmins and Bungalows

Travels through South Indian History

KAVITA WATSA

PENGUIN BOOKS

PENGUIN BOOKS

Penguin Books India (P) Ltd, 11 Community Centre, Panchsheel Park, New Delhi 110 017, India
Penguin Books Ltd, 80 Strand, London WC2R 0RL, UK
Penguin Group (USA) Inc., 375 Hudson Street, New York, NY 10014, USA
Penguin Books Australia Ltd, 250 Camberwell Road, Camberwell, Victoria 3124, Australia
Penguin Books Canada Ltd, 10 Alcorn Avenue, Suite 300, Toronto, Ontario M4V 3B2, Canada
Penguin Group (NZ), cnr Airborne and Rosedale Roads, Albany, Auckland 1310, New Zealand
Penguin Books (South Africa) (Pty) Ltd, 24 Sturdee Avenue, Rosebank 2196, South Africa

First published by Penguin Books India 2004

Copyright © Kavita Watsa 2004

Passages quoted on pp 159-61 from *The East India Company: Trade and Conquest from 1600* (1999) by Antony Wild are reprinted by permission of HarperCollins Publishers Ltd, UK, copyright © 1999, Antony Wild

All rights reserved

10 9 8 7 6 5 4 3 2 1

For sale in the Indian Subcontinent and Singapore only

Typeset in *Perpetua* by Mantra Virtual Services, New Delhi
Printed at Baba Barkha Nath Printers, New Delhi

This book is sold subject to the condition that it shall not, by way of trade or otherwise, be lent, resold, hired out, or otherwise circulated without the publisher's prior written consent in any form of binding or cover other than that in which it is published and without a similar condition including this condition being imposed on the subsequent purchaser and without limiting the rights under copyright reserved above, no part of this publication may be reproduced, stored in or introduced into a retrieval system, or transmitted in any form or by any means (electronic, mechanical, photocopying, recording or otherwise), without the prior written permission of both the copyright owner and the above-mentioned publisher of this book.

*This book is written with much
affection and gratitude
for*

*My family
whose faith in me has outlasted my every errant scheme*

and

*Rohit
who makes homecoming the best part of any journey*

Contents

Prologue: Over the Bungalow Wall — *1*

The Heart of Anglo-India

Srirangapattana: The Isle of Lost Dreams — *11*

Mysore: A Large and Handsome Town — *43*

Bangalore: The Vanishing Cantonment — *65*

Along the Arabian

Padmanabhapuram: A Palace Made of Wood — *87*

Devbagh: Beyond the Realm of Prose — *109*

Goa: Five Hundred Monsoons Now — *125*

Coromandel Colonies

Madras: The Forgotten Fort — *153*

Pondicherry: The Empire That Never Was — *177*

Tranquebar: Day of the Danes — *195*

The Temple Trail

    Hampi: City of Victory   *213*

    Mamallapuram: Masons and Moonrakers   *236*

    Thanjavur: In the Womb of the South   *252*

Kodaikanal

    Epilogue: Woodsmoke and Roses   *273*

Prologue
Over the Bungalow Wall

*If the first education is, as it were, a second birth, I am able to say that
I came into the world with a desire to travel.*
—Jean-Baptiste Tavernier, Paris, 1676

If plotted on a graph, my early childhood in Mysore would yield a straight line drawn with a firm and steady hand; for it was largely spent in my grandfather's bungalow, where the placid equanimity of the older generation created an atmosphere of such serenity that the very clocks ticked softly lest they seem too obtrusive. It was only on the odd afternoon when the family was dozing peacefully indoors and the cook was catching forty winks on the veranda that I could escape the pleasant confines of our garden, with a surreptitious creak of the old wooden gate and a muted thud from its falling latch. Wandering a little way down the street, kicking stones and trailing patterns in the dirt with my bare toes, I would think wistfully of the town zoo less than a mile away, its rows of caged attractions lined up in eternal tantalization. The guttural grumbling of a restless lion often kept me awake late at night, for I was certain that it was only a matter of time before the great, soft-footed cat found a way out of its moated playground and wrought havoc in the neighbourhood. In short: prolonged solitude, with a little help from these frequent nightly imaginings, caused the concept of confinement to make a considerable impression on me. I was always pleading to be allowed to play in the large, grassy maidan opposite the bungalow, or to be taken up the hill some distance away, or even, when I sensed that my family was particularly well disposed towards me, to be accompanied to the zoo itself. My polite requests were usually brushed away with the reminder that a large garden with plenty of fruit trees was quite sufficient entertainment for a child of my age.

There would, however, be an occasional windfall in the form of an unsuspecting elderly relative, who, visiting for a week or two, could be inveigled into sacrificing a morning's plans on my account. The outing that ensued—utterly splendid from my point of view—was much frowned-on by my family at large, who took collective exception to having to minister, on our return, to the migraine of the visitor in question.

'You really are a nauseating child,' my Aunt Margaret was once heard to say as she carried a cold towel to one such unfortunate soul, '*exactly* as your father was at your age, and what you deserve for going to the zoo without my permission is a good hiding on your skinny behind.' Unmoved by this remark, I informed my ever-forgiving aunt, not without a note of triumph, that there was a new tapir in the tapir pen.

It was during a particularly vacant summer that, by an unkind twist of fate, it was I, not a visitor, who suffered heatstroke and fell quite ill after a morning with the macaques. The immediate consequence of this sad turn of events was that the zoo, along with all the other interesting destinations in the neighbourhood, was struck from my list of legal amusements. The days grew long, boring and finally altogether vile, the hours hanging heavy as I took up residence in the garden, making countless mud pies and rolling listlessly in the gravel with the dogs. All the children who lived nearby had gone away for the holidays, and so had Hugh Warren, the middle-aged Englishman who was one of our few regular callers.

There was just one redeeming event that summer, an expedition that opened my eyes to the World at Large. It took place at considerable risk to my reputation, not to mention my skinny behind; but it broadened my horizon a few critical centimetres, and for this I am a great deal obliged to my great-uncle, whose proper name I did not know at the time, for we all somewhat disrespectfully called him 'Buncle', a silly abbreviation of 'Baba-Uncle'. Though christened David, my grandfather's youngest brother was promptly nicknamed Baba—little boy.

This aged but somewhat delinquent individual was by far the most curious member of the family. He was the perfect foil to my grandfather, who was about as straight-laced and upstanding as his brother was eccentric and unpredictable. About once every six months, we would hear a massive tarpaulin-covered lorry rumbling to a halt outside, following which my grandfather would grunt philosophically and walk out to the gate. I was always enthralled by my great-uncle's arrival; for apart from bringing a whole *lorry* with him, he would say and do the most outrageous things, to the family's ill-concealed vexation and my secret glee. And he would always tell me about far-off places like Poona and Cochin, which I had not visited and thought I never would, so distant and mysterious did he make them sound.

One day, having exhausted the limited possibilities at home, Buncle was bored. As evening fell I could see his disenchantment growing, and finally he rose from the ground, where he had been sitting on his haunches, smoking his way through a roll of foul-smelling bidis.

'Come on,' he said casually. 'Do you want to help me look for an arrack shop?'

I looked at him in disbelief. Arrack was something that people of low birth drank when they couldn't afford anything else; and while I knew of Buncle's affinity for alcohol, I hadn't known that he drank anything as dreadful as this. I was shocked, to say the least, but hopelessly fascinated, and very tempted to join him.

'We'll go in a jutka,'[1] he said, neatly snipping the last thread of my resistance.

'All right,' I heard myself say, giving up the struggle with a conscience that appeared to have shrunk in the wash. I set off with him down the drive—again asking no one's permission—in a state of poorly suppressed excitement, wondering what an arrack shop was like.

'Now,' said Buncle impressively, 'follow me'—and he vaulted over the compound wall. I had been about to unlatch the gate, but he helped me scramble over the wall instead, thus correcting my foolishly orthodox ideas on how to exit the garden. 'When you're going somewhere without telling anybody,' he said sternly, 'you have *got* to jump over a wall.' Delighted at having accomplished this all-important step, I followed him as he imperiously hailed a jutka and we set off down the road, soon passing stately Government House at a reasonably fine pace.

'I don't mind jutkas,' declared Buncle presently. 'When you drive a lorry all the time, it's quite stylish to get a chauffeur to take you about town. A bit of a change, don't you think?' I nodded rather tepidly, wondering what a chauffeur was and inspecting the back of the jutka-wallah's neck for anything out of the ordinary. It was dreadfully hot and stuffy in the carriage, and I was growing dizzy from looking out through the opening at the back as we jolted along relentlessly. In the failing light, it was hard to see much of the neighbourhood we were passing through, but I could tell that we were in a part of town where the streets were narrow and smoky and people hung about in shifty, straggling groups. A few more sharp turns to the left and right and I began to feel distinctly nervous and disoriented. This was a completely unfamiliar part of town, deep in the heart of some old mohalla far removed from Theobald Road, the Boulevard and all the other friendly places I knew. Robbed of my sense of direction, I was momentarily stabbed by a memory of someone telling me that it was only *very* stupid people who ever lost their way. Yet my guardian seemed to know where we were headed, judging by the regal instructions he issued to the driver from time to time.

Miraculously, we passed the back wall of the convent school I attended and a wave of relief swept over me. At least we were still in *Mysore*, I thought. Things were not entirely out of control.

'Did you go to this school too?' I asked by way of conversation, knowing that my father had gone to the convent before me.

'No,' he said, a bit shortly. 'I went to school in a town far away from here, and then I went to England.'

'What did you learn in England?' I persisted, intrigued.

'How to drive a lorry, of course.'

I turned this information over in my head and decided I would rather believe my father, who had once told me a yarn about Buncle having been a king's commissioned officer in the army until he decided to leave, a move that the army, being an old-fashioned sort of institution, did not much appreciate. I puzzled over it for a while but still didn't understand how the lorry fitted in. I was about to ask, but Buncle seemed a bit subdued now. Smoking moodily, he stared down hard at the road we were leaving behind us.

In a few minutes, we stopped short of a dingy hut. A couple of tables were set up on the street, and at these sat some distinctly ragged and unsavoury people.

'Wait here,' Buncle said, and there I waited obediently for a good half hour, the jutka-wallah expectorating loudly at intervals. My sense of adventure was now beginning to wilt, hampered considerably by the interrogation of my companion, an aged Muslim, who asked me if my grandfather knew where I had gone. Though I hastily said yes, he wasn't fooled for a moment.

'Cannot be,' said he, scratching his beard, for everyone in the town knew my grandfather. 'This is a bad place, and that . . . that person is a lunatic to have brought you here.'

And then, warming to his theme: 'Now that you've been seen near such a place, your reputation is ruined. Nobody will marry you when you grow up.' I sniffed hard at this, more from humiliation at such crude discussion of my personal affairs than from any real dread of spinsterhood.

'Don't fret, silly child,' he added in Urdu, seeing that I was close to tears. 'I'll look after you.' I was not consoled.

At this sensitive moment the 'lunatic' returned, his spirits flamboyantly restored. 'Oh, I say!' he exclaimed. 'I'd forgotten all about you!'

'Don't mention it,' I replied, quivering with indignation at the long wait in the dark with the excessively familiar old man and the horse-fleas. After an unnecessarily jovial conversation with a man who sidled up and tried to sell us something, we creakily turned around and started back the way we had come. I clambered up through the front end of the box to where the jutka-wallah sat, preferring his remonstrations to Buncle's now considerably sharpened wit. It was a treat to look out at the world from that position, what with the shenanigans of the horse, a recalcitrant beast that stopped every now and then just to delve into its bag of greens. Great was the chivying, prodding and cursing of its mother to get it moving again when it decided to halt for sustenance.

'Please,' I begged the jutka-wallah, swallowing my pride, after we made yet another unwilling start, 'may I hold the reins for a while?' He handed them to me without a word and took out some tobacco, which he rolled thoughtfully between his palm and thumb.

'Thank you,' I managed to whisper, afraid to so much as shift my weight in case the horse realized it was only a little girl at the reins, not its gruff old master. It was an incredible moment, holding those worn leather ropes for the first time and watching the blinkered horse clip-clopping along, none the wiser. I felt a sudden and intoxicating feeling of release. This was what I had been waiting for, this satisfaction of having gone somewhere and done something.

'You're doing quite well—for a girl,' said the jutka-wallah meditatively as he leaned against the wooden frame of the carriage, his great belly rolling from side to side with the jerky motion of the horse. Spurred by such high praise, I concentrated on the road ahead, sitting up very straight so as to make an impression in the event that any of my friends saw me, unlikely though it was that they were out and about at eight o'clock at night.

There was, of course, a considerable commotion when we arrived at the bungalow. Buncle returned me to the custody of the rest of the family with the air of one who had tried to rescue a child from savages and failed. We skulked about in disgrace the next morning, for the family was unanimous and vocal in their disapproval and we could scarcely get a word in edgewise. In the afternoon, I heard a scuffling in the pantry and found Buncle in there on all fours, extricating several plastic bags of arrack from under the larder where he had stored them for safe keeping. I was a little annoyed with him for all the trouble we had gotten into, but I stuck my hands in my pockets and went away without a word, pretending I had not noticed what he was doing. He looked at me crookedly, with the air of a conspirator, and I had to struggle hard not to give in and smile. Leaving him to his own devices, I found my Aunt Margaret in the bungalow, and tried to worm my way prematurely back into her good books by asking whether she was going to church in the morning, and whether I could go with her.

'Yes, I should think I'm going to church,' she replied, 'but not with a young booze-bird like you.' Nettled by the gross injustice of this accusation, I managed only to retort that she knew very well I hadn't drunk anything at the arrack shop. I was in any case, I informed her, much too small to drink!

'Fancy worrying about *that*,' said my aunt, pocketing the last word with expert ease. 'It's only a matter of time.'

That afternoon, after a late lunch consumed with the cook in the outhouse, Buncle collected his belongings in a little bag and marched purposefully down the drive without saying goodbye to anybody. I went out to the gate, dismayed, and watched silently as he climbed into the impossibly high cabin of his mustard-coloured lorry. The engine started with a roar and I could stand it no longer.

'*Buncle!*' I screeched at the top of my voice. 'Where are you going?'

The engine stopped and he poked his head out of the window and grinned.

'Women can't stay quiet for long,' he said. 'More's the pity.'

Ignoring this provoking remark, I repeated my question. The idea of someone leaving for an *unknown* destination was still too alien to bear. He pointed over his shoulder to the mysterious load the lorry was carrying under its tarpaulin.

'I have to drop off that lot in Calicut. Do you want to come?'

Beaming from ear to ear, but shaking my head in refusal, I clung to the old wooden gate with both arms as Buncle pulled a face of mock disappointment and drove off, slowing down with a great crashing of gears as he negotiated a curve at the end of our road. Swinging to and fro on the violently creaking gate, I wondered how long it would be before it was my turn at the bend.

Note

1. 'Jutka . . . The native cab of Madras, and of Mofussil towns in that Presidency; a conveyance only to be characterised by the epithet ramshackle, though in that respect equalled by the Calcutta cranchee . . . It consists of a sort of box with venetian windows, on two wheels, and is drawn by a miserable pony. It is entered by a door at the back.' Henry Yule and A. C. Burnell, *Hobson-Jobson, The Anglo-Indian Dictionary* (1886; reprint, Ware, Hertfordshire: Wordsworth Editions Ltd, 1996), p. 474.

The Heart of Anglo-India

Srirangapattana
The Isle of Lost Dreams

The old fortress of Seringapatam remains in much the same state as it was left in after the siege nearly a hundred years ago. The formidable fortifications have stoutly withstood the ravages of time, while the breach made in the curtain is still visible from the opposite bank of the river, where two cannons fixed in the ground denote the spot on which the English batteries were erected. Inside is shown the gateway on the northern face where Tipu fell in his death-struggle. The whole island is now insalubrious. A few wretched houses only remain where once there was a great capital, and the ancient temple of Vishnu looks down, as if in mockery, on the ruins of the palace of the Muhammadan usurper.

—Lewin B. Bowring, *Haidar Ali and Tipu Sultan*, 1893

When I was a child, the faded green top of an ancient Fiat regularly appeared alongside my grandfather's garden wall on Sunday mornings. This sight held much promise: it meant that Hugh Warren had come to ask if I could go with him on a picnic. At the age of seven, it did not strike me as the least bit odd that a mottled old Englishman who worked at the Wesley Press was my most faithful friend and playmate, separated though we were by at least fifty years. It was yet the age of innocence in our town, for although the seventies had dawned, my grandfather's house remained entirely unaffected by their intrusions. Our entertainment still came from such means as we could devise by ourselves, and a day out on Srirangapattana, an island in the nearby Cauvery, was far and away the best diversion there was.

Once my Aunt Margaret had consented, I would tear madly from room to room gathering jam jars and a butterfly net. Garments would be flung with abandon out of my chest of drawers and on to the floor as I searched for an old pair of bloomers and a vest that could be used as a swimming costume. Then Uncle Hugh and I would get into his friendly old car, with its fascinating knobs and dials, and drive through the silent town into the countryside, where the hot summer air came alive with the buzzing of insects and the shouts of village children as they splashed in wayside streams. The paddy fields on either side of the road were entrancingly green and my friend would gaze at them dreamily, his wispy, toffee-coloured hair flying in twin streams behind his ears. In the back seat an odd assortment of objects, including a tin of watercress sandwiches, banged and rattled as the old car gathered speed down the undulating road.

Presently, we would drive across the south branch of the Cauvery on a little bridge that also served as an aqueduct and, before reaching the fort on the western part of the island, turn off on to a cool mud road flanked on both sides by tall shade trees. It would not take long to arrive at Scott's Bungalow, an old English house by the river, and make our way down the damp, dark path to the water. We would hear the river before we reached it—little gurgling sounds would give away its presence as it flowed busily between banks heavy with undergrowth. I would race down the stone steps cut into the bank and hundreds of little guppies would swim through the shallows to my feet, crowding around my ankles and nibbling gently at my toes. Uncle Hugh would tread gingerly down behind me, unbeautiful in a pair of vintage swimming trunks that might, in their younger days, have been described as pea-green. He would light up quickly, hide his pouch of tobacco beneath a stone, and float gently on his back into the middle of the river, pipe in mouth and a hat over his eyes. I would play in the shallows under the protection of a fretwork of overhanging branches, shrinking back only when a brown water snake writhed past, leaving a delicate pattern of ripples. Thus we remained, each lost in a silent world, for the rest of the day.

When the sharpness of the sun began to diminish and birds swooped low overhead, strangely malevolent, I would quickly release my jam-jar aquarium of guppies back into the river and disappear behind a bush to change into dry clothes; for when the trees started to cast cold, forbidding shadows on the water, the river turned inky and frightening. 'Better be going,' my friend would say at last as he shivered, unearthed his tobacco, and filled his pipe for one last smoke on the stone steps by the river.

Strangely, in all the years Uncle Hugh drove me to Srirangapattana, it did not seem to have occurred to him to take me inside the fort or any of the 'tombs and things' that lay strewn about. Our activities were always confined to that corner of the island on which Scott's Bungalow stood among the trees. Perhaps he thought I would be happier playing among the reeds, and did not wish to inflict on me his interest in things historical. Only well after I had left Mysore did it dawn on me that people as far afield as Calcutta, where I moved with my mother at the age of ten, knew more about Srirangapattana than I did. It was hard to conceal my dismay upon learning that Tipu Sultan, the ruler most widely associated with the island fort, was *dead*, and had been that way for two hundred years. I had honestly thought he was an old man who lived in his fort on the Cauvery, leading, like almost everyone else I knew, a peaceful retired life. I had also assumed that the British siege of the fort had occurred when my grandfather was young, a time when war seemed to have occupied everyone's attention. Why, I wondered, had Uncle Hugh, despite telling an occasional story by the river, never told me that Tipu had been killed a long time ago?

It was likely that he had omitted this detail simply because the sultan had been Indian, and his slayers British. Uncle Hugh was always delicate about such things; he would say words such as 'Independence' with enormous gravity, clearing his throat awkwardly afterwards and inspecting the tops of his weather-beaten sandals. The rare reference he made to England was almost apologetic; Mysore and its environs were clearly his home.

Although I eventually returned from Calcutta (where, in fact, the descendants of the sultan live in ignominy) and put down roots in Madras, it was only a decade later that I felt inclined to revisit my old haunt on the Cauvery and piece together my memories of the island with its absorbing history, an understanding of which I had tried to acquire in the interim. My Aunt Margaret, who still lived in Mysore, and my father agreed to accompany me on this jaunt. As the two of them had also whiled away many a pleasant hour by the river in their youth, we were all armed with a proprietary interest in the island as we drove out of Mysore one Saturday. The road was quite as I remembered it, except that the paddy fields on either side were now marred by commercial hoardings that had sprouted out of them with an almost agricultural determination.

As we crossed the aqueduct bridge that led to the island, I craned my neck to see Scott's Bungalow, but it was now hidden by trees that had, understandably, grown taller in twenty years. I looked away, half relieved that it was invisible, for my plan was to explore the island in an academic manner with the aid of the Reverend E. W. Thompson's excellent little book *The Last Siege of Seringapatam*,[1] which, among other things, describes those historical structures that were still standing in 1923. I did not, however, remain unsentimental for long; it was impossible to be unmoved by the condition of the island. Judging by the abysmal state in which we were to find many of the structures in and around the fort, the latter-day British in India, of which breed

Uncle Hugh must have brought up the rear, were the last to have taken a heartfelt interest in the island they once called Seringapatam. Lewin Bowring, once chief commissioner of Mysore, wrote in 1893 that 'To an Englishman few places in India are more replete with interesting historical associations than Seringapatam.'[2] The tragedy of this statement is that while the island should, by rights, be just as fascinating as it always was, it now stands forlornly in the river, its historic fort callously neglected. Many an old structure has fallen by the wayside, or been preserved in such a crass and unimaginative manner as to effectively bury the zeal of all but the most persevering to acquaint themselves with its associations.

The island seems to have sprung suddenly into importance in the eighteenth century, when Hyder Ali and his son Tipu Sultan took dramatic command of it. Although it might appear that the history of Srirangapattana began when the activities of the famous father and infamous son raised the hackles of the traders at Fort St. George— the pair sparred often with the British during the thirty-eight years that they struggled determinedly for power in the South—the story of the island goes back a good deal further. The evidence is sturdy enough: the Sri Ranganathaswamy temple, one of the few intact structures in the fort, is more than a thousand years old. It was enlarged in the fifteenth century, when the region paid allegiance to the Vijayanagar empire. Inscriptions in the Pampapati temple at Hampi refer to King Narasa having crossed the Cauvery and captured Srirangapattana, and to this great achievement being praised 'in the three worlds'.[3] When the Vijayanagar empire fell in 1565, the king of Mysore, Vira Chama Raya, became virtually independent and ruled for twelve years, until a relative, Raja Udaiyar, seized power.[4]

Eventually the house of 'Wodeyar' grew weak, and the power of its diwan, or chief minister, increased overwhelmingly. An ambitious Muslim named Hyder Ali Khan became commander-in-chief of the army, and by 1761 he had taken over the government and the revenue of the kingdom. Thus was Muslim rule established on Srirangapattana, and its repercussions would be considerable: the names Hyder and Tipu became known from Kabul to Cape Comorin, from Bombay to Burma, in the furthest outposts of the European colonies, in the splendid courts of Versailles and Constantinople and, not least, in the busy streets of London and the dark closes of Edinburgh, where tales of the young sultan, suitably embellished, found their grisly telling.

Under Hyder Ali, the extent of Mysore's influence widened as the poligars[5] of the South began to yield him territory. This caused the Marathas and the nizam of Hyderabad, not to mention the British, considerable consternation. The British, who allied with the Marathas and the nizam against Mysore in the first Anglo-Mysore war, were faced with an unexpectedly powerful force; they suffered heavy losses and finally accepted the peace that Hyder dictated in 1769. This trend of resistance, and refusal to acknowledge British dominance, was continued more famously—and often less rationally—by Tipu Sultan, who in a very short time proved a different breed of ruler from his relatively circumspect father. With Hyder and his son subjugating all around them, the little island in the Cauvery staged more than its fair share of drama in less than four decades. Rev. Thompson points out that in the conflict with the British, Srirangapattana came to the fore thrice: first during the second Anglo-Mysore war of 1780-84, when a number of British soldiers were captured and subjected to an infamous imprisonment in the fort; in 1791-92, when Lord Cornwallis took Ganjam, the pettah[6] adjoining the fort, in the third Anglo-Mysore war and forced Tipu into the Treaty of Seringapatam, a peace too unhappy to last; and finally in 1799, when the fort was at last besieged, taken, and its brave, rebellious master put to the sword. After this, the last Anglo-Mysore war, the fort was occupied by its new colonial overlords, who, to give them their due, ensured that Tipu had a proper and honourable funeral. The Hindu Wodeyar prince was reinstated—not on the island but in nearby Mysore, where a grand palace still stands though the monarchy has long been replaced by dreary democracy.

Set as it is on a rocky, attractive stretch of the Cauvery, the Srirangapattana fort is still ruggedly beautiful, though only when seen from certain angles from a passing train or one of the bridges leading to the island. Perhaps time conspired with the elements to conceal its tragic history and make the fort picturesque again, for the sad old stones are now overgrown with greenery, their even, grey severity softened by gentle sprays of colour. The surrounding countryside is ever lovely, with mauve heads of sugarcane waving in the breeze against a smoky watercolour sky. Rev. Thompson once observed of the southern rampart: 'The massive ramparts overgrown with vegetation, the deep ditch, the river with the old bridge, and Chamundi hill in the distance, form a picture which is not easily surpassed.'[7]

At present, however, such views are mightily reduced, and passing visitors might be pardoned for wondering what the good padre was going on about—assuming, of course, that they notice the fort in the first place, for the road that runs past its two main gates is lined with that peculiar breed of wanton concrete construction that despoils so many historical monuments in India. All that remain inside the fort are a temple, a mosque and some desultory ruins, precisely the combination to disappoint pilgrims of history, for there is no dearth of temples or mosques elsewhere. Yet even in the absence of most of the original palaces and buildings in and around the fort, their crumbling ruins and vanished outlines tell a story to those who care to listen. There is no denying that the island has a certain sadness about it, the air of a place that is trying to soldier on in an age when neither romance nor refinement find appreciation.

Instead of starting with the neglected fort, we began our exploration of the island with the relatively well preserved Darya Daulat, Tipu Sultan's summer palace and one of the few visual reminders of his day. We turned eastward from the Bangalore Road and drove across to Daulat Bagh, the garden Tipu once destroyed before Lord Cornwallis could get to it (while that gentleman was planning, during the third Anglo-Mysore war, a siege that did not ultimately take place). The garden spreads over a portion of the northern part of the island, and even now is beautiful and reasonably well tended. My father and aunt, who were somewhat affected by the afternoon heat and had seen the garden palace before, chose to stay outside in the shade of the plentiful trees. A jutka had halted there, too, making a pretty picture as its horse bent to inspect the yellow blossoms that had fallen like a carpet on the road.

I made my way down a stairway into a sunken wooded area dotted with benches upon which lovers sat, arms entwined. In the heart of this great space was the Darya Daulat, protected from the heat by massive green blinds that enclose it on every side. The intact survival of this square palace owes a great deal to the fact that Colonel Wellesley (later the Duke of Wellington) occupied it for a time after the eventual fall of the island in 1799. The following year, the colonel wrote from Trincomallee, Ceylon, to an officer at Seringapatam to say that his brother Lord Wellesley might visit the next season, and if he did, he proposed to stay at the Darya Daulat: 'Although I think it very probable that the plan will never be put into execution, I shall be obliged to you if you will now and then take a look at my house, and urge forward the painting of it.'[8] Fifty years later, when Lord Dalhousie, Governor-General of India, visited Seringapatam in the mid-nineteenth century and saw that the summer palace was no longer in use, he too ordered that the building be kept in good repair, and that the faded murals be restored by those who could recall them as they had been.

I wandered about the building, straining to examine the wall paintings in the dim, shuttered light. They seemed to be on a dramatic scale, with entire armies represented in a single work. In 1800, the traveller Francis Buchanan wrote of what he called the *Durria adaulut Baug* that the paintings in Tipu's favourite retreat-from-business represented both the political and the social: Hyder and his son in procession, the defeat of Colonel Baillie at Pollilur near 'Conjeevaram' in 1780, the costumes worn by various castes and professions common in Mysore. That Buchanan had a relentlessly low opinion of the skill of the local painters was evident from his comment on a crudely executed Seringapatam illustration included in his book: 'The annexed Drawing ... of a Brahman, his wife, and child, done by one of the best artists at Seringapatam, and fully equal to the paintings on the walls of this palace, will convey to the reader a more exact idea of the progress made there in the art of painting, than words could possibly express.'[9] Really this is most misleading, and rather unkind of the Company-sponsored writer; for the paintings at the Darya Daulat, now preserved by the Archaeological Survey of India (ASI), are boldly and colourfully done, gripping despite their lack of refinement. Even if one condemns them on technical grounds, only the stuffiest viewer could fail to appreciate their value as period art. Bowring was able to see, for instance, that the defeat of Baillie was 'a most amusing caricature, that General being shown reclining helplessly in a palankeen, while Tipu on horseback is calmly smelling a rose and giving orders to his troops'. He did add in all honesty that '[the] perspective is ludicrous— legs, arms, and heads flying off in all directions, and considerable research is needed to find the corresponding bodies.'[10] Admiring the eccentric old paintings, I found myself thinking that they served as an epitaph of sorts. They gave a remarkable impression of the Anglo-Mysore tussle from the Muslim perspective, and an insight into the spirit of the times. To my eye, the only thing ludicrous about them was the poor quality of the ASI captions. I wondered idly what Buchanan might have reported if he had lived to read those.

The meticulous Buchanan had travelled extensively through Mysore, Canara and Malabar with the intent of investigating, under the orders of the imperious Marquis Wellesley, the 'agriculture, arts, and commerce; the religion, manners, and customs; the history natural and civil, and antiquities' of these regions. While it is hard to understand his dour and prosaic dismissal of local art, I could sympathize with his view, circa 1800, of the whole island as a 'sink of nastiness',[11] with 'a most ugly, dreary appearance' consisting mainly of 'naked rock, and dirty mud walls', and his scathing description of the fort as 'an immense, unfinished, unsightly and injudicious mass of building'.[12] Buchanan had visited Seringapatam almost immediately after the bloody and decisive siege of 1799, by which time most of its glory had been reduced by the strain of conflict. Today (and apparently even two hundred years ago), it is almost impossible to believe that a large and attractive garden called the Lal Bagh once covered the island's eastern end, or that a brilliant, richly decorated palace once stood in it. It was Lord Cornwallis who ordered the destruction of the great garden; he had camped on the island, outside the fort, during the second Anglo-Mysore War. As Mark Wilks, that detailed chronicler of Mysore history, recorded, the time between 7 and 16 February 1792, while Cornwallis waited for General Abercromby to join him, was 'industriously employed in the formation of materials for the siege, by the reluctant, but indispensable ruin of the extensive and beautiful garden of the Lall Baugh'.[13]

Wilks was much moved by this historical spot, for he took care to mention that the Lal Bagh was lovely by the old-fashioned English standard: 'beautiful, according to the ancient taste of our own country, when it had not begun to abhor straight lines, and imitate nature'. In its heyday the garden was not just a pleasure grove of stately cypress, but also a princely nursery for the produce of Mysore—Wilks quoted Lieutentant Rodrick Mackenzie as observing that

> trees bearing apples, oranges, guavas, grapes, plantains, cocoanuts, beatlenuts, as also sandalwood, sugarcane, with cotton and indigo plants, rose out from the several enclosures . . . Plants of mulberry too, from the extraordinary attention with which they were treated, discovered that the Sultaun had set his mind on the manufacture of silk.[14]

Like Wilks, I was quite taken by the romance of this garden. While Aunt Margaret watched the steady stream of life emerging from a village on the island's eastern side, past the ancient pettah of Ganjam, my father and I walked down through what was left of the splendid garden towards the gumbaz, or mausoleum, of Tipu and Hyder. Where the Lal Bagh once flourished, nothing but a few rows of trees remain, and a stretch of lawn that someone was trying, with a marked lack of success, to grow. At the end of it stands the bulbous, ivory-coloured resting place of the two Muslim rulers. This modest monument evidently met with Buchanan's approval, for he described it as handsome—as indeed it still is—and 'ornamented with misshapen columns of a fine black hornblende, which takes a most splendid polish'.[15] The pillars, I feel compelled to record, still gleam two hundred years later, astonishingly beautiful in the afternoon sun. The double doors, ebony inlaid with ivory, were given by Lord Dalhousie a good half century later,[16] which explains why Buchanan did not refer to them in his description; he did, however, mention that the tombs were covered by 'rich cloths at the Company's expense' and that there were 'moulahs' to offer up prayers and musicians to perform the 'Nobat'.[17]

The Company kept up these practices well after the fall of the fort, as did Mysore state for decades thereafter. Even today, the gumbaz has an air of sanctity and the rare appearance of being carefully tended. On Tipu's tomb is inscribed: '*Nur Islam wa din z'dunya raft, Tipu ba wajah din Muhammad shahid shud, Shamsher gum shud, Nasal Haidar shahid akbar shud*' ('The light of Islam and the faith left the world; Tipu on account of the faith of Muhammad was a martyr; the sword was lost; the offspring of Haidar was a great martyr').[18] Many of the visitors to the gumbaz are Muslim; I saw family after family walking around the tombs to pay homage. In the late nineteenth century Bowring had written,

> During the perilous days of the Mutiny, it is said that bigoted Musalmans congregated at this spot to say their prayers and breathe secret aspirations for the re-ascendancy of their faith. As one stands in the tomb, words faintly uttered resound in hollow reverberations in the lofty dome, and one cannot help

feeling a momentary compassion for a Sovereign who, tyrant and usurper as he was, died a soldier's death.[19]

It was in the Lal Bagh that a grand, two-storeyed palace once stood, by all reports uncommonly beautiful. Buchanan noted in 1800 that, although built of mud, the palace possessed 'a considerable degree of elegance' and was in fact the 'handsomest native building' he had ever seen.[20] The building must indeed have been striking, for this was high praise from Buchanan. Although Colonel Wellesley had it repaired and readied for a British officer, who occupied it for a time, it fell into complete ruin after the officer left for Mysore, and only its woodwork was saved for use in St. Stephen's Church in Ootacamund.[21] My father said the palace had been razed to the ground, probably within a decade of the siege.

Determined to find the palace's former site and see whether any part of it remained, I followed an old map that showed a spot a little to the east of the tomb. A path led into some fields that had been cultivated on the historic site. Just as we were about to give up looking for anything out of the ordinary, we found that we were walking towards the remains of an ancient gate—or what appeared to be an ancient gate, for the gate itself was missing but the gateposts and the small sections of wall on either side were unmistakably those through which Tipu must have passed from the palace to his father's tomb. We stood by the remains of the entrance for a long while, lost in contemplation of the eerily green paddy; here, where the green stalks stood deathly still in the afternoon heat, had stood a palace so grand that its inner walls, with their floral motifs in paint and gilt, had given the appearance of porcelain. A French general wrote that at about half past six in the evening, bearers of flambeaux gathered to illuminate finely crafted chandeliers.[22]

Of course, it is challenging to get a sense of the former grandeur of such a palace from the fields that grow on its grave, especially with no help from a signboard to acknowledge the site nor any attempt to preserve the remains of the gate. All that is left here is an unmistakable sense of melancholy. From a distance, Karigatta hill looks down apologetically on the gumbaz, the invisible outlines of the ghost palace, and the garden it betrayed; for it was from this modest height that Lord Cornwallis directed some of the key action and destruction in 1792.

Returning silently from the gumbaz, and pausing to collect my aunt before halting for tea at a nearby village, we proceeded towards the fort by way of the pettah of Ganjam, with its still-standing church of Abbé Dubois, and crossed the busy Bangalore road to enter the fort itself. The first structure that we looked for, and found in a state of downright ruin, had been something of an oddity in its time. It was not connected with any event historical, but was simply quirky, and wonderfully representative of the colonial facility for innovation. Thomas de Havilland, an engineer officer stationed at the fort during the British occupation, had—presumably to ease the boredom when there was no more threat of war—decided that it would be possible to build an incredibly low brick arch with a span of 112 feet. He proceeded to erect, in the compound of his bungalow, a strange bridge-like edifice that became known to all and sundry as De Havilland's Arch. My father had delighted in this odd construction as a child, saying somewhat wistfully that he remembered jumping on it and feeling it bounce beneath his feet. Weakened, no doubt by several generations of such juvenile attentions, the bouncing arch collapsed in the 1950s, and all that remains is a peculiar oblong cluster of collapsed bricks overgrown with thorns and shrubbery, rather like an abandoned railway carriage. Some of the bricks have been removed, and it is not hard to see where they were next used: near the arch, on a litter-strewn swell, is a scruffy little village of small houses, with hens pecking listlessly in the dirt and a couple of mongrels growling in warning at anyone who approaches. If only the arch itself had had such zealous guardians, I thought as I sidestepped a clump of garbage to take a photograph.

Close to the northern wall of the fort is a raised platform upon which another palace, Tipu's palace-in-the-fort, once stood. This building was mercilessly pulled down during the British occupation of the fort (only its foundations survive), but a description of it survives in Buchanan's report. At the time when he visited the island, part of the palace was being used to house the occupying troops; and if one is to believe him, the present day has not lost much by way of its absence.

> The palace of the Sultan at Seringapatam is a very large building, surrounded by a massy and lofty wall of stone and mud, and outwardly is of a very mean appearance. There were in it, however, some handsome apartments, which have been converted into barracks; but the troops are very ill-lodged, from the want of ventilation common in all native buildings.[23]

The front of this palace was a revenue office, and it was from here that Tipu sometimes gave audience to the public. The main entrance to the sultan's private apartments was through a narrow passage guarded by four tamed tigers. Tipu was evidently highly wary of attack, for his bedchamber held a hammock suspended in such a manner that he should be invisible from the windows while he slept—and in this hammock were found, after the sultan's death in the siege of 1799, a sword and a pair of pistols. The only other passage to Tipu's apartments was from the zenana, which, Buchanan reported, had survived the siege 'perfectly inviolate under the usual guard of eunuchs'. In its prime the zenana contained about six hundred women, of whom eighty belonged to the sultan while the rest were slave girls and attendants kept in equally strict confinement. 'I have sufficient reason to think,' said Buchanan of the harem, without, unfortunately, specifying this reason, 'that none of them are desirous of leaving their confinement; being wholly ignorant of any other manner of living, and having no acquaintance whatever beyond the walls of their prison.'[24] Women seem to have held little importance in Tipu's scheme of things; in

1786, he directed his commander Burhan-ud-din to cross the Tungabhadra and 'leave the women and other rubbish, together with the superfluous baggage of your army, behind.'[25]

A third palace—this is indeed an island of vanished palaces—that met the same fate was the royal residence of the Wodeyars, Tipu's Hindu predecessors. This palace, which Buchanan described as being in a 'ruinous condition', had once stood between the two temples on the western part of the island.[26] The old raja had been imprisoned there by Hyder and died childless, after leaving in his wife's care a relative whom he had adopted as his son. This young man died soon, but his infant son remained and the boy was eventually reinstated by the British, who chose him as a safer puppet king than any of the sons of Tipu. To keep things in perspective, although the royal family might not have been treated with the care to which they were accustomed, they were at least allowed to live in their palace for a few years even as Hyder ruled from within the same fort, and every year at Dasara, the main Hindu festival in Mysore, the young raja was allowed to preside over the ceremonies. A European held captive in the fort recalled in his prison diary that during the Dasara festivities of 1783, the raja watched the games and fireworks from a throne on the balcony. By 1796, the royal family had been moved from their palace to a small house, and the royal residence was converted to an armoury and storehouse and greatly neglected.[27]

At the time of the siege of 1799, the royal family, by then living in much diminished circumstances, was trying to cope with the sickness of the child heir, whose condition had worsened after bad treatment. They knew little of what was happening outside and nothing of the glory that was soon to be theirs again; upon the British attack, they feared for their safety and barricaded themselves in the temple of Sri Ranganathaswamy.[28] After the conclusive siege, the British decided against restoring the palace on Srirangapattana, for the island was of greater use to them as a military station, and instead reinstated the Wodeyars in Mysore. The following year, the old palace of the Wodeyars was pulled down, and not a trace of it remains except a small part of the old fortification around it.[29]

The temple of Sri Ranganathaswamy is much older than the town and fort on Srirangapattana, having been built by the Ganga king Tirumalaiya in the ninth century and later enlarged by a Vijayanagar viceroy. Like a great many ancient Indian temples, it is still used; as we approached, a mass of visitors were milling around it and a temple chariot stood outside, looking for all the world like a carriage waiting to carry the lord away to take the air. The gopuram, though not dazzlingly large, is an absorbing enough sight with its many reducing tiers; it was probably completed in the fifteenth century under the patronage of Vijayanagar. To distinguish this island temple from another on Srirangam, much further down the Cauvery near Trichy, it is called Paschima (western) Ranganatha Kshetra, while the temple at Srirangam is called Purva (eastern) Ranganatha Kshetra, as both are centres of the same Vaishnava faith. This classification can be a little confusing as there are not two but three such island shrines to Ranganatha, the other at Sivasamudram. The shrines are sometimes more clearly called Adi (first), Madhya (middle) and Antya (last) Ranga, with Sivasamudram occupying the centre position.[30] At Srirangapattana, the great god Ranganatha reclines as usual on his serpent Adisesha, but his usual consorts are nowhere to be found. There is only a figure of the goddess Kaveri, at whose request Ranganatha is said to have come to rest on the island, sitting at his feet and holding the lotus that is usually seen springing from his navel.

It is rather odd to see this ancient and deeply Hindu architecture perfectly intact in a fort made famous by a sultan, where so much else has been torn down; evidently neither the Muslims nor the British dared to tamper with it. Though Tipu was indisputably a bigot, he did have enough grace to make several gifts to this temple and others. Although his ancestors came from the North, Tipu was Mysorean and must have retained some respect, however grudging and minimal, for the dominant religion and erstwhile rulers. No story endorses his

Hindu superstitions more strongly than one that Aunt Margaret told me about a temple in nearby Nanjangud, where a desperate Tipu asked the deity Nanjundesvara to heal his favourite war elephant when it took ill. The animal recovered, and such was the sultan's gratitude that he gave a grant to the Nanjangud temple and thenceforth referred to its deity as Hakim (Doctor) Nanjunda.

Just as prominent as the temple in the fort is a large and rather attractive cream-coloured mosque with slender minarets, a contribution from Tipu. The visual tussle between the Jame Masjid and the temple of Sri Ranganathaswamy for dominance of the fort's interior is another reminder of the strange brand of equivocation that Tipu often employed in his dealings. He asked for favours from the local gods when in need, and retained in his service a Hindu called Poorniah, diwan under the former Mysore raja in his minority; yet he is also said to have demolished the tower of a nearby temple merely because it overlooked his palace.[31] His closest confidant remained a Muslim, Meer Saduc, whom Buchanan described as a 'monster of avarice and cruelty'.[32] The people may not exactly have loved Tipu, yet it was this minister they seem to have blamed for most of their misery. When Saduc died, apparently while trying to escape through the gates during the siege, it was suspected that he was killed by some of Tipu's own soldiers. His corpse lay where he had fallen while people insulted it, spat on it or threw slippers at it, so great was their anger at his corrupt, exploitative behaviour during the sultan's reign.[33]

As we looked up at the pigeon-holed minarets, around which dozens of birds wheeled, my aunt told me of a curious local belief: that the Cauvery rises and falls according to the level of the water trapped in the receptacles at the top of the minarets, and that this level is determined by the amount of water the pigeons drink. It was one of those Sindbad-like tales that made me stop and shake myself, for anything was believable on this island, and the noisy, circling pigeons did seem to wear a distinctly proprietary air.

Moving past the exposed foundations of Tipu's palace, we skirted the northern margin of the fort and came to its famous dungeons, adjoining the ramparts. Leaving my aunt in the car, my father telling off a healthy-looking saffron-clad beggar, and a woman selling slices of green mango and cucumber generously covered with chilli powder and flies, I climbed a mud slope to get to the entrance, then took the stairs down. It is said that Europeans were imprisoned here, many of them captured during various battles between 1780 and 1784. One of the most famous of these was fought at Pollilur, near Kanchipuram, where Hyder's army forced the surrender of a British division that included the First Battalion of the 73rd Highlanders, commanded by Colonel Baillie. Those who survived the terrible battle were held captive in Hyder's camp before being pushed to Srirangapattana in irons, and among these unfortunate men was Colonel Baillie himself. After the long journey from Arcot, they arrived in March 1781 at the fort that was to be their unpleasant home for the next three years. The length of an individual's imprisonment depended essentially on whether or not he survived the ordeal. There is considerable doubt, however, as to whether the dungeons at Srirangapattana were the actual site of imprisonment, and whether subsequent prisoners were actually brought here, for as Rev. Thompson argues, their construction also suggests use as a bomb-proof shelter.[34]

Site of so much legendary torture, the dungeons today look almost modern, for although the damp seeps in from the river, there is fresh-looking plaster on the solidly built walls and the roof appears to have been reconstructed. All that connects the single large room to history is a large cannon lying embedded in the floor—it once fell through the roof, and, being too heavy to move, was simply left there.

As I looked around for anything of interest apart from the cannon, I was joined by a company of about forty school-children from Kerala, under the tutelage of an adolescent master with a cloth bag over one shoulder.

'Tipu Sultan defeated the English in *this* room,' he announced in a thick Malayali accent. 'See his gun!' I listened to this nonsense from behind a pillar as the children crowded round the cannon noisily, most of them interested, a few too busy eating peanuts from paper cones or exchanging hair slides to be bothered with Tipu or his gun.

'He *chased* them out from here and they were *so* frightened, they *jumped* over the wall and *fell* into the river,' continued the master with the air of one who, despite many trials, was deeply committed to the cause of education.

'And then they all drowned?' asked a small boy, hopefully. The master glared at him, indignant that the climax to his tall tale should be thus purloined.

'No,' he said flatly, 'they . . . they . . . they swam to the other side and escaped.'

The din in the claustrophobic dungeons was painful, for another boy had been trying to stand on the cannon and was now being pulled off by the class monitor while his peers cheered in a cacophonous mixture of Malayalam and English. The teacher, dramatically clapping his hands over his ears, retired outside for a smoke.

I followed, and walked away along the ramparts until I could see the beautiful old Wellesley bridge across the north branch of the Cauvery. Dedicated to the 'other' Wellesley, Governor-General of India in 1804, 'as a lasting monument of the benefits conferred on the people and country of Mysore',[35] the bridge still spans the river two centuries later, though a more modern bridge is used by twenty-first-century vehicles. To the west, beyond the railway bridge, once stood an even more ancient bridge, now visible only as a faint line of ripples where the rocks had fallen into the river. I wished I could bring the children up to the ramparts and tell them a few of the fort's stories, but it was getting late, and when I returned to the car, which had been baking in the heat, my aunt made a mild remark on the general subject of imprisonment.

To return to the prisoners of Seringapatam, it appears that several officers were held in houses, choultries[36] and prisons at various locations within the fort, rather than the dungeons themselves.[37] The prisoners' living conditions were very uncomfortable: an anonymous officer of Colonel Baillie's detachment recorded that the 'Expenses of fitting up a Prisoner newly arrived at Seringapatam' included a piece of coarse cloth, enough to make two shirts; leather and tape for galligaskins; straw for pillows and half a piece of 'dungeree'[38] for pillow cases and towels; and an earthen 'chatty' to eat off. Certain articles of luxury were also sometimes 'obtained by the Opulent after a Length of Saving', among which were a penknife, sweetmeats 'per stick', fruit, 'dressing a hubble-bubble per week', and materials to make a pack of cards. Speaking of how the ill-treated prisoners took heart, the same officer wrote: '[R]ecollecting we were Britons, we endeavoured to resume our usual gaiety of mind, determined by the help of Providence, to live out every difficulty.'[39] Their endurance was sorely tested, for by the time the temporary peace of 1784 brought release, the number of prisoners had shrunk. Several had died from the poor conditions and lack of medical care, including Colonel Baillie, to whom a now-forgotten memorial stands near the gumbaz. Wilks wrote, 'the spratts nut, cassia fistula, jaggery, tamarinds, and a rude blue pill, formed by the trituration [sic] of quicksilver with crude sugar, constituted the whole extent of their materia medica . . .'

The plight of the Indian sepoys was much worse, for they were meted out such treatment as their captors thought befitted those who had fought against their own countrymen. Wilks reported that they were 'kept at hard labour, and these faithful creatures, whenever they had an opportunity, sacrificed a portion of their own scanty pittance to mend the fare of their European fellow soldiers . . . many of them sustained the severest trials with a fortitude which has never been surpassed in the history of any country.'[40]

A number of Europeans, those kept separate from the officers, were not released in 1784. Some of these were prisoners—many just children—who had been handed over to Hyder in 1782 by the French general Suffren. These unfortunate boys had been forcibly circumcised, enlisted as military slaves drilled by a Sergeant Dempster (a deserter from the Bengal army), and made to wear a silver pearl in the right ear. It is very sad that their release was not included in the terms of peace; possibly British negotiators did not know of the existence of this second body of captives, which Tipu had discreetly removed to Mysore when the negotiations were in progress. It is clear that Tipu intended they should never leave, for he even organized their mass wedding to young girls who had left the Carnatic with their families when Hyder had attacked that region. A description of this event by James Scurry, a Devonshire boy who after much travail returned home to run, of all things, a grocery store in Plymouth, is both comic and pathetic:

> Some of these poor creatures were allotted for us; and one morning, we were ordered to fall into rank and file, when those girls were placed one behind each of us, while we stood gazing at each other, wondering what they were going to do. At last the durga[41] gave the word 'To the right about face;' with the addition (in the Moorish language) of 'take what is before you'. This when understood, some did, and some did not; but the refractory were soon obliged to comply...When this ceremony was completed, we were ordered back to our square, and on our return with our young black doxies, we had the bazaar, or public market to pass, where the crowd was so difficult to penetrate, as to separate us. This laid the foundation for some serious disputes afterwards, many insisting that the women they had, when they arrived at the square, were not the same they had at first. This scene was truly comic, for the girls, when we understood them, which was many months afterward, had the same views that we had; and were frequently engaged with their tongues on this score, long before we could understand the cause of their disputes. Our enemies seemed to enjoy this in a manner that would have done honour to a British theatre.[42]

It was, however, the British who had the last laugh when, several years later, the fort was breached and taken during the famous siege of 1799, and Tipu killed in action. The best way to view the site of the breach—later bricked up by the British—is to drive out of the fort towards Mysore, and look to one's right at the fort wall running along the north bank of the river. It is easy enough to identify the breach, for the masonry used by the British is quite distinct from the older stones around it. Alexander Beatson, who served in more than one war with Mysore as surveyor-general to the army in the field, described the crossing of the Cauvery and the ascent of the breach in his *View of the Origin and Conduct of the War with Tippoo Sultaun,* a highly academic and official-sounding first-person account:

> The passage across the river from our advanced trench, was by no means difficult; it was a smooth rock, having two or three small streams, twelve or fifteen inches deep; and when arrived at the stone glacis, the troops ascended by the slope which terminates the glacis before the north-west bastion, to the top of the retaining wall which forms the outer part of the ditch. In the inner part of this wall are steps, made by single projecting stones, by which they could descend into the ditch without using scaling ladders; but these were employed by the right column, in getting over the retaining wall. The water in the ditch, directly opposite to the Breach, was only about knee deep, although much deeper on either side. The Breach was wide and the ascent easy; and when upon it, unless at the very summit, the troops could not be seen from the west cavalier. As the defences to the right and left had been silenced by the batteries, the Breach was, in fact, a place of safety: the danger was in getting to it. Being arrived at the summit of the Breach, a formidable ditch appeared between it and the cavalier, or the second wall: but as the enemy had not cut off the Breach, and were unable to defend the inner rampart, on account of the destructive fire of the enfilading battery, it was only formidable

in appearance. This rampart is of mud, and seems to be the remains of the ancient Fort of Seringapatam.[43]

Fortunately, other accounts of that fateful day in May have also survived, and from them a more human view of the proceedings may be obtained. Although Beatson made the crossing sound disarmingly easy, and indeed the breach was attempted just before the monsoon when the river was at its lowest, the crossing was not without difficulty. The river was not quite as shallow as Beatson reported, for a Thomas Beveridge, writing home to his mother in Kinross, Fife, breathlessly described the progress across the Cauvery thus:

> We remained in the Trenches till about one o'Clock, when orders were given to commence the Assault, we immediately rushed out of the entrenchments and advanced about 400 yards to the Breach exposed to a most heavy and continued discharge of fire arms and rockets of every denomination, which killed and wounded a considerable number, especially in crossing the river which runs round Seringapatam, the bottom of which is composed of huge rocks which rendered the passage very tedious and difficult in some places the water did not reach to our knees, and in others many were obliged to swim over, by which means their ammunition was entirely destroyed, so that the Bayonet was the only defence after getting up the breech [sic] which was soon cleared of the Enemy . . . I have been very well considering the bad water, provisions and fatigue that we were exposed to during a long and tedious march, and thanks be too [sic] God I did not receive the least hurt during the storm or siege . . . We expect to remain in this part of India for some months until the Country is divided between the Nizam and the Company.[44]

Whether the passage was in fact easy or tedious, the outcome was what the British wanted: the resistance was broken, the enemy began to retreat and soldiers to attempt escape, and finally the sultan himself was put to death, an act that marked the absolute end not only of a remarkable life, but of Muslim power in south India.

East of the dungeons was a horribly tasteless modern memorial— a mere lump of cement surrounded by a carelessly designed metal fence—to the Tiger of Mysore, which did little to recall the manner or circumstances of his death. I looked at it with disgust and tried to reconstruct, in sheer self-defence, the final events of that fateful day.

The sultan had been killed near a gate that led into the fort through the inner rampart, which was later demolished and thrown into the ditch by the British less than a year after they took possession of the fort. At the time when he was slain, Tipu was perhaps attempting to return to his palace, and a Major Allan said that when his body was brought from under the gateway, 'his eyes were open and his body was so warm, that for a few moments Colonel Wellesley and myself were doubtful whether he was not alive; on feeling his pulse and heart, that doubt was removed.'[45] The sultan had been wounded in four places, three in his body and one in his temple, and his turban was lost. His body was carried in a palanquin to the palace for conclusive identification, and the subsequent funeral was held with due attention to custom and attended by four flank companies of Europeans as a show of respect.

Earlier in the afternoon, when my father, aunt and I had halted for tea at a little shop at the entrance to the gumbaz, my father had read aloud from Rev. Thompson (to the deep interest of the shopkeeper and a couple of long-bearded idlers) the chapter on Tipu's funeral. It had sent shivers up our spines, for my father read well, and we were fully aware that the hangers-on at the tea shop might have been the descendants of those very people from the pettah and the fort who had witnessed the sultan's interment.

The preparations for the funeral of Tippoo Sultaun were

superintended by the principal Cauzee of Seringapatam; every article was provided according to his direction, that the ceremony might be performed with as much pomp as circumstances would permit. The bottom of the state palankeen served as a bier, in which the body was laid, wrapt up in muslins, and covered by a rich brocaded cloth . . . The streets, through which the procession passed, were lined with inhabitants, many of whom prostrated themselves before the body, and expressed their grief by loud lamentations. Meer Allum, and the chiefs of the Nizam's Army, met the body at the entrance of the Loll Baug, and after paying their respects to the prince, fell into the procession. When the body had reached the gate of Hyder's mausoleum [My aunt's face was transfigured now, as she listened] the grenadiers formed a street; and presented arms as it passed. The usual service being performed, the body was placed near to that of the late Hyder Ali Khan; and a *keeraut,* or charitable gift, of 5,000 rupees, was distributed by the Cauzee to the different facquirs, and to the poor who attended the funeral: and to add to the solemnity of the scene, the evening closed with a most dreadful storm, attended with rain, thunder, and lightning, by which two officers and some others in the Bombay Camp were killed, and many severely hurt.[46]

A fitting conclusion, perhaps, to the death ceremony of a man who had proclaimed that in this world he would rather live two days like a tiger than two hundred years like a sheep.

History has created two caricatures of Tipu Sultan, the ruler of this fort-in-ruins: that of an irrational, vainglorious bigot and that of a brave, self-sacrificing freedom-fighter. It would be naïve to try and fit him into either, for in truth he was a bit of both, and much more. Of his personality, so much has been written that it would be impossible to do it justice without dwelling on the subject at length. There are, however, two perspectives that offer radically different views: that of

Wilks, pragmatic as ever, commenting on Tipu's conduct at Mangalore in 1783, and another, more romantic view expressed some decades later, that of Sir Walter Scott. Wilks spoke very harshly of Tipu's attack on Mangalore after his French allies had informed him that they would no longer side against the British due to a European declaration of peace:

> It is not intended to express surprise at the dark stupidity which could induce Tippoo Sultaun, however mortified and foiled, to think that under such circumstances he could obtain an accession of military fame by determining to persevere by whatever treachery and whatever sacrifice of men, of time and of honour, to obtain the fort of Mangalore, before concluding a peace which would give it to him without an effort, and we can only explain this strange political suicide by the miserable pride of attempting to shew that he could achieve by himself an exploit, which French troops could not accomplish.[47]

This was not exactly high praise, and it burned in my head long after I had read it; yet as I stood at the crassly beautified spot where Tipu fell, it was Sir Walter Scott's words that came more sharply home. In the context of Napoleon's abdication in 1814, Scott had written, 'although I never supposed that [Napoleon] possessed, allowing for some difference of education, the liberality of conduct and political views which were sometimes exhibited by old Haidar Ally, yet I did think he might have shown the same resolved and dogged spirit of resolution which induced Tippoo Saib to die manfully upon the breach of his capital city with his sabre clenched in his hand.'[48]

Disappointed by the unromantic 'memorial' to the controversial sultan, we had little else to do but go back the way we had come, and we drove out through the Mysore gate, once the fort's main entrance. In its heyday this entrance was a series of gates, of which three still stood in 1923. There was not much left of any of them now except fallen stones and skeletal pillars, and the road that passed between them was straight—definitely British in construction, for in the sultan's time, it had wound from one gate to the next. All these gates had been very high, so that elephants crossing the deep ditch by the drawbridge could easily pass through them. Rev. Thompson reproduced thus the translation of the Persian inscription on a slab let into the inner gate of the outer rampart:

> In the Name of God the Merciful, the Padshaw [emperor] began the construction of the fort . . . when the heavenly bodies were auspicious and in good conjunction with each other . . . under the influence of these stars this fort is filled with ornaments, articles of consumption, and wealth (i.e. all the requisites of war, peace and greatness), and the fort by the grace of God will ever remain free from all misfortune.[49]

Nothing could have been more wishful than this sentiment, for the fort had come to grave misfortune soon enough, and time had been cruel to both vanquished and victor. Just across the road from the Mysore gate lay the British Garrison Cemetery, one of two such spots on the island that are filled with the stones of Europeans who died here.

Squeezing through a hole in the cemetery's wooden gate, I searched for a grave belonging to the Scott family. Just over the old wall flowed the Cauvery, less than a mile downstream from Scott's Bungalow, where I had spent so many hours with Hugh Warren. Pausing to read old inscriptions on graves belonging to the regiment De Meuron, which had fought in the siege, and keeping an eye out for snakes in the tangled undergrowth, I was reminded very strongly of Uncle Hugh, and of the sudden depression to which he would fall prey. Often, as the sun began its downward journey, he would lean back against a tree trunk and sigh almost imperceptibly. On such evenings by the river, he would tell me the story of 'old Scott', the British officer who had first lived in the bungalow two hundred years ago. It was a sad story, as were many that Uncle Hugh loved to tell.

Colonel Scott had held charge of the gun-carriage factory in the fort, and eventually became commandant of the fort itself. It was the raja of Mysore who built the bungalow for him, and there he set up house in the early nineteenth century. Many local legends described his fate and that of his family. Some said that Scott's wife and young children caught the cholera, and he found them dead one day upon returning from parade. A nineteenth-century Anglo-Indian poet, Aliph Cheem, wrote in his *Lays of Ind* that Scott killed himself in a fit of grief by riding his horse into the river, after which tragedy the house lay uninhabited for decades, its furniture and upholstery decaying bit by bit. As Uncle Hugh looked over his shoulder at the house behind us, he would stop, shudder briefly and proceed to explain, with austere Anglican regard for the truth, that the real story lay buried in the nearby garrison cemetery, where I now stood among the stones.

It was my father, of course, who found the grave I was looking for, for he had been exploring quickly and efficiently while I was distracted by the guava trees and pretty old stones. There it lay, a sombre stone memorial to Caroline Isabella Scott, who had died along with her infant in 'childbed' in 1817. Her husband, in his unhappiness, had simply ended his service and returned home.

As we made our way out of the cemetery and towards the aqueduct, and as the sun prepared to set and hasten us on our return to Mysore, the memory of another drive home on that road returned. I remembered leaving the island on a deep-green evening; the smell of pipe smoke came back strongly, for I would often slide down on the springy front seat of Uncle Hugh's car and fall asleep, my nose close enough to the pouch of tobacco in his pocket to sniff its strong, comforting smell. Prompted by this far-off thought, I hesitantly voiced an idea that I had been toying with all day: to visit Scott's Bungalow itself, for the current lady of the house still lived there. My aunt was discouraging, for it was too late to visit unannounced, and I abandoned the notion. For years it had haunted me that Uncle Hugh had died in that very house after a swim in the river, shortly before he was due to return unwillingly to England to live out a lonely old age. Lines from Aliph Cheem repeated themselves over and over in my head—a verse that referred to Scott's Bungalow being left to ruin after the legendary death of its master—and although I tried to reason that it was just an old story, that the house was still inhabited and indeed being well cared for, the image of ruin and abandonment persisted.

> The mouldering rooms are now as they stood
> Nearly eighty years ago,
> The piano is there,
> And table and chair,
> And the carpet rotting slow;
> And the beds whereon the corpses lay
> And the curtains half time-mawed away . . .[50]

No, I did not insist upon going to Scott's Bungalow, for the day had left me with a sense of penetrating pathos. In such a frame of mind, I did not want to get any closer to that company of people, now long forgotten, whose dreams had been lost on Seringapatam.

Notes

1. Reverend E. W. Thompson, *The Last Siege of Seringapatam* (1923; reprint, New Delhi: Asian Educational Services, 1990). The author kindly includes a guide to the island 'for the convenience of visitors'.
2. Lewin B. Bowring, *Haidar Ali and Tipu Sultan* (1893; reprint, Delhi: Idarah-I Adabiyat-I Delli, 1974), p. 205.
3. P. V. Jagadisa Ayyar, *South Indian Shrines* (New Delhi: Rupa, 2000), p. 752.
4. Robert Sewell, *A Forgotten Empire (Vijayanagar)* (1878; reprint, New Delhi:

40 brahmins and bungalows

Asian Educational Services, 1986), p. 269.

5. 'This term is peculiar to the Madras Presidency. The persons so called were properly subordinate feudal chiefs, occupying tracts more or less wild, and generally of predatory habits in former days; they are now much the same as Zemindars in the highest use of that term . . . The word is Tam. *palaiyakkaran,* 'the holder of a *palaiyam,*' or feudal estate; Tel. *palegadu;* and thence Mahr. *palegar*; the English form being no doubt taken from one of the two latter.' Henry Yule and A.C. Burnell, *Hobson-Jobson, The Anglo-Indian Dictionary* (1886; reprint, Ware, Hertfordshire: Wordsworth Editions Ltd, 1996), p. 718.

6. *Hobson-Jobson* defines a pettah as 'Tam. *pettai*. The extramural suburb of a fortress, or the town attached and adjacent to a fortress' (p. 702). It was to the pettah of Ganjam that many Mysoreans were forced to relocate when Tipu destroyed the town. Here, too, once lived a priest by the name of Abbé Dubois, who came after the fall of the fort in 1799, and remained in Mysore for twenty-four years. Among other things, he introduced the practice of vaccination, and wrote a book on *Hindu Manners, Customs and Ceremonies*.

7. Thompson, p. 70.

8. Quoted in ibid., pp. 71-72.

9. Buchanan, *A Journey from Madras through the Countries of Mysore, Canara, and Malabar* (1807; reprint, New Delhi: Asian Educational Services, 1999), vol. I, p. 74.

10. Bowring, *Haidar Ali and Tipu Sultan*, pp. 206-207.

11. Buchanan, vol. III, p. 417.

12. Buchanan, vol. I, p. 62.

13. Mark Wilks, *History of Mysore* (1810; reprint, New Delhi: Asian Educational Services, 1989), vol. II, p. 547. Colonel Wilks served as Acting Resident in Mysore in 1800, and in 1810 published this exhaustive history of the kingdom.

14. Lt. Rodrick Mackenzie, *Sketch of the War with Tippoo Sultaun* (Calcutta, 1794), quoted in Wilks' *History of Mysore,* vol. II, p. 547. Betel nut is the common—but, alas, incorrect—name for the areca nut, a hard nut that is often chewed with betel leaf.

15. Buchanan, vol. I, p. 74. Hornblende is a 'dark brown etc. mineral constituent of granite etc.' (*Oxford Dictionary & English Usage Guide,* 1996, p. 337).

16. Jagadisa Ayyar, p. 752.

17. Buchanan, vol. I, p. 74.
18. Bowring, p. 227.
19. Ibid.
20. Buchanan, vol. I, p. 73.
21. T.P. Issar, *The Royal City* (Bangalore: Mytec Ltd, 1991), p. 157.
22. Ibid.
23. Buchanan, vol. I, p. 69.
24. Ibid., p. 73.
25. Bowring, p. 217.
26. Buchanan, vol. I, p. 67.
27. Thompson, pp. 15-16.
28. Buchanan, vol. I, p. 67.
29. Thompson, p. 15.
30. Jagadisa Ayyar, pp. 751, 753.
31. Thompson, p. 64.
32. Buchanan, vol. I, p. 71.
33. Ibid., p. 65.
34. Thompson, p. 14.
35. Ibid., p. 65.
36. According to *Hobson-Jobson*, the choultry is 'Peculiar to S. India ... A hall, a shed, or a simple *loggia*, used by travellers as a resting place, and also intended for the transaction of public business.'
37. Thompson, p. 16.
38. *Hobson-Jobson* defines 'dungaree' as 'a kind of coarse and inferior cotton cloth ... The finer kinds are used for clothing by poor people; the coarser for sails for native boats and tents.'
39. Anonymous, *Memoirs of the Late War in Asia, with a Narrative of the Imprisonment and Sufferings of Our Officers and Soldiers* (1788), quoted in *The Tiger and the Thistle: Tipu Sultan and the Scots in India* (National Galleries of Scotland, 2000; www.nationalgalleries.org.uk/tipu).
40. Wilks, vol. II, p. 272.
41. Daroga, head of a government department.
42. *The Captivity, Sufferings and Escape of James Scurry* (London, 1824), quoted in Thompson, pp. 26-27.
43. Quoted in Thompson, p. 37.
44. 'Original manuscript letter from THOMAS BEVERIDGE at Seringapatam to his Mother Mrs Beveridge, Bridge-Stone, Kinross, No Britain. Camp.

near Seringapatam 12th June 1799.' National Library of Scotland, Acc 9250. Quoted in *The Tiger and the Thistle: Tipu Sultan and the Scots in India* (National Galleries of Scotland, 2000).
45. Thompson, p. 47.
46. Ibid., pp. 54-55.
47. Wilks, vol. II, pp. 219-20.
48. Quoted in *The Tiger and the Thisle: Tipu Sultan and the Scots in India*.
49. Thompson, pp. 67-68.
50. From *Lays of Ind*, quoted in Thompson, p. 69.

Mysore
A Large and Handsome Town

But the city, if much of it is modern, is not garish. Indeed, in many of the streets, and before many of the buildings, the chief impression is of something serenely and enduringly beautiful, of a reticent yet gracious charm . . . May the visitor who sees a clean and beautiful city, a pleasant and peaceful countryside, see behind it something of the steadfast purpose of great statesmen, something of the loyal work of her people . . .

—Constance E. Parsons, *Mysore City*, 1930

All over the world, there are towns and cities that first blossomed under royal patronage, their plush palaces and noble neighbourhoods rubbing shoulders with the extrusions of a later day. Nowhere, however, is there a princely city with as uniquely blended a heritage as Mysore—not even elsewhere in Anglo-India, where East meets West as routinely as breathing in and breathing out.

This quiet setting of my early childhood was once the capital of a kingdom built under the simultaneous direction of two committed masters—one the maharaja of the historic house of Wodeyar, who ruled from a palace at the town's heart, the other a British Resident, modestly ensconced in a house built at a discreet, respectful distance from the royal stronghold. Together these men and their wives, over 150 years, created a capital that embodied two fundamentally different cultures, their distinctions reflected in the often colourful aesthetics of the local ruler and the more understated dignity of the British. Part of the magic of Mysore is that the mixture survived as a single entity rather than a quilt of mismatched squares. As early as 1801, hardly two years after the fall of Srirangapattana, Colonel Arthur Wellesley wrote to his brother Lord Mornington: 'Mysore is become a large and handsome town, full of inhabitants; the whole country is settled and in perfect tranquillity.'[1] Over the years, the splendid palace and classical mansion, the simple *agrahara* (street of row houses) and the dainty boulevard, the tiled and gabled bungalow and the elegant, flat-roofed house of the Indian noble all became symbols of integration, of stability and peace and, more subtly, of a sense of contentment among the citizens that, even a century after the creation of modern Mysore following the death of Tipu Sultan, did not fail to be noticed and commented on. In 1892 Lord Lansdowne, Viceroy of India, observed, 'There is probably no State in India where the ruler and the ruled are on more satisfactory terms, or in which the great principle, that government should be for the happiness of the governed, receives a greater measure of practical recognition.'[2]

Yet another century later, in the late 1970s, the city where I spent my first seven years in my grandfather's tranquil bungalow was an ageing, somewhat neglected masterpiece. Both royalty and Resident had vanished, but had left a series of remarkable, if rapidly fading, impressions. Their influence lingered about the streets and lanes, as if an unseen bugler stood at a corner and piped a melancholy strain after the rest of the band had marched away. This plaintive melody could be heard throughout Mysore—on the terrace of the ice-white Lalita Mahal on a still, shimmering summer afternoon, up gracious old Chamundi hill in the dead of night, beside the statue of the maharaja under his gilded sunshade, in the echoing corridors of the lavish public buildings, under the gables of the bougainvillea-draped bungalows, in the jasmine-scented courtyards of the old noble mansions; along quiet colonial streets lined with shady trees, and even, if you listened hard enough, above the din and chaos of the parrot-infested Sayyaji Rao Road,[3] which runs past the large market in the heart of the town. It was, of course, heard like a clarion in my grandfather's house, where the family still spoke of palace doings with fondness and familiarity, almost as if the royal family still lived in their former state of glory. Our old albums held photographs of the princesses and the solitary prince when, as children, they had been under my grandmother's tutelage; old biscuit tins spilled out piles of picture postcards that the last maharaja, Jayachamarajendra Wodeyar, had sent my grandmother, addressing her respectfully by her full name but signing himself 'Jaya'. On the old German piano stood silver-framed portraits of Queen Elizabeth, her husband and, of course, of Nehru.

With its dual affiliations, Mysore was just the sort of city to nurture such an unusual couple as my grandparents. My grandfather was three-quarters Indian and one-quarter Portuguese, while my grandmother was the only daughter of a large English family to have chosen to stay in India after Independence, and to survive the new order and the changes that accompanied democracy and socialism. Together, my grandparents had braved the differences of culture and race—admittedly not very many, considering the somewhat anglicized Indian Christian world from which my grandfather had emerged, lean and handsome in a hat and coat—and had been married in St. Bartholomew's Church, Mysore, in 1939. The home they proceeded to establish was furnished entirely in the colonial style, with furniture of rosewood and rattan, and meals served with brown sauce and pudding. Of course, there was plenty of Indian influence as well, for my grandfather would often wear a vest and a crisp white mundu at home, a throwback to his Mangalore and Calicut upbringing, and my stout, jolly grandmother would occasionally discard her severe frock in favour of a soft, clinging sari. They had philosophically survived the long separations of the Second World War, during which my grandfather had served in the British army, and in the post-war period enjoyed the privileges of both royal and government service. They were pillars of St. Bartholomew's Church, lending their support to such august bodies as the women's fellowship and the pastorate committee, and seem to have taken quiet pleasure in their shrinking community. My grandmother was often heard ordering my grandfather to make himself scarce when the church ladies were expected to tea.

'Hop it, Sid,' she would say, firmly, 'or I'll fling you out on your ear.'

The house from which my grandfather was periodically flung in the early years stood in the great grounds of Government House, where he had worked years before I was born. My father and aunt had a lot of affection for this old British building, as they had spent their childhood playing in its compound, but I was always a little frightened when I passed its arched gateway and deserted garden on my way to school. Government House was once the British Residency, dreamed up in 1800 by the historian Mark Wilks, then the acting Resident in Mysore, and completed in 1805. Its exterior is unremarkable—in this city of palaces and mansions, it was never much more than a dignified old house with an extravagant porch—but tucked away in its interior is 'the hall', a brilliant piece of architecture for its time. This large banquet hall was commissioned by Sir John Malcolm, Resident of Mysore from 1803, supposedly as a wedding gift for his wife; and he chose for its execution none other than Thomas de Havilland, the versatile architect of the bouncing brick arch on Seringapatam.[4] Says Constance Parsons, author of a guide to Mysore written in 1930,

> Sir John, evidently determined that the hall should not only be handsome and imposing, but unique, sent for an engineer who had already 'by Satanic aid' . . . achieved the apparently impossible. To disprove the assertion that he could not make a stable arch of country brick of a span of 100 feet, he had built,

in his own garden in Seringapatam, the great arch of 112 feet . . .
So Captain de Havilland was called from the bungalow in
Seringapatam . . . and we may imagine how gleefully he
attempted and achieved another feat—the building of the largest
room in South India of which the roof is unsupported by pillars.

In this remarkable hall, Parsons continued, 'Royalty and viceroyalty—all the viceroys—governors and generals, princes, prelates and presidents, statesmen and men famous in the world of letters and of art—have sat under Lady Malcolm's unsupported roof, and most of them sat upon it, to view the fireworks usually made in the city.'[5] The unostentatious Residency indeed received many distinguished visitors, including the British royal family and Monsieur Clemenceau, and I could not help wondering if they had been nervous about the strength of the roof while sitting beneath it, or indeed on it. Perhaps they trembled only inwardly while enjoying the legendary Mysore hospitality and admiring de Havilland's daring designs.

Government House is not as beautifully maintained as it used to be, but at least it does not wear the same air of inexorable decay that many of Mysore's other colonial buildings do. One of the most pathetic of these ramshackle structures, forming part of the vague architectural consciousness of my childhood, stands across the road from Government House in a state of severe disrepair. This is Wellington Lodge, its name sadly incongruous in view of the broken windows and grass-tufted masonry of the one-time residence of the man who would become Duke of Wellington. Though the lodge was a plain, almost ugly structure to begin with, I cannot but marvel at the crassness of a modern administration that pays so little attention to historicity. As a child, I skipped past the lodge almost every day with absolutely no knowledge of either its name or its former function—yet here the celebrated Colonel Wellesley had lived for two years, from 1799 to 1801, when he was given political charge of Mysore while the raja was reinstated on the throne. Wellington Lodge was intended to be a temporary home and headquarters until the Residency was built, hence its economical, godown-like design; yet thanks to its solid construction, it still stands after two centuries despite an almost complete lack of recent maintenance. The only feature that gives away its high birth is the twin-winged stairway to the east, for this is a stately embellishment, tagged on almost as an afterthought to an otherwise unadorned structure. Up and down this majestic open stairway the distinguished officers Wellesley, Harris, Kirkpatrick and Close must have trod, the first commissioners of Mysore after the return of the house of Wodeyar. Standing in a small compound that now houses an educational institution, the lodge that bears Wellesley's better-known name is in no danger of being remembered by future generations.

It was in this quiet, slowly crumbling neighbourhood that I grew up, for after my grandparents' days at Government House were done, the family moved into two adjacent bungalows a little way down the road. The one I lived in was a typical Mysore bungalow set in a pretty, tangled garden, with a high ceiling to coax away the summer heat, a central living room with bedrooms on either side, and verandas at the front and back. My memories of this old house are filled with that same sense of gentle, inexorable decay that pervades the city, much like the feather-soft, half-brown bougainvillea blossoms that cling to its bushes in summer. I used to share a room with my great-aunt, who, stricken by polio in her youth, could usually be found lying on her narrow cot, reading or humming patiently to herself. Often she would turn her neck sideways on the pillow and begin to sing, her soft, clear voice blending with the silence rather than breaking it.

Now the day is ended
Night is drawing nigh
Shadows of the evening
Steal across the sky

The old hymn would touch every corner of that homely room

with its comfort, from the roughly laid Cudappah stone floor to the thick Burma-teak beams and rafters overhead.

My grandfather would while away the hours in a ponderous armchair in the drawing room, a heavy volume open on his knee. Books were his companions, his way of alleviating loneliness, though with my grandfather loneliness had an odd sort of dignity, as if it were not quite an unpleasant thing. All would be saintly silent where he sat, save the sucking and bleeping of the old radio, with its big white keys and large dials, and the drunken whirring of insects around the single ceiling lamp. Evenings were a particularly lovely time in the bungalow, for, having baked gently in the heat of the day, its rafters exuded a warm woody smell when the sun went down over the bund. It was greatly comforting to return at night to the serene old house as it glowed gently in the garden like a giant, dreaming firefly, shedding around it a pool of amber light. After dark Aunt Margaret often sat in the backyard on a little wicker stool, and I was sometimes allowed to linger with her long past my bedtime. We would both watch the moon hanging enticingly out of the night sky, outlining the bungalow and its many-levelled roofs almost as clear as day. Suddenly, its luminescence would disappear behind a cloud and the tiles would blacken again, their orange-red tints dispelled by the returning dark. At length, my aunt would stand up with a sigh, but not an unhappy one, for she, like the others in the bungalow, and indeed throughout our quarter of the town, had long since ceased to question the quiet, unchanging tenor of their lives.

The centre of our uneventful existence was St. Bartholomew's, a squat but interesting little church that was walking distance from the bungalow. Initially built for Mysore's increasing Anglican population in the early nineteenth century, St. Bart's continued to serve the Indian Christian community after the colonial era (which in Mysore ended in the late nineteenth century, when authority shifted to the maharaja). Its belfry was the most intriguing structure I had ever seen, standing by itself in a large and twiggy compound, supported by a profusion of wooden beams laid against each other at odd angles. On summer Sundays we often had Bible lessons outdoors near the belfry, with newspapers spread out beneath us to absorb the damp from the grass, for which they would compensate by leaving interesting black patterns on our behinds. Clad in our best church clothes, starched stiff and ironed crisp, as uncomfortable a body of children as ever sat through a warm morning, we would sit and gaze up at the bell. The teacher would tinkle on sweetly about Jesus, as only a Sunday-school teacher can, while we twisted and fidgeted impatiently, and relieved the tedium by picking the burrs out of each other's socks. Inside the sun-baked church, the congregation rose and sat, drowsily following the timeless cadences of worship. Occasionally snatches of hymns would drift across the grass to where we sat, and the older children hummed along to the more familiar tunes.

The old church was always full, despite the summer heat and the unbearable stillness. The old pews would creak and groan as parishioners shifted uneasily in their seats, perhaps more than one wishing that they, too, were outdoors, under the shade of the old rain tree while it dropped its blossoms like blessings on the cool earth below. When the service was over, the elders would hobnob a while on the porch, cups of coffee in hand, and then we would walk home again, looking forward to porridge and eggs with all our might.

Our mohalla, or neighbourhood, was deeply historical, but visitors would need more than their share of imagination to conjure up scenes of the past in its comatose streets. Who would believe today that the maidan, the bungalows and the alleys behind them stood on the site of a dramatic, even violent past? In the eighteenth century Tipu Sultan tore down the buildings of 'old' Mysore, including the greater part of the ancient palace of the Wodeyars, and planned the construction of a new city and fort that he named Nazarbad. Neither city nor fort fully materialized, but our humdrum old neighbourhood still bears the name of the sultan's dream. As a child, I had not known there was anything remarkable about Nazarbad, with its handful of quiet mansions and dozens of humbler houses tucked away behind them. The bazaar at the heart of the dusty colony has long been somnolent and monotonous, unlike the one near the palace, which even today flaunts great mounds of yellow and vermilion powder and glittering stacks of bangles. I must admit that all the charm Nazarbad ever held for me was contained in the hole-in-the-wall shops on the narrow main street, where men sit on their haunches selling puffed rice and roasted lentils, which they give you in a paper cone bound with jute string. The maidan was simply my extended garden and playground; I would sit on the bund for hours with our dogs, a motley crew of mongrels and a lone Silky Sidney, and watch village women prise dried dung cakes off an old brick wall, throw them into the cane baskets they held at their hips, and slap on fresh dung with a sickening squelch. In short, I thought Nazarbad a bit dull, even at the age of seven, when places are apt to seem considerably *more* interesting than they actually are.

It was twenty years later, when I was reading the travels of Francis Buchanan through the Mysore dominions of the early nineteenth century, that I stumbled on a reference to Nazarbad, and could scarcely believe that Buchanan was referring to the unpretentious neighbourhood I knew so well. With predictable condemnation of Tipu's schemes, Buchanan wrote:

> *Tippoo,* with his usual policy of destroying every monument of the former government, had razed *Mysore,* and removed the stones of the palace and temples to a neighbouring height, where he was building a fort; which, from its being situated on a place commanding an extensive view, was called *Nazarbar.* The fortress could have been of no possible use in defending the country, and was probably planned merely with the view of obscuring the fame of *Mysore,* the former capital. At a great expense and to the great distress of the peasants working at it, the Sultan had made considerable progress in the works of this

place, when he began to consider that it afforded no water. He then dug an immense pit, cutting down through the solid black rock to a great depth and width, but without success; and when the siege of his capital was formed, the whole work was lying in a mass of confusion . . .[6]

I couldn't help thinking that Tipu would have been thoroughly apoplectic if confronted with such a view of his efforts. Colonel Wilks also mentioned Nazarbad in his *History of Mysore*, commenting on Tipu's destruction of Mysore in the faultless philosophical prose that distinguishes the historian from the mere observer:

The town and fort of Mysoor, the ancient residence of the rajas, and the capital from which the whole country derived its name, was an offensive memorial of the deposed family, and [Tipu] determined that the existence, and if possible the remembrance, of such a place, should be extinguished. The fort was levelled with the ground, and the materials were employed in the erection of another fortress on a neighbouring height, which he named Nezerbar: and it is a curious example of that vicissitude in human affairs, which history so often preaches in vain, that the very same stones were re-conveyed to rebuild the same old fort of Mysoor, in 1799.[7]

In a footnote, Wilks added that he had been told by two of Tipu's secretaries that the sultan had intended the name of the new city to mean 'the place visited by the eye of the Almighty'.

On a recent visit to Mysore, I wondered aloud if anything was left of the incomplete fort of Nazarbad, even after its stones had ironically been used to reconstruct the seat of the Wodeyars.

'Oh, yes,' my father said casually, 'there's a bit of the old wall left near the Van Ingen bungalow.'

I could not believe my ears, for I had passed that bungalow a thousand times as a child, stopping to pet the old horse that often came up to the gate and sniffed at my outstretched hand. When we drove there later that day, I found that a section of the fort wall does indeed survive, rising along an incline and separating the Van Ingen residence from the family's long-closed factory next door, where they had carried out the odoriferous task of taxidermy after the maharaja's hunts. Perhaps at some other time I would have found the old factory (and all it evoked) deeply fascinating, but the crumbling fort wall took precedence, for its few remaining mighty stones are all that remain of Tipu's jealous dream, so vain and bloody in its execution that he destroyed all that lay in his path before starting afresh. I left with a sense of amazement that I had spent so many years blithely kicking stones past historic fortifications and playing hopscotch on the steps of an old maidan mansion that, I now realized, stands on the site of the sultan's imagined palace. Perhaps anything erected in that space was ill-fated; for Chamundi Vihar, the mansion later built for the yuvaraja, has been in a state of advanced dilapidation for as long as I can remember, with cattle lowing mournfully in its grounds and village children playing, as I did, on its steps. The eye of the Almighty, it appears, has been averted from Nazarbad ever since Tipu was so brash as to demand its undivided attention more than two centuries ago.

Other parts of Mysore still thrive, however, particularly the palace precinct at the heart of town. The marvellous palace of the Wodeyars is reasonably well maintained, perhaps by divine favour but more likely on account of its high visibility and value as a tourist magnet. Rebuilt more than once on the ruins of the dwelling that Tipu destroyed, Amba Vilas Palace quite overwhelmed me as a child. The building was simply too wide and too tall for a little girl to take it all in while sitting on the front bar of a bicycle and being squashed by the rider as he zigzagged through the bazaar. Only when I revisited Mysore as an adult did the full Indo-Saracenic splendour of the onion-domed pile become apparent. The Amba Vilas, I realized, is relatively modern, as the palace rebuilt for the reinstated Wodeyars was destroyed by fire in 1897.[8]

Unlike its predecessor, which had been erected in a hurry and lasted less than a century, the 'new' palace, begun in 1897 and completed in 1911-12, was built to last; indeed, it has outlasted the very concept of royalty. Though no longer a functional palace, it still dominates the townscape, drawing visitors by the hundred thousand, causing the most sedate Mysoreans to catch their breath when it is illuminated on Sunday evenings, and relentlessly firing the imagination of local children. I remember pretending that our bungalow was the palace, and trundling my young cousin Yohan, shrieking for help, around it in a wheelbarrow that was supposedly the maharaja's Rolls.

The palace was designed by Henry Irwin, architect of the Connemara Public Library in Madras and the stately Viceregal Lodge in Simla. It was an emblem of its time, a magnificent and bewildering blend of architectural styles and embellishments, a whole infinitely greater than the sum of its many parts. T.P. Issar, author of *The Royal City,* wrote that its features were 'a profusion of rounded and slightly curved arches, arcuate canopies, slender-columned colonnades—some very Byzantine and some with conspicuous Hindu hoods in the Rajput style—consoled parapets, marble architraves, bay windows and a variety of foliate capitals and mouldings'.[9]

From the moment of its birth, with an extravagant fairy-tale design and great durbar hall, Amba Vilas Palace became one of the most daring and romantic of Mysore's images, and received bouquets and brickbats alike—people either loved it or hated it. It was not surprising that the palace evoked strong reactions; it was impossible to be indifferent to a structure possessed of such amazing self-assurance, such a marked refusal to apologize for its flamboyantly hybrid origins.

'Whatever the school or schools represented,' wrote Constance Parsons, who thought the palace one of the loveliest new buildings in India, 'the result is admirable . . . Domes, walls, floors, balustrades, pillars, cornices, pierced screens—whether of red, black or grey granite, of porphyry, of grey-green soap stone, of blue pot stone, of pale flesh-coloured feldspar, of green and white marble or of black hornblende—all are inexpressibly lovely.' Countering some of the Western criticism that was levied at the new palace, she added in an indignant footnote,

> It is true that there have been Westerners so insular that they judge the palace by Western standards only: who are blind to the beauty of the Oriental massing of rich colours which, tawdry as they might look in a villa in Tooting, are pure and beautiful in the translucent air of India: men who feebly rant of it as 'the most painfully inartistic building in the world', who superciliously condemn silver, ivory and rosewood as material for doors. To men so narrow, so unable to see and appreciate beauty, one is tempted to offer Turner's oft-quoted retort to the woman 'who had never seen such sunsets as he painted'. 'No Madam, I am sure you never have, but don't you wish you could!'[10]

To me, and to most others who had lived in Mysore for any length of time, the palace—we spoke of it as if it were the only one in the world—was simply ours, and being ours, its sheer magnificence took precedence over its defects. The building belonged to us as much as we belonged to the town, and it still attracts swarms of visitors during the October festival of Dasara, which celebrates the victory of good over evil.

It was at this time of the year that people used to gather by the thousand to watch the ceremonial procession of the maharaja through the city on elephant-back, in a howdah covered with beaten gold— now on display inside the palace.[11] Those of the older generation, having witnessed this annual ritual in its original splendour, have assured me that today's procession is much watered-down.

'It's a *travesty* of what it used to be,' said Aunt Margaret. 'You should have seen the attention to detail: all those rituals for the state elephant, and for the pure white horse, all those carriages and chariots taken out especially for the day. The trappings—the caparisoned elephants with huge embroidered cloths over them, and the beautiful uniforms of the palace guards . . . those same old things are worn even today, but it all looks so faded, so jaded. It's a sad reminder of the glory that was. And it's not only appearances—in those days the procession was not just grand, it had *meaning*. The maharaja was considered the provider, you see, so people came from the villages to pay homage, some in the belief that if they saw him, the rains would be good that year. It was such an event that army contingencies attended, and people came from all over the world. Respect was shown to the state of Mysore.' She paused for a while, thinking, no doubt, of dignity past. 'Take England now. The monarchy has no power there, either, but they haven't lost their sense of history. Here, after the maharaja died, it all petered out. Earlier, the people of Mysore would all come out and line the streets for the procession; now I can't even bear to look at it. Nobody's bothered about the past, you know, we have such a poor sense of history. Everybody's busy galloping into the future. I can't understand how you can advertise something all over India, call it the "grand Mysore procession", and hold such a ragged event. About the only sensible thing about it is that they carry an image of Chamundeshvari on the elephant instead of putting somebody else there in the maharaja's place.'

What I did remember about October—as no one deemed it worthwhile to take me to the procession—was the annual Dasara 'exhibition', erected on the bed of an erstwhile lake once famous for its reflection of the palace amid the beautiful flame, casuarina and eucalyptus trees that lined it. The city must still regard the exhibition with mixed feelings; children look forward to it for months with unholy glee while their parents dread it with equal intensity, knowing they will be called upon to spend at least one evening in the overexcited company of their offspring at this ultimate celebration of kitsch and gaudiness. Year after year I dragged my aunt there, clinging to her arm like a limpet while we wandered from popcorn and cotton-candy stalls to giant wheels and merry-go-rounds. The air was thick with sensations: the hot, strong smell of butter-brushed corn and the irresistible aroma of roasting gram; the high-pitched inveigling cries of vendors as you walked past their wares in pretended disdain; the clouds of dust that rose from the feet of those gathered to watch the great wheel as it moved its half-crazed cargo of children around in the sky. I always refused to go home until well past nine o'clock, for even though my stomach churned from the unaccustomed snacks and nauseating rides, there was always more to be seen and done. However late it was, I insisted on popping into the large tent that housed bearded ladies, hideous contortionists who could twist their bodies into impossible shapes, and people with more than their fair share of arms and legs. Then, eyes falling out of my head, I would agree that it was probably time to go, and my aunt would send up a silent prayer of thanks that such entertainment came to town but once a year.

Chamundi *betta*, the hill that provided the backdrop to the Doddakere maidan—and indeed to the rest of the old city—was a highly evocative sight, for it was saturated with associations of Mysore's early history as well as the colonial era. Of this long, flat ridge that was haunted by tourists in the day and jackals at night, Parsons wrote,

> Mysore owes so much of her loveliness to her tutelary hill that the first sight of her great isolated granitoid mass causes the returning Mysorean more than a little thrill; the last backward look, as he leaves her, a little stab of pain. Cloud-capped at dawn, rose-flushed at sunset, star-spangled with her 'torrent of gems from the sky' through the night; her mountain sides, green and gold and grey, Chamundi, as a background to the city she guards, is perfectly and perpetually satisfying.

The 'little stab of pain' was familiar enough. I had even felt it as far from home as the Persian Gulf, for while visiting my mother there in the nineties, we had driven into the oasis town of Al Ain and seen a great craggy mass overlooking it—an arid but unmistakable desert twin to the hill I knew so well. There are two ways to reach Chamundi's summit: walk up the thousand steps that lead to the Chamundeshvari temple, or drive up a narrow, winding road. In days gone by, royalty and viceroyalty were carried up the hill by *dhooly* (shaded litter) or taken up on elephant-back; Parsons wrote that either way it was a 'long, hot and tiring expedition'. One lady of high birth, she continued, described it thus:

> After lunch we went to the top of a very high hill, which I ascended in a *jhampan* [another type of carried chair], borne by 12 men, who chanted as they went up the thousand steps; it was a wild sort of song, which sounded very inspiriting. D—— rode up the other side of the hill and we met at the top, where we admired the view of the country, and a fine specimen of a Hindu temple which crowns the hill . . . our descent was very fatiguing, as the thousand steps were very slippery.[12]

A penchant for getting to the top of the hill was passed down the generations among the British—Hugh Warren had driven me up countless times—and was now continued cheerfully by college students, judging by the number of motorbikes now parked along the hairpin bends and the empty beer bottles strewn about.

The gopuram of the Chamundeshvari temple, built to honour the goddess who slew the demon Mahishasura, stands atop Chamundi and can be seen for miles around. A huge and terrible statue of Mahishasura stands near the temple, and while people tend to dismiss it as vulgar and unnecessary, I have to say that it made me quake when I was younger, and to regard the top of the hill with superstitious dread. Although the temple tower was built fairly recently—by Krishnaraja Wodeyar III in 1826—the temple itself is very old, dating from the eleventh century. Before the existing tower was built, another had been erected by Chamaraj, who is said to have been struck by lightning while worshipping here in 1573, and to have escaped miraculously—except that he lost all his hair in the bargain, and earned the title 'Bola'. A little way down the hill, along a road that leads off from Rice Circle, is a massive stone Nandi, or sacred bull, said to be more than three hundred years old. It is said that if you stoop to walk through a stone passage under the bull's bended knee, your wishes will come true.

As a child I was fascinated by the Nandi, but what actually attracted me most about Chamundi hill was the stately Rajendra Vilas palace on its crest, built in 1938 to replace a similar building dating from 1822. The palace was eventually converted into a hotel—one of many that rested in my grandfather's care, for hotel management had been his last task for the royal family. I used to love going there with him, and playing on the grounds under the supervision of an aged and turbaned bearer. Sadly, the hotel no longer functions and the palace is not open to view; indeed, on a recent drive I was dismayed to find the great iron gates locked and the garden half reclaimed by the surrounding scrub. I was reminded for a moment of the fairy-tale trees in the castle grounds in *Rip Van Winkle*.

There is much about Chamundi, however, that has not changed— the dark, forested slopes slipping gently down into the night, the shimmering pinpricks that illuminate the town below, and the lights in the windows and along the broad pavilion of the Lalita Mahal in the distance. Lalita Mahal is a splendid white mansion, built in 1931 in the classical style for the comfort of the maharaja's European guests. Standing at the edge of the city on a low ridge, the mahal has a perfectly proportioned exterior and a plush interior with a glorious staircase made of Venetian marble. Philip Davies, in *Splendours of the Raj*, observed that the Lalita Mahal is 'nothing less than a bold attempt to transpose St. Paul's Cathedral to a South Indian setting'.[13]

One must refrain, however, from taking this remark to heart, for the soul of Mysore and the spirit of its builder-kings are complex. The city, while technically part of south India, is yet far removed from it in a way that is not readily understood. Suffice it to say that the Lalita

Mahal's classical lines might well be out of place amid the paddy fields of the deep South or the laterite extrusions of the west coast, but in Mysore, they belong: and in the 1930s the city's social calendar was full to the brim with both European and Indian affairs. There is, to my mind, no pleasure quite as sharp as the first sight of this mansion; it is always startling, cool and milky against the warm, red Mysore soil and the deep-green hill that towers to its south. The view from the palace was once lovely, across the small valley between the city and the hill, but today houses spring up like mushrooms in the night.

Standing on Chamundi that night, I was prompted by a slight drizzle and a flirtatious breeze to notice that the weather was typically pleasant. At an altitude of 2500 feet, Mysore was undoubtedly a comfortable place for the British to visit, for even at the height of summer it was not nearly as stifling as other southern cities. Constance Parsons had written most evocatively of the seasons here:

> Her weather from November to the end of February is calm, clear, cold and sunny. March, April and May are hot months, tempered by thunder showers and hail storms; heavy rains (usually at night and never all day long) are followed by glorious weather in August and September. Then come the tank-filling downpours of October, heavy but intermittent, glorious cloud-masses and perfectly wonderful sunsets. Indeed, the translucent delicate colouring of earth and sky, at dawn and sundown, and especially of the 'afterglow', in the winter months are inexpressibly lovely.[14]

Looking out towards our old bungalows, just visible from where I stood, I recalled the most spectacular storm I had ever witnessed in Mysore. All evening the wind had blown mercilessly and then the hail began, with stones the size of golf balls crashing into the tiles. In the garden, the plants were beaten to the ground, and creepers torn off the walls; guavas and pomegranates fell from the boughs before their time; dogs and cats cowered, wet and miserable, under the kitchen stove and near the great brass boiler in the bathroom. The thunder grew louder and louder and I lay under several layers of quilts, pulling them over my head to shut out the relentless sound of the rain. When I awoke, it was to such a morning as I had never seen before—a morning when my grandfather did not sit as usual in the drawing room, hunched over his newspaper, but stood at the front door and silently looked at the garden, or what was left of it. It was like a lake on the boil, with more than a foot of bubbling, swirling, brown-and-white flood water. The bund had burst during the night, and storm water from the maidan was flowing fiercely across the road into the bungalows on our side, leaving each family marooned in an inundated compound. Although we had to struggle to revive the garden after the water had been drained through a hole in the compound wall—and it was a sorry sight for weeks thereafter—the 'flood' was followed by several blissful days of pretty purple-and-white weather, with gentle night showers that seemed to apologize for the dreadful fit of temper that had gone before.

It was heartwarming to be back on Chamundi's familiar rise, thinking old forgotten thoughts, and seeing in the distance some of the old Mysore haunts. I associated these places strongly with Hugh Warren and his old Fiat, for he would take me out on a drive every other evening to keep me amused. One of our favourite places was Karanji Kere, a picturesque lake that was really little more than a pond but made up for its diminutive dimensions with sheer character. In the seventies there were always a couple of boats moored there, and we would take one gingerly out on to the delicately rippled water, manoeuvring through clumps of lotus and water hyacinth until we reached the middle. There we would stop rowing, and examine the water spiders and other long-legged insects skimming lightly along the surface. In time, this lake became part of the neighbouring zoo, and that was probably a good thing; it was saved from becoming a 'tourist' spot, and its bottom is yet uncluttered with plastic or other debris.

Another place Uncle Hugh and I haunted was the Boulevard, along which can still be found some of the prettiest and best-preserved bungalows in all of Anglo-India. From the headquarters of the mounted police (originally built for the maharaja's bodyguard) and the race-club buildings to the smaller but equally delightful bungalows built in the early twentieth century to house English jockeys and palace officials, all the buildings on the Boulevard—with only one or two modern exceptions—celebrate that old Anglo-Indian style of architecture of which so little evidence now remains. Gabled porches, carved green woodwork, red tiles faded to a delicate hue, and above all the distinctive 'monkey-top' windows are laid out almost uninterrupted along this stretch of road, freezing the cuckoo clocks and plunging you deep into India's colonial past.

Descending from the hill and driving along the Boulevard, I thought of Mysore's other distinctive, somewhat narrower streets: the traditional agraharas, rows of neat, modest houses that originally took their name from the villages that royalty assigned to Brahmins for their maintenance. Agraharas in the modern sense are planned neighbourhoods within the town limits. Several of those built in the late nineteenth century still bear names such as Cheluvamba and Lingamba, Laxmivilas and Ramvilas. I was more than familiar with the ins and outs of the local agrahara, for there was one such row of houses just behind our bungalow, with a typical long, shared veranda from which each doorway led to a private inner courtyard. Many of my friends lived in these compact dwellings, so I spent a good bit of time playing on that common veranda, writing on old slates with bits of *balpa* or chalk, or tearing splinters off the firewood that was often stacked outside each door. Sometimes, as on our backstreet, the row of houses was the frontage of a poorer neighbourhood, and into these even narrower streets I occasionally wandered in search of our cook, who would welcome me warmly into her house and bid me eat a ball of ragi served with thin vegetable curry. It was fascinating to fritter away an afternoon there, to watch the cycle-man pump air into his antediluvian bicycle tyres, or the butcher whack his axe down on a carcass placed lovingly upon a huge round slab of wood while puppies fought at his feet for the scraps, or to buy a fistful of peppermints from the tiny shop at the corner.

I remember, on such an evening in the late seventies, joining a pair of Nazarbad children as they sat on the bund and threw sticks and stones into the stream, talking nineteen to the dozen in two languages. One was a plump, pretty Hindu girl from the agrahara, who spoke the loud and colourful local Kannada; the second a delicate, fine-boned Muslim girl who lived next door and preferred her native Urdu. They smiled tolerantly when I arrived, for I was younger than they were and not quite fluent in either language, but managed with an English insertion when words or grammar failed me. It did not strike any of us, of course, as the sun came down on our little cluster of heads, that we were a living representation of the many ingredients that had gone into the making of our town—that in us and in our descendants, something of Mysore's character would live on despite the slow, steady crumbling that set in when the maharaja's day was done.

Notes

1. Quoted in Constance E. Parsons, *Mysore City* (Oxford University Press, 1930), p. 20.
2. Mark Wilks, *History of Mysore* (1810; reprint, New Delhi: Asian Educational Services, 1989), vol. II, p. 774 (footnote).
3. Sayyaji Rao was a ruler of Baroda, from a royal family that was closely connected to the Mysore Wodeyars.
4. Thomas de Havilland also designed the beautiful, large-domed St. Andrew's Kirk in Madras.
5. Parsons, pp. 15-16.
6. Francis Buchanan, *A Journey from Madras through the Countries of Mysore,*

Canara, and Malabar (1807; reprint, New Delhi: Asian Educational Services, 1999), vol. I, pp. 67-68.
7. Wilks, vol. II, p. 312.
8. The original Amba Vilas Palace was built in the Hindu style, with a painted front supported by carved pillars. The *amba vilas* itself was an upper-storey room in which the maharaja received European guests and did his day-to-day business.
9. T.P. Issar, *The Royal City* (Bangalore: Mytec Ltd, 1991), p. 24.
10. Parsons, pp. 22-23.
11. *Hobson-Jobson* has a wonderful entry for 'Howdah (vulg. Howder)': 'A popular rhyme which was applied in India successively to Warren Hastings' escape from Benares in 1781, and to Col. Monson's retreat from Malwa in 1804, and which was perhaps much older than either, runs:

> *Ghore par hauda, hathì par jìn*
> *Jaldi bhag gaya Waren Hastìn / Kornail Munsìn!*

Which may be rendered, with some anachronism in expression:

> Horse with howdahs, and elephants saddled
> Off helter skelter the Sahibs skedaddled.'

12. Parsons, pp. 44-45.
13. Philip Davies, *Splendours of the Raj: British Architecture in India, 1660–1947* (London: Penguin, 1987).
14. Parsons, pp. 7-8.

Bangalore
The Vanishing Cantonment

If, as a little boy in the 1920s, I had been asked what I was, I would have said I was English. Everything in Bangalore, the British cantonment on the Deccan, the south Indian plateau where I was born, served to make me feel so. The weather, especially in December, was cool and often wet and misty, transporting me in mind to the England that I used to read about in the book I invariably got for Christmas. I thought and spoke in English, as did everyone else in our essentially Anglo-Indian town. My dress and habits were western, and my education, perceptions and loyalties British, as was, indeed, the entire cantonment atmosphere of the time. The notion that I might have been Indian never entered my mind . . .

—Eric Stracey, *Growing up in Anglo-India*

Although my family lived in Mysore until the early eighties, we always felt an intimate connection with Bangalore, the larger city eighty-seven miles away and more than five hundred feet higher. It could be reached either by a road so familiar that we knew the streams and fields between every milestone, or by a slow, sedate train drawn by steam engine along a metre-gauge track. One of my earliest and most powerful memories is that of watching a colossal, soot-encrusted engine belching smoke as it pulled the Bangalore train out of the quaint little Mysore station.

Our familiarity with the city at the other end of the narrow track, flanked on either side by tall fields of sugarcane and flat green paddy, was several generations old. My grandmother's family had lived there at various points of time in the colonial era, as church registers and tombstones testify, and members of my grandfather's clan had made their way there from various towns on the west coast, abandoning its scenic delights for the cosmopolitan advantages of the British cantonment. Indeed, Bangalore had an almost magnetic effect on south India's Europeans, Anglo-Indians, and Indian Christians, no doubt because of its decidedly Western orientation and its educational infrastructure. My father, for instance, was sent to Bishop Cotton's School—a premier Protestant institution modelled as a British public school, where the headmaster and many of the staff were British nationals well past 1947—as soon as he was old enough to board. In fact, the entire cantonment, the sprawling military station established in the early nineteenth century, retained a good measure of its British character long after the British had left, and was for many a place of comfort and refuge—a reserve of sorts, where something of the old way of life could still be found. When my grandfather retired from service in Mysore, and we of the bungalow at last fell to contemplating change, it was logical that we moved to Bangalore cantonment, as my father had already lived and worked there for some years, revelling in the shirtsleeves weather and the feeling of cultural affinity.

At the age of eight, I thus found myself transplanted into the Hutchins and Wheeler Road area, where a grid of narrow streets formed a vivacious stronghold of middle-class Anglo-India. The families here had Indian, British, and Portuguese blood, and nurtured lifestyles that reflected all three in various degrees. Here, to my surprise, everyone spoke English, ate all kinds of meat including beef and pork, wore only Western clothes in public, and had great-aunts who taught the piano. My grandfather fitted in perfectly, being inclined to wear a grey suit, complete with hat and cravat, even to go down the road to post a letter, and to stroll eccentrically down the middle of the street with no regard for the occasional vehicle that veered into the gutter to avoid him. Although local habits were Western, there was a markedly Indian warmth to everything, and it took us no time at all to make friends and be adopted by several kind neighbours. Far from feeling like an insignificant cog in the wheel in this new, much larger neighbourhood, I soon found myself playing cricket in the street, setting up make-believe houses and shops in shady corners of other people's gardens, and raiding the gooseberry and guava trees of the larger bungalows. Sunday lunch could be had at anybody's table, for the lines between family and friends were often blurred. I hardly realized that people from other parts of the country thought Bangalore cantonment slow and somnambulistic; for me, it brimmed with life and activity. There was no pleasure greater than cycling wildly with half a dozen others down the sloping streets of Cooke Town and Fraser Town, and occasionally into the forbidden market in Cox Town where there was real traffic, shrieking as we swerved and wobbled past rickety, front-engine auto-rickshaws manned by sour old men from Russell Market. We were joined by goats being driven unwillingly to the slaughterhouse on nearby Pottery Road, Iranian students with deliberately loud motorbikes and pointed patent-leather boots, and pretty Anglo-Indian girls taking the air in dresses cut faithfully to pre-Independence fashions.

Catapulted into this environment from the Mysore of the seventies, where I believe the very concepts of quietness and retirement were invented, I found Bangalore gay and sophisticated, if not downright bohemian. It soon became home and has remained so ever since, though two decades have passed since I actually lived there. Today one rarely hears any such accusation of quietness levelled at Bangalore, for at three thousand feet above the sea, on the great hard rock of the

Deccan, it has become, for such an altitude, an unexpectedly large and commercially inclined metropolis. Unbeknownst to many, this new identity owes much to the British military base that dominated the area for 150 years.

Bangalore's old mud fort, built by the chieftain Kempegowda in the mid-sixteenth century, prospered and grew into an important military centre in the eighteenth century under Hyder Ali. It was rebuilt with strong masonry, some of which still survives in the crowded City Market area, though one is apt, in the general confusion and congestion, to miss it altogether. In 1791, during the second Anglo-Mysore War, Lord Cornwallis and his army marched to Bangalore and occupied the fort, which was

> of nearly oval form, with round towers at proper intervals and five powerful cavaliers: a faussebray, a good ditch and covered way without palisades, and some well finished places of arms . . . There were two gateways, one named the Mysoor, the other the Delhi gate . . . the petta or town, of a great extent to the north of the fort, was surrounded by an indifferent rampart and an excellent ditch, with an intermediate berm, if such it may be called, of near one hundred yards wide, planted with impenetrable and well grown thorns.[1]

Into this place—from which the local population had quickly removed their valuables—marched the men and their commander, and within it they saw, according to Wilks, 'bales of cotton and cloth in every direction' that 'indicated a great manufacturing town'.[2] The effect of a large occupying army and its animals must have been disastrous, but after Cornwallis moved on five days later, the fortunes of the fort dipped even lower, and the last decade of the eighteenth century brought more misery upon Bangalore and its inhabitants. Tipu, who had already cut commercial ties with Arcot and Hyderabad—states he disliked—lured the inhabitants back after Cornwallis left. Before long, however, he accused them of having been 'friendly' towards the British, surrounded Bangalore with troops and proceeded to exploit the town ruthlessly, making the women part with 'their most trifling ornaments'.

Francis Buchanan, who passed through in June 1800, saw a town that was limping back to normal after the nightmare of the 1790s. Then, he wrote,

> The inhabitants, not knowing whom to trust, immediately dispersed, and for some months the place continued deserted. The people, however, are now flocking to it from all quarters; and although there are few rich individuals, trade and manufactures increase apace; and the imports and exports are estimated to already amount to one fourth of what they were in its most flourishing state. The manufacturers and petty traders are still very distrustful and timid; but the merchants, many of whom have been at Madras, and are acquainted with British policy, seem to have the utmost confidence in the protection of our government.[3]

Here, after the Mysore wars at last concluded with the siege of Srirangapattana in 1799, arose a military cantonment that would later hear, along its regular streets, the very heartbeat of Anglo-India. Although Marquis Wellesley is said to have opposed the idea of shifting troops from the island, it was only a matter of time before this became a necessity, as the malarial swamps of Srirangapattana posed a severe health hazard. Bangalore, with its cool temperatures and relatively healthy environs, was judged the best alternative. The construction of the cantonment had an undoubtedly positive effect on law and order, on commerce, which had dwindled in the preceding decades, and most of all on the general townscape, which took on a decidedly picturesque aspect. Military precision and uniformity were tempered with soft, warm, residential architecture and plenty of greenery.

When they first arrived, the troops were stationed in the fort, which quarter they must have found exceedingly disagreeable. More than five years before they descended on the fort that had been rebuilt by Hyder 'after the best fashion of Mussulman architecture', Buchanan had walked through it on a typically 'cool and pleasant morning' and found not much more than ruins: '[The fort] was destroyed by [Hyder's] son, after he found how little it was fitted to resist British valour . . . In the centre of the fort are still visible the ruins of the mud wall that surrounded the small village which occupied the place before Hyder founded the city.'[4]

The British were quick to express the need for new barracks; this was not a good enough place to house large numbers of troops. The maharaja of Mysore, with whom they had negotiated the shift, agreed to give them land, and by 1809 space was found for all the Srirangapattana troops. The cantonment was born, and over the decades it was beautifully laid out. By the end of the nineteenth century it had grown into a sizeable settlement, bounded (very roughly) on the north by Benson Town, on the east by the still-functioning Isolation Hospital, where my grandmother's brother died of smallpox as a child, on the west by the racecourse, and on the south by an area that extended well across the Sarjapur road.[5] The Indo-Saracenic style so popular in other parts of India did not take root here; the classical European building was preferred, flanked coyly by that most British of creations, the bungalow. The cantonment was extremely handsome, and it is nothing short of tragic that, just two hundred years later, only a fraction of its architecture survives.

There was, of course, a military air to everything. The streets bore—and still bear—names such as Infantry Road and Cavalry Road, and there were barracks, lines, messes, officers' quarters, and a large parade ground that remains the cantonment area's nerve centre. Of all the thousands of Europeans who passed through here, and of the many who recalled it in their memoirs, none achieved a fraction of the fame that would come to Winston Churchill, who lived in Bangalore in 1896 with the 4th Hussars. He described the lifestyle of a young

British officer's life with characteristic colour, writing that officers were not provided accommodation by the army; instead, they were given an allowance

> which together with their pay and incidentals fills each month with silver rupees a string net bag as big as a prize turnip. All around the cavalry Mess lies a suburb of roomy one-storeyed bungalows standing in their own walled grounds and gardens. The subaltern receives his bag of silver at the end of each month of duty, canters home with it to his bungalow, throws it to his beaming butler, and in theory has no further material cares.

In a Cavalry regiment, Churchill wrote, it was a better idea to supplement 'the generous rewards of the Queen Empress' with an allowance from home that was three or four times as much; as he must have been able to do easily, belonging as he did to one of England's more distinguished families. Throwing in his resources with those of two others, Barnes and Baring, Churchill proceeded to elevate himself from the hoi polloi by renting

> a palatial bungalow, all pink and white, with heavy tiled roof and deep verandahs sustained by white plaster columns, wreathed in purple bougainvillaea. It stood in a compound or ground of perhaps two acres...We built a large tiled barn with mud walls, containing stabling for thirty horses and ponies. Our three butlers formed a triumvirate in which no internal dissensions ever appeared. We paid an equal contribution into the pot; and thus freed from mundane cares, devoted ourselves to the serious purpose of life. This was expressed in one word—polo.[6]

Driving through the old cantonment, you might still chance upon a red-tiled, warm-walled bungalow or two; a few such houses remain near Cantonment Station, some near Richards Park, and a handful more scattered across the 'towns'. A year ago, when I accompanied an aunt to an appointment on Halls Road, I volunteered to sit in the car while she attended to her business, for the sheer pleasure of parking under a tree for half an hour and looking over the wooden gate at an old bungalow set back from the road in a tidy garden. Memories of my childhood flowed back unfettered, and I revelled in the gracious lines and wooden gables that have now become so rare. People seeing Bangalore for the first time must find it hard to imagine that the whole cantonment was once dominated by this charming style. With the scores of flashy new buildings that have come up in the last twenty years, and the unfortunate amount of vehicle pollution in the air, the fragrances that wafted lazily through the colony of old have been all but obliterated—yet in this little residential pocket where the past struggled to the surface, I was touched to find that they were still there: the faint scent of roses from the yard, the heady, half-fermented smell of sun-ripened fruit, the pleasant sensations given off by damp earth in a newly watered flowerbed, the passing aroma of meat being cooked on a slow fire in a kitchen at the back of the house, and the occasional scent of soapsuds and the thwack of clothes on an old-fashioned outdoor washing stone.

The odours of poverty sometimes intruded on this pleasant domesticity, particularly from the nearby slaughterhouse area with its open drains. Historically, every upper-class neighbourhood in the cantonment had given rise to a poorer quarter close by, where the maids, watchmen, gardeners and vendors lived. Eric Stracey, a resident of Richmond Town in the pre-Independence period, described the divisions between the residential areas intended for the gentry and those for their servants and the poor:

> Bangalore had its own segregated areas. There was usually a servants quarter or 'patch', our abbreviation of 'patcherry', the nearest we got to the Tamil word parr-cheri (pariah locality). Richmond Town had two such patches, one named

Akithimmanahalli and the other Pudhuparrcherry. They backed on to open fields and consisted of huddles of mean houses in which our servants and others of their class lived. These were mostly lower-caste Tamilians, Christian converts descended from the camp-followers of the Company's army who had settled locally after the Mysore wars.[7]

The residential areas that developed within the cantonment (which was also called 'Laskar' Town[8]) were called 'towns', and even today bear British names such as Langford, Fraser, Richmond and Benson. Their large bungalows were set in generous gardens, and the townscape was dotted with tastefully designed parks, churches, clubs, schools and shopping areas. One of these establishments, the Bangalore United Services Club, still functions as the 'Bangalore Club', and its pillars, verandas and simple but elegant proportions constitute an excellent example of the architecture that was popular in the mid-nineteenth century. It was at this originally white male preserve that Churchill left an unpaid 'due' of thirteen rupees, which the club eventually wrote off as irrecoverable. By the twentieth century, the cantonment was so distinct from the rest of the city that it might as well have been another world, separated by a wide strip of land that eventually became, according to Eric Stracey,

> a wide belt of undulating green that in my time was a place of parks, lakes, orchards, golf courses and playing fields, interspersed with a few handsome official residences and public buildings. Here were the library, museum, courts and secretariat, mostly built in Greek classical style, as also the more modern Residency and Flagstaff house. Here too was the Raja's Bangalore palace, a handsome building which he rarely used, for he normally lived at Mysore, his state capital. Near by were the extensive palace orchards that have long since been sold and are now an elite, private residential area. This green belt,

which fortunately remains largely untouched even today, also served the cantonment as a cordon sanitaire against any contagion, especially political, emanating from the congested city and its nationalist-minded population.[9]

The old fort area had been kept at arm's length from the new military settlement from the very beginning, and the results of this insularity were visible long after Independence, when the 'Bangalore Civil and Military Station' was given to the Indian government. For almost two centuries there had been a razor-sharp distinction between the cantonment and the 'city', or old Bangalore, and although people were now free to live wherever they pleased, the Western-influenced population still chose to inhabit the cantonment while the more orthodox Hindus occupied the huge extensions of the city. As late as the early 1980s, I found that life on one side of the line was entirely different from life on the other. Though my heart belonged in the cantonment, I spent most of my time with my mother, one of the few cantonment-type people who had chosen to live in a city-type neighbourhood. Here my friends were different, my schoolmates were strange, and the language spoken was usually Kannada. Some of our neighbours were friendly enough, but others were downright hostile and watched our activities with a mixture of curiosity and suspicion. I was virtually adopted by a Mrs Urs, who encouraged me to play with her three children in their neat yard, flattened with a mixture of earth and cow dung, and welcomed me into her home to offer me everything that was cooked in her kitchen. She even taught me a Sanskrit sloka. There was, however, another lady who disliked my associating much with her children; it was hard to forget the evening I asked her for a glass of water and then watched her, after she handed it to me reluctantly, pour the entire contents of her earthen pot over the wall, fearing I might somehow have contaminated it.

On the positive side, I learnt that there was much more to traditional culture than I had previously imagined. What I'd learnt in the backstreets of Mysore did not amount to more than a sketchy knowledge of the local language, and a consciousness that the girls of our mohalla wore skirts down to their ankles, while my frock barely reached my knees. In Bangalore city, the differences were far more obvious; all around me there was a sense of pride in being Indian, and in Indian dance and art forms. Despite having lived there for three years, and having attended a 'new' city school (unlike the old British-style schools) where the children were more likely to speak Kannada during recess than English, I found it hard to identify with the city neighbourhood west of Chord Road. In subsequent years, when I thought of Bangalore as home, it was always the Anglo-Indian neighbourhoods that came to mind. I had little cause ever to go back to the 'city'.

An amusing adult perspective on this divide comes from the writer Peter Colaco, whose family settled permanently in the cantonment in 1958, when he was thirteen. The Bangalore of this time, he wrote, had clearly defined ethnic areas:

> City referred to the orthodox Hindu area, what was once the Maharaja's Bangalore. Cantonment was the hold-out of regimental British Bangalore, English-speaking, meat-eating and supposedly delightfully wicked . . . The cultural divide from Fraser Town to Basavangudi or Jayanagar was greater than to London or New York . . .

When he once announced at home that he was going to spend the day in Jayanagar, a large city neighbourhood, 'it caused a flutter.'

> My parents were apprehensive, my younger neighbours wide-eyed with admiration. I might have been Columbus setting off on a bicycle to discover the edge of the world . . . Cantonment people used to think that the City was a distant native settlement.[10]

The people of the city were apparently no less exclusive in their attitude, for when Colaco referred to himself as an 'old Bangalorean' in his column, written almost forty years after his expedition into the city on a bicycle, a friend who had lived in Basavangudi all her life greeted his claim with amusement, and dismissed it: 'Imagine calling yourself an old Bangalorean . . . you lived in Cantonment. That's not Bangalore!' To her, wrote Colaco, the cantonment was nothing but 'an irrelevant colonial enclave'.

Though sentiments on either side of the line rose and fell, and mutual suspicion lingered for decades, Bangalore is no longer so divided. The sudden rusting and falling away of the invisible barbed wire happened in the early 1990s, when the entire city—including the cantonment—was flooded by a wave of new business from all over the country. When the waters at last stilled, citizens awoke to find that their city had changed irrevocably and its new appearance, for better or worse, was more cohesive than the old. Disoriented old-timers who searched for the familiar dividing line found it buried a mile deep, under vintage architecture that had fallen with the flood.

The old 'pensioners' paradise'—an odious but common term for the cantonment—was replaced with incredible rapidity by a lively, congested metropolis driven forward by a youthful, prosperous workforce. Some neighbourhoods became virtually unrecognizable in the space of ten years. There was a time when this metamorphosis was indigestible, when those who knew and loved the cantonment ached deeply for its disappearing quaintness and character, and refused to be impressed by the smothering trappings of progress, the mushrooming of wealthy new suburbs in every direction and the great filling out of the 'city' areas. In the late nineties, each time I went back to Bangalore, there it was: the gaping hole left by the destruction of another old building, the open, rubble-filled grave of another landmark that had vanished to create space for a glassy, unromantic high-rise. Change was, of course, inevitable, but the question of whether something might have been done to prevent it from occurring in such a barbaric manner remains unanswered. Perhaps the worst blows, to my mind, were the demolitions of scores of old bungalows and gardens in the 'towns' to make way for charmless constructions; the murder of the facades that made South Parade (now Mahatma Gandhi Road) one of the most charming streets in India; the ruthless felling of the seven-layered tiled and gabled roof of Cash Pharmacy, arguably one of the cantonment's prettiest buildings; and the destruction of Elgin Mills, whose warm-blooded red-brick architecture belonged more to a fairy castle than to an industrial compound. Many who loved these buildings shared my grief and outrage; this sort of change was akin to someone going somewhere in a hurry, knocking down a living creature on the way, and disappearing, whistling insouciantly.

In recent years, if one can forgive the senseless attrition of heritage architecture, it is possible to appreciate the stable urban identity that has developed after a period of careless growth, an identity that borrows much from the character of the old cantonment in its leaning towards the West and its taste for the good life. Today's Bangalore owes much to the liberalism that was in vogue here long before the Indian economic revolution of the early nineties. Here, globalization was not contrived; it was merely a matter of repackaging an old tradition in twenty-first-century wrapping, and allowing Westernization to spread out of the cantonment and into suburbs once known for their orthodoxy. People who move to the city, even the freshest of settlers, now tend to discard their prior identities and become Bangalorean with ease. Although there is a tendency for new Bangaloreans to behave as if they invented the city—and who can blame them, for so little is left to remind anyone of the old days—it is a pleasant and sought-after place, and people who live here for a time often find it hard to adjust to city life anywhere else in India. Their reasons are the same as those that historically drew Anglo-Indians and Indian Christians: predominance of the English language, excellent schools, relative freedom from the domination of any religious or linguistic group, and, of course, fine weather. There are new reasons as well: opportunities for employment, chiefly in the burgeoning technology sector; a government that has made genuine attempts to improve infrastructure; a lively and tolerant social structure in which background and community do not matter to a large extent; and, not least of all these, the charming custom of stopping to down a beer, even in the middle of the day.

One of the most obvious distinctions of life in modern Bangalore is its heady pub-and-club atmosphere, with dozens of such establishments in the heart of the old cantonment. New pubs open every time I visit; there seems an ever-growing need for watering holes, some tasteful and elegant, suggesting the cantonment in its heyday, but most catering expressly to the nouveau riche. However flashy these places are, there is no denying that they have their charms, including the fact that they are more laid-back than other such establishments in Bombay and Delhi, and cosmopolitan enough for women to feel comfortable without male company. Provided one does not intrude upon the cheaper, all-boy sorts of places, Bangalore's friendly barmen and waiters will happily stop and chat for a minute. People who are new to the city look upon its pub culture as a product of the nineties, but the cantonment actually had this culture for decades without bothering to give it a label. My father fondly remembers such places as Greens Bar, Tom's Billiards Parlour, and Bascoe's at the top of Brigade Road, and The Old Bull and Bush at the foot of the same street. The new places, to the eye of an old Bangalorean such as he, are crass imitations. Of these older establishments, only one is left— Dewar's Bar, which seems to have shouldered the long, bleak stagnancy of the post-Independence economy simply because it is quiet and unobtrusive, devoid of any pretension. While no new Bangalorean would be seen dead inside 'that old place', it is still an experience to fritter away time there on a lazy afternoon. Nothing about it has changed, despite the upheaval all around; it has the same cane chairs, and serves the same mutton-liver fry as it did in the old days.

Because the cantonment always had a fair sprinkling of Western-oriented restaurants, caterers and confectioners, Bangalore today has a tradition of eating out that goes well beyond the expensive and generally excellent restaurants around Mahatma Gandhi Road. Every neighbourhood has a string of restaurants, again usually very good, and their prices are reasonable. In the old days, the cantonment had Baccala's, originally an Italian-owned pastry shop that later became a caterer; The Three Aces, a wildly popular club-and-restaurant; and Koshy's, where you can still eat some of the dishes that were served decades ago. The 'city' had its famous Mavalli Tiffin Rooms near Lal Bagh, which still draws so many people at lunchtime that there are queues outside its door. Today, there are so many establishments that it's difficult to name even the best of them; suffice it to say that Bangalore is home to some of the best restaurants in India, and you could easily spend months in the city without trying them all.

The one restaurant I dearly loved, and to which I would have directed any traveller without wasting a second, no longer exists: it was appropriately called The Only Place, and was situated in a dreary compound at the bottom of Brigade Road, sandwiched between a guest house so liberal that it allowed one lady to live there with a dozen pet snakes, and Snaize Brothers, the local undertaker's. None of the existing restaurants, sophisticated though they are, could ever rustle up enough savoir-faire to serve beefsteak followed by peach pie in a tiny bougainvillea-clad bower, even as carpenters hammered nails slowly into half-finished coffins strewn about within view. The people who frequented The Only Place were characters all, from long-boned socialites with diamond earrings who fished insects gingerly out of their wine, to sad-faced Americans who lingered in the cantonment for months or even years in search of the meaning of life. There is no OP's now; yet another shopping mall has been erected in the old compound. The restaurant did resume its activities briefly in one of the mall's boring corridors, but in this new location, and with its new clientele, we all agreed it might as well have been called Pizza Hut.

The cantonment had more than its rightful share of characters. There was at one time an African-American called Gunboat Jack, who was reputed to have fought in the world heavyweight championship and who, according to my father, used to spend his later days begging on the pavement outside Bascoe's. Apparently, during the war days, when Bangalore was overrun with soldiers, Gunboat Jack was a motorcycle stunt man in an amusement park that had been set up to cater to the needs of the suddenly enlarged population. Then there was Milton Reeves, who acted in a James Bond film, which must have been something to write home about. In my own experience there was P.K. Srinivas, a journalist and intellectual of considerable repute. As a young girl had I heard my father talk about him, particularly about bumping into him regularly at a certain bar, so I was delighted when, one day in a tiny, dimly lit Chinese restaurant near Mosque Road, my father suddenly said, 'P.K.!' and shook somebody warmly by the hand. Srinivas was a quiet, soft-spoken person, heavily under the influence, but to listen to his conversation was simply delightful, and I was fortunate to have met him and to have felt that unspoken benediction for my own career when I did, for a few months later we heard that he was dead.

These, of course, were the more visible characters; there were some in every neighbourhood who added considerably to the colour of the cantonment. I recall with more than passing fondness an old man who carried about a badly framed picture of the Virgin Mary and sang hymns loudly and tunelessly down Hutchins Road every afternoon; and a young boy who was so captivated by the Michael Jackson phenomenon of the eighties that he slicked his hair down, dressed like the star, and was frequently seen leaning on a bicycle on Wheeler Road, which activity earned him the nickname Cycle Jackson.

These stories and a thousand others will linger for as long as Bangaloreans remember them and pass them on, but something of the old cantonment does exist more tangibly in its buildings, particularly in those that are preserved and maintained by the army or the church. Lovely stone constructions still grace the road to the north of the parade grounds, with St. Andrew's Kirk nestled in their midst; the old Tract and Book Society building at the top of St. Mark's

Road still stands (though it is now home to a rather loud pub); each old school and college has its share of heritage architecture; and one or two old shop fronts still await the executioner on Mahatma Gandhi Road. The prettiest church in Bangalore is arguably All Saints, a cottage-sized structure hidden away on the Hosur Road, notable for its exposed stone surfaces and the lovely angle of its roof. There are other fine churches—St. John's near Coles Park, St. Mark's Cathedral at the top of Mahatma Gandhi Road, Trinity Church at the bottom—but I am perhaps biased about All Saints, as an ancestor of mine was responsible for building it. Apart from the military property, the churches and Bangalore Palace itself, modelled along the lines of Windsor Castle but set in regrettably dusty grounds, the most glorious public building is the long, low, brick-red High Court, or Attara Kacheri, at one end of Cubbon Park. The High Court's aspect has been spoiled to some degree by Vidhana Soudha, the massive, less elegantly proportioned secretariat built across the road in 1956, still trying unsuccessfully to match the glowing lines of the older building it looks down on with envy. Attara Kacheri, beside which a rather unhygienic smoked-corn and fruit-selling area has now come up, was completed in 1868 at the instigation of Bowring, one of Bangalore's better-known commissioners. The building originally housed eighteen public offices; it was only in 1956 that these were moved to Vidhana Soudha.

Behind Attara Kacheri is a remarkable park named after Mark Cubbon, Bowring's predecessor. The green expanse was designed by Richard Sankey, chief engineer of Mysore at the time, for the precise purpose of providing a suitable setting for the court, and Bangalore remains grateful that this little bit of England has been preserved. Despite the crowds that flock to it at lunchtime and in the evening, it is a pretty and orderly place that becomes absolutely spectacular after the rains, when the road that runs through it is thickly carpeted with fallen yellow and purple blooms. One part of the park is a children's amusement area, which I remember well: it was the high point of a weekend to be taken there and allowed to ride the toy train, which took reluctant adults and beaming children through forests of bamboo, past stone elephants and little ponds and streams. I remember the first time I was encouraged to ride the train alone, without my father beside me, and the feelings of sheer panic as the train pulled away and carried me for what seemed like an eternity through this miniature world. As an adult, it is easy to notice that Cubbon Park is not as well-maintained or beautifully tended as it once was; some of its trees have been axed to make way for new buildings, and the children's park itself, though delightful to ten-year-olds, could make better use of its space. Given the tendency for open spaces to be filled with ugly concrete construction, it is a wonder that so much of the original park does remain, if not with perfection in every blade of grass. Together with Lal Bagh, Cubbon Park is almost all that remains to uphold Bangalore's old reputation as a garden city.

The Lal Bagh, a large, high-walled triangular park at one end of the cantonment, was originally two gardens, one the creation of Hyder Ali (one of three that he designed in his lifetime, the other two at Malavalli and Srirangapattana) and the other an extension laid out by Tipu Sultan. Today's combined botanical garden is a much-needed green space, home to a lake and dozens of species of plants and birds; the only defect in its design is the wall that prevents the pleasant trees from being seen while driving past. The gardens of Hyder and Tipu were once divided into square plots, separated by avenues of cypress, with Hyder's watered by a reservoir while his son's was served by three wells from which water was drawn by a pair of bullocks. Buchanan was not terribly impressed by the Lal Bagh when he visited Bangalore in 1800, for two obvious reasons: he passed through in May, when water was scarce, and in 1800, by which time Srirangapattana had fallen, and neither the British nor the maharaja had settled down enough to start attending to horticulture. 'The Mussulman fashion,' wrote Buchanan, 'is to have a separate piece of ground allotted for each kind of plant. Thus one plot is entirely filled with rose trees, another with pomegranates, and so forth. The walks are not gravelled, and the cultivation of the whole is rather slovenly; but the people say that formerly the gardens were well kept.'[11] It was the British who resuscitated the Lal Bagh—the East India Company's botanist gifted it to the Governor-General in 1819, and the garden was then looked after by the botanical gardens of Calcutta. Eventually it was returned to the Mysore administration and in 1856 it became a government botanical garden, which it remains today. Although the park's present upkeep and the pollution of its lake are matters of concern, the value of the Lal Bagh as an oxygen pocket in modern, congested Bangalore cannot be underestimated.

Much as the desecration of its architecture and the congestion of its streets still bewilder me, there is always a sense of homecoming when I return to Bangalore, for wherever my interest in travel has subsequently taken me, I have found no other city in the world to match its particular charms, and no other such concentration of like-minded people. Some aspects of the city come to mind at the oddest times, bludgeoning me in some unfamiliar place where nothing but a map connects me to reality, and all of a sudden my heart fills with a great desire to go home again: to sip a lime juice at Koshy's and listen to the conversation of college students and journalists; to watch the low, violet clouds of the monsoon roll in across the plateau in early June, transforming the hot weather overnight to something akin to Scotland in summer, and reminding me that the British used to call Bangalore a hill station; to catch my breath while driving past a park in full bloom with jacaranda and frangipani. As long as there is still a high bank of flowers on one side of South Parade, and a few bungalows left to uphold a gracious aesthetic; as long as there are old-timers to mourn the passing of the old days, yet accept the new with lightness of heart; as long as I can walk into a restaurant and order a beefsteak without batting an eyelid; and long as the night train still pulls into a little grey and green station in the chill of a Bangalore dawn, there will be reason for me, and hundreds like me, to return to the vanishing cantonment for a few decades yet.

Notes

1. Mark Wilks, *History of Mysore* (1810; reprint, New Delhi: Asian Educational Services, 1989), vol. II, pp. 430-31.
2. Wilks, pp. 433-34.
3. Francis Buchanan, *A Journey from Madras through the Countries of Mysore, Canara, and Malabar*, vol. I (1807; reprint, New Delhi: Asian Educational Services, 1999), pp. 193-94.
4. Ibid., p. 44.
5. As seen in a Survey of India map published in Maya Jayapal's *Bangalore: The Story of a City* (Chennai: East West Books, 1997), p. 53.
6. Winston Churchill, *My Early Life* (1930; reprint, Fontana Books, 1985), pp. 111-112.
7. Eric Stracey, *Growing up in Anglo-India* (Chennai: East West Books, 2000), p. 17.
8. *Hobson-Jobson* says the word is originally from the Persian *lashkar*, 'an army', 'a camp'.
9. Stracey, p. 15.
10. Peter Colaco, *Bangalore: A Century of Tales from City and Cantonment* (Bangalore: Via Media Books, 2003), pp. 56-59.
11. Buchanan, p. 46.

Along the Arabian

Padmanabhapuram

A Palace Made of Wood

[A]t the place called Travancor, where this Kingdom of Koullam terminates, there begins another Kingdom, taking its name from this very Travancor, the king of which our people call the Rey Grande, because he is greater in his dominion, and in the state which he keeps, than those other princes of Malabar . . .'

—João de Barros, 1553
(quoted in Hobson-Jobson)

I awoke one morning in Thiruvananthapuram, walked to the window of the tenth-floor apartment at which I had arrived the previous night, and reeled. Below me was a sea of green, a great, rippling, rocking sea of green. The illusion created by the thickly clustered lime- and emerald-fronded coconut palms swaying in the breeze, and the uneven hilly ground on which they grew, was so powerful that it detracted from the view of the real sea, which shimmered lazily on the horizon, waiting its turn to be admired. I paid my respects to it perfunctorily, for one did not under any circumstances ignore the Arabian, but there was not a moment to be wasted. I dressed in a hurry, pulling a long red kurta over my jeans in deference to the fact that this was Kerala, and ran downstairs and up the drive.

This burst of athleticism did not meet with the approval of the watchman at the gate, who looked at me with frank disdain as I rushed past. Momentarily disconcerted, I continued to hurry, for this was the same gentleman who had spearheaded a roadside toddy party that had awakened me in the wee hours the previous night. In no time, this unsavoury person and his midnight shenanigans faded from my mind, for the day had a great deal in store.

It had always been on my wish list to go to Padmanabhapuram, capital of the rajas of Travancore, and I could scarcely believe I was now on my way there. As luck would have it, work had brought me to Thiruvananthapuram, the modern capital of Kerala, and the old seat of royalty was only fifty-odd kilometres away, an easy detour at a town called Thuckalay on the Kanyakumari road. After a week of visiting film and audio production houses, theatres and studios, the prospect of a drive into rural Kerala, and a halt at one of the most refined palaces in the world, was welcome indeed. Between meetings with various production-world personalities, I had also somewhat unwisely given myself the entire, undiluted Malayalam film experience at a local film festival, and had come to realize that both courses of action would have been infinitely more interesting had I actually been able to speak or understand Malayalam. The time had now come to spend a morning doing something peaceful in a place where I would not have to converse with anyone except the ghosts of an old royal residence.

Thiruvananthapuram is close to the tip of Kerala, this startlingly green and self-contained state, and indeed to the southernmost point of the Subcontinent: Kanyakumari, a town that belongs not to Kerala but to Tamil Nadu. Though now culturally and politically distinct, these two states share a significant part of their ancestry, having once been part of a larger kingdom. The early history of the territory we know as Kerala is not particularly well documented, for much of it is derived from the Puranas and other texts that are heavily mythological.

However, the districts of modern Kerala were definitely once part of the larger Chera territory, of which something is known from Sangam poetry[1]—the earliest surviving Tamil literature—and from archaeological evidence. The Chera kingdom was, with the Cholas and the Pandyas, one of the three ancient Dravidian kingdoms. K.A. Nilakanta Sastri, in his history of the South up to 1565, writes:

> The monarchies of the Cheras, Cholas and Pandyas were believed, at least in subsequent ages, to be of immemorial antiquity; and the poems of the Sangam attest the anxiety of all of them to connect themselves with the events of the Great War between the Kauravas and the Pandavas. The first Chera monarch we hear of, Udiyanjeral (c. AD 130) is said to have fed sumptuously both the armies of Kurukshetra, and thereby earned for himself the title 'Udiyanjeral of the great feeding'. Perhaps it is best to look upon this as a conventional attribution to him of an achievement of some remote ancestor.[2]

This kingdom of the Cheras, for which historians have been able to construct only a brief genealogy, had its capital at inland Vanchi—identified with present-day Karur—and Tamil was clearly its predominant language. Malayalam was the last of the southern languages to evolve; it grew gradually from Tamil, borrowing also from Sanskrit. Sanskrit learning was widely encouraged in Kerala; Sastri speaks of a college and hostel being set up by royal endowment for the maintenance of ninety-five Vedic students in the middle of the ninth century:

> [They] were admitted after an entrance test in Vyakarana (grammar), Mimamsa (exegetics), Paurohitya (priestcraft) and Trairajyavyavahara (Law and usage of the three countries, perhaps Pandya, Chola and Kerala). The college was to function in a Vishnu temple at Parthivasekharapuram in South Travancore,

and indeed, the many temples of the land as well as the mathas and sattras tended each in its way to become a centre of learning of the gurukula type.[3]

Thus, despite being a mountain-bound region and in some respects insular, Kerala seems to have been fairly well connected with the rest of the South. The region also had ties further afield, since the south Indian coast attracted a great deal of trade including a flourishing link with Rome from as early as the reign of Augustus. The anonymous author of the *Periplus of the Erithraean Sea* describes this trade in detail in the first century AD, mentioning the west-coast harbours of Tyndis (Ponnani), Muziris (Kodungallur), Nelcynda (near Kottayam), and Naura (Kannur) and reporting that the Romans sent vessels there to trade in pepper and malabathrum.[4]

> There are imported here, in the first place, a great quantity of coins; topaz, thin clothing, not much; figured linens, antimony, coral, crude glass, copper, tin, lead; wine, not much, but as much as at Barygaza; realgar and orpiment, and wheat enough for the sailors, for this is not dealt in by the merchants there. There is exported pepper, which is produced in quantity in only one region near these markets, a district called Cottonara. Besides this there are exported large quantities of fine pearls, ivory, silk cloth, spikenard[5] from the Ganges, malabathrum from the places in the interior, transparent stones of all kinds . . . diamonds and sapphires, and tortoise-shell . . .[6]

There are corresponding descriptions in Sangam poetry of ships coming into Muziris laden with gold in return for pepper. Apart from literary mentions, there is plentiful archaeological evidence of an early connection with the West, for large numbers of Roman gold coins have been unearthed at various places in Kerala and Tamil Nadu. There was even a Roman 'factory' at Arikamedu, south of Pondicherry.

As we drove at breakneck speed down the narrow tropical roads of Thiruvananthapuram, the car swerved past the usual early-morning pedestrians spilling untidily off the pavements. There were countless school-children running down the road with their bags strapped over their foreheads and their ageing grey socks held up by elastic bands, coy groups of college girls waiting at bus stops, men and women returning from the temple with fresh *pottu* on their forehead, and young nuns hurrying self-consciously along in drab brown habits, trying to ignore the rest of the world and not quite succeeding.

Kerala's multi-religiousness is not the product of a sudden wave of settlement, but has evolved slowly over the centuries: the ships that first skirted the northern Subcontinent to reach the palm-fringed southern coast, and in later times boldly sailed across the Arabian, carried more than just merchandise. The Jews of Cochin, now but a tiny fraction of the colony that once flourished there, believe that Jews originally came to Kerala as refugees after the destruction of the second temple of Jerusalem in the first century AD. There is no evidence for this, but it is certain from copper plates preserved in the Cochin synagogue that the Jews did arrive very early. Ravi Varman I, who ruled from AD 962 to 1020, granted one Joseph Rabban the village of Anjuvannam (near Kodungallur) and its revenue and allowed him to use a parasol and a palanquin, both of which were prerogatives of rulers. When the Moroccan traveller Ibn Battuta explored Kerala in the fourteenth century, he found a colony of Jews midway between Calicut and Kollam, which discovery he reported with disappointing blandness in his otherwise colourful chronicle:

> On the fifth day of our journey we came to Kunji-Kari, which is on top of a hill there; it is inhabited by Jews, who have one of their own number as their governor, and pay a poll tax to the sultan of Kawlam.[7]

'Kunji-Kari' refers to a stretch of water called Kanjirapuzha, east of

Chennamangalam, an old Jewish settlement near Cochin.[8] Although the tiny Jewish quarter in Cochin is a relatively modern settlement, it is still an experience to walk down the narrow street to the synagogue, built in the sixteenth century and rebuilt a hundred years later after it was destroyed by Portuguese fire. The building has an air of old dignity about it, and one cannot help mourning the near extinction of the community today: there are probably less than twenty Jews left in Kerala, most having emigrated long ago.

The Syrian Christians, a large and thriving Kerala community, claim that their ancestors were converted by St. Thomas the apostle. 'Doubting Thomas' is said to have come to India and been martyred in the neighbourhood of modern Madras. Although this remains unproven and the history of the earliest Christians in Kerala is shadowy, we know that they came as settlers from Mesopotamia between the third and ninth centuries, had their liturgical centre in Edessa, and used the East Syrian liturgy in their churches. Whatever the community's origins, its members take justifiable pride in their ancient heritage. One afternoon, in conversation with friends in Bangalore, I was asked, after I had divulged that a part of my ancestry was Keralite, whether I was a Syrian Christian.

'Oh no,' I said, hastily, 'I'm just an ordinary Christian.' This impulsive declaration was greeted with considerable amusement, and I have often thought back to it and smiled.

The age-old worship of the Syrian Christians was shaken to some extent by the Portuguese, who wanted to establish jurisdiction over them. Roman Catholicism spread along the west coast from the sixteenth century onward, most successfully in the Konkan but also in Malabar and further south. The Abbé Carré, a traveller to the west coast in the late seventeenth century, noted in his journal, with some disgust,

> I have also written of two Portuguese monks, whom I met some years ago at Cannanore on the Malabar coast. They were

> so occupied with Hindu heathen traders that in my presence they refused to help a large number of poor Christians who ran after them, begging for the Sacrament of Penance, as they had been without priests for over a year. I was so exasperated at this lack of charity . . . that I resolved to stay some days amongst them to help them and administer the Sacrament, which these monks had so unkindly refused.[9]

Today Christianity in Kerala is a bewildering mass of sects and subsects, and Christians are about one-fifth of the population.

A thriving Arab connection ensured that Islam followed in the path of early Christianity, for by the ninth century there were Muslim settlements on the Malabar coast. Today's Mapillas have their roots in this early community: their military and equestrian knowledge found favour with the local powers-that-be, and they were free to marry local women and integrate with society. This was one of the first Kerala communities I had come into contact with as a child in Mysore, for a mango-seller who visited us regularly with a head-basket full of the fruit was known universally as 'the Map'la', with scant regard for the fact that he might have had a name. By the fourteenth century, when Ibn Battuta visited India, it was clear that Islam had come to stay, for there were mosques not only in Kerala but along the entire west coast. Battuta described the road through Malabar, from Goa to Kollam, as being of two months' duration and running the whole distance:

> . . . beneath the shade of trees, and at every half mile there is a wooden shed with benches on which travelers of every kind, whether Muslims or infidels, may sit. At each shed there is a well for drinking and an infidel who is in charge of it. If the traveler is an infidel he gives him water in vessels; if he is a Muslim he pours the water into his hands.[10]

While suffering such minor discriminations, Battuta noted with something akin to gratitude that when he passed 'infidels' on the road at night, they stood aside to let him pass, and that in general Muslims were shown the 'highest consideration' in this country—except that Hindus did not allow them into their houses and did not eat with them. Food was sometimes served to Muslims on banana leaves, for if they ate from vessels, these would have to be broken or given to them to take away. When the traveller reached Mangalore, he found there a colony of four thousand Muslims, and in Calicut, he broke journey as a guest of the Hindu king. Travelling further south by river, he arrived in ten days at the port of Kollam, which he described as one of the finest towns in Malabar. Muslims, he wrote, were 'honoured and respected' there.[11]

As we left Trivandrum behind and began to negotiate the winding road to Thuckalay, fragmented memories of earlier, less solitary visits to this green sliver of a state returned. I remembered my first visit at the age of three or four, when, after a night journey by bus from Mangalore, my mother and I had arrived at Calicut in the pouring rain and visited an aunt who lived in an old house with a wooden trap door that had terrified me as I climbed up and down its old stairway. All through our stay it had rained, the coconut trees had bent this way and that, and incessant streams of water had poured off the tiles into the gutter that ran around the house. In later years there had been several drives along Kerala roads with my father, who, after having eaten an inordinate quantity of plump, masala-fried sardines for breakfast, accompanied by a generous mug of gently fermenting toddy,[12] would pull up in the afternoon and catch forty winks by the wayside. Kerala had offered many things at intervals in my youth—lazy holidays at Kovalam beach, nights passed in old ancestral houses with courtyards full of the sounds of the night, peaceful evenings by the green and brown, deathly still backwaters, visits to various friends and relations that meant a suffusion of seafood and coconut-rich sweets.

All these were pleasant enough, but I am convinced I would have enjoyed it all a great deal more had we actually lived here for any length of time. Although we had roots in Malabar—Calicut and Cannanore—the ties had been more or less severed with my grandfather's generation, and there was little sense of any real affinity. Despite its early cosmopolitanism, Kerala is a curiously closed society; Malayalis tend to leave their home state in droves in search of employment and a more worldly lifestyle, but the opposite is not true—not many people move south to settle in Kerala. In recent years there has been a great wave of tourism, particularly to the backwaters in the Allapuzha–Kottayam area and the massage experience at Varkala, and this has injected the economy with some much-needed spirit as well as softened attitudes towards outsiders; but claims to Kerala ancestry are never taken seriously unless one can break out into fluent colloquial speech.

I was reminded suddenly of my shortcomings in this direction when the driver drew my attention back to the road. With much adjustment of the rear-view mirror and caressing of his shock of springy, glistening curls, this mundu-clad gentleman informed me in an excellent, incomprehensible south Kerala drawl that we were now approaching Thuckalay. At least, that is what I assumed he said, for all I had caught, while trying not to meet his faintly flirtatious eye in the mirror, was the name of the place, pronounced with great relish in a series of prolonged and treacle-coated syllables.

Looking out at the milestones, gleaming white against the green backdrop of banana plantations, I realized we were getting very close to Padmanabhapuram. The princely state of Travancore had developed out of the historical district of Venad, which in the ninth century was one of the feudatories of the Perumal, overlord of a revived Chera territory. Tradition dates Travancore as far back as AD 311, when King Veera Kerala Varma is said to have been crowned at Veerakeralapuram, near Thiruvithamcode, the 'dwelling place of prosperity' of which the name Travancore is a corruption. The first inscriptional evidence of a Venad king, however, goes only as far back as the ninth century, mentioning an Ayyan Adikal Thiruvadikal who ruled from Kollam in

849. Literature of the thirteenth and fourteenth centuries also refers to the kings of Venad ruling from Kollam, and it is not known when exactly the seat of power shifted further south to a place called Kalkulam, later renamed Padmanabhapuram.

In the mid-sixteenth century, Travancore was evidently a power to reckon with, for the Portuguese writer Barros describes its ruler as the 'Rey Grande' (Great King), superior to all the other princes of Malabar. There is evidence that Kalkulam fort—at first a modest mud structure—was built in 1601, and that the Darpakulangara palace inside it may have been built even earlier. This complex would later come to be called Padmanabhapuram. By the early seventeenth century, however, Travancore had dwindled to a tiny, weak kingdom of no great significance. It was only in the first half of the eighteenth century that the modern princely state revived—during the reign of Marthanda Varma, arguably the greatest of the Travancore rajas.

Dasa Vanji Pala Marthanda Varma Kulasekhara Perumal—whom in the interest of the rainforests we shall continue to call Marthanda Varma—was thirteenth among the fourteen kings who ruled from Padmanabhapuram. He ascended the throne when he was very young, at a time when the shrunken kingdom was threatened both within and without. It was an environment in which he would clearly either sink or swim, and he was determined to strike for shore. What the young king inherited, according to Sir T. Madava Row, a diwan of Travancore during the British era, was 'a small territory, full of anarchy and disorder' in which, in the earlier days of his reign, 'his life was often exposed to the hand of the assassin.'[13] Yet from this disadvantageous position, the ambitious king rose to such considerable heights that Fra Bartolomeo, a Catholic priest who spent several years in Travancore, wrote of him in his *Voyages to the East Indies*:

> The kings of Travancor had hitherto been insignificant princes, whose territories extended only about fifteen or twenty miles up the country from Cape Comari; and were, besides, not very

fruitful. The sovereign of this district, at that time Vira Martanda Pala . . . was a man of great pride, courage and talents; capable of undertaking grand enterprises, and from his youth had been accustomed to warlike operations. As he had concluded an alliance with the king of Madura, it needs excite no wonder that, agreeably to his character, he should conceive the idea of making conquests and of enlarging his unproductive dominions by the acquisition of new provinces.[14]

Despite his youth and the extreme measures he had to take for his personal safety, such as travelling in disguise, Marthanda Varma succeeded in subjugating rebellion in his kingdom and bringing together all the dynasty's branches—Attingal, Nedumangad, Kottakara and Kollam—not to mention annexing the petty kingdoms around him and extending the northern boundary of Travancore as far as Cochin. In doing so, he inevitably upset the Dutch, who had established themselves on the coast between Kolachel and Cochin and viewed his rising power with suspicion. While Marthanda Varma was busy suppressing a territory called Kayemkulam, the Dutch intervened, asking him not to declare war. This request was politely declined by the raja on two occasions, after which the infuriated Dutch threatened to invade Travancore. A somewhat childish exchange followed, with the raja reminding the Dutch of the improbability of their success in such a scheme, and of the forests into which he could tantalizingly retire should they actually succeed. The Dutch, not to be outdone, threatened to follow the king wherever he went, to which the raja amicably replied that he would then consider invading Europe with his boats. That this was not so much tall talk was proved by the siege of Kayemkulam, where Dutch opposition was routed; however, their reinforcements soon landed at Kolachel from Ceylon and began to attack Travancore's coastal outposts while planning a siege of the palace at Padmanabhapuram. The raja, then at Thiruvananthapuram, rushed back to Kalkulam and organized his forces to meet the Dutch. In

August 1741 the battle of Kolachel was fought, and Travancore was clearly victorious.

In 1744, Kalkulam fort and palace were renamed Padmanabhapuram, and in 1750 Marthanda Varma dedicated his newly enlarged kingdom to Sri Padmanabha.[15] From then on, the rulers of Travancore were considered servants of this god, and ruled the kingdom in his name. As the royal family was matrilineal, the kings were succeeded by their sisters' sons, who ruled from Padmanabhapuram until the close of the eighteenth century, when they shifted the capital to Thiruvananthapuram. Commenting on Marthanda Varma's political and military achievements, Shungoonny Menon, a Travancore historian of the late nineteenth century, observed that in the course of about fifteen years, Marthanda Varma had brought under his control the whole area from Edavaye to the Periyar, releasing the people from their tyrannical overlords. Those who had been conscripted were released from military service and allowed to return to their neglected fields.

It was to the heart of Marthanda Varma's world that we were driving, speeding dangerously down the narrow, thickly populated road to Thuckalay. Roads in Kerala tend to feel as if they pass through one long village or town, and this is not an illusion, for it is one of the most densely populated states in India. Even Ibn Battuta noticed this more than seven centuries ago:

> On this road, which, as we have said, extends for a two months' march, there is not a span of ground or more but is cultivated. Every man has his own separate orchard, with his house in the middle and a wooden palisade all round it. The road runs through the orchards, and when it comes to a palisade there are wooden steps to go up by and another flight of steps down into the next orchard. So it goes on for two months. No one travels on an animal in that country, and

only the sultan possesses horses.[16]

Yet this crowded state is still picturesque, with its impossible greenery and miles upon miles of rivers and backwaters.

When we arrived, I found that Padmanabhapuram had been built in a fittingly beautiful spot, with the Veli hills rising behind it and sprawling acres of fertile, undulating land at its feet. Tall granite walls constituted the fort's outer boundary, and I remembered that these had been constructed during Marthanda Varma's reign as part of an effort to strengthen fortifications across the kingdom. Oddly enough, he had entrusted the supervision of this task to a European—Eustacious D'Lanoy, a prisoner of Flemish origin who was taken when the Dutch were defeated at the battle of Kolachel, and in whom the enemy had seen great potential. Swearing allegiance to the Travancore king, Marthanda Varma, D'Lanoy rose quickly in his favour and soon became a general and commander-in-chief of the Travancore army, then to be known as the Valia Kappithan (Great Captain). With the help of the king's able dalawah, Rama Iyen, he erected a number of defensive constructions with exemplary speed and economy. The mud fort at Padmanabhapuram was replaced by the strong granite one I saw before me; a larger fort was built at Udayagiri, where an iron foundry operated to cast cannons, mortar and balls for the army; and another went up at Aluwakaray, south-east of the temple at Kanyakumari. D'Lanoy also strengthened the skills of the existing Travancore army, which then numbered about fifty thousand troops whom he had already trained by European methods. They were armed largely with weapons procured from the English, with whom Travancore had always been very cordial, and the Dutch, with whom friendship had been once again established. The general divided these troops and placed them under the command of Europeans, Eurasians, Nayars and Pathans. The main army was cantoned in three places: Padmanabhapuram, Thiruvananthapuram and Kollam.

Despite the fortifications still evident at Padmanabhapuram, it is hard to associate the place with any sort of military activity, for its narrow streets bear a somnolent, unspoilt village air. Down this street, or one very like it, must have wearily come the good Fra Bartolomeo, who had once hastened to Padmanabhapuram on church business when Portuguese clergy had begun to impose fines on Christian fishermen, thus causing no end of trouble in their congregations. That day was nothing like the present, for in the late eighteenth century Kerala was still in the vice-like grip of the caste system.

> At Tiruvandaburam my coolies or palanquin-bearers ran away; so that I was obliged to travel twelve miles on foot on the king's high road, named Madacava, which none but the Brahmans and nobility dared to tread. As soon as I approached Padmanaburam, I repaired to a very small church on the south side of the castle; for the gates were shut, and no person belonging to the inferior casts, in which the Europeans are commonly included, was suffered to enter the city.[17]

Marthanda Varma's successor, Rama Varma, was inclined towards tolerance, for he sent for the priest the next morning and attempted to sort out the difficulty between his Christian subjects and their Portuguese priests. However, he met the priest in his secretary's house, for on that particular day he could not grant audience in his own palace for fear that it would be defiled.

I had heard a great deal about the unique aesthetic of this very Hindu palace complex, but I was still taken aback at its simplicity and elegance. At first sight, from the gate, it looked like the large and beautifully maintained mansion of a person with incredible good taste—nothing like a palace in the conventional sense. The longer I stood and stared at the complex, to which successive rulers had added more and more structures, the stronger this feeling grew, for the buildings were utterly unpretentious, yet possessed of impressive style and a certain delicacy. Many of Marthanda Varma's structures clearly bore his stamp; as Madava Row had observed,

> His benevolence was unbounded, though of course it flowed in the channels which the Hindu shastras prescribed or the Hindu public admired . . . It was that very benevolence that induced a life of frugality and abstemiousness as a means of increasing the resources to be employed in the exercise of that virtue. The Maha Rajah was far from indulging in that magnificence which is the characteristic of Courts oriental. His tastes were simple. His dress and equipages were almost primitive; his mansions displayed no great architectural splendour; and his court and all that appertained to it showed that what was useful was decidedly preferred to what was showy or gorgeous . . .[18]

Padmanabhapuram, built almost entirely of local material—wood, granite, burnt brick, laterite and lime—was, in fact, a splendid architectural representation of all that constituted the simple Kerala aesthetic. It belonged wholly to a land whose women often dressed (and still dress) in plain white cotton by choice. This simplicity of attire is the subject of much comment in the rest of the country, where white is generally considered the colour of widowhood. Even if the colour had not been questionable, it was the way the women draped their garments in Kerala. I remember having felt, as a girl in Bengal, distinctly angry one evening when my plump Bengali tutoress made the uncharitable—and no doubt faintly envious—observation that Malayali women had no 'shame'. In Malayalam films, she said, they wore white blouses with no chador or veil wrapped across the chest, even when there were men present. In other Calcutta circles, the more modest version of the Kerala costume had been much admired; people shook their heads in appreciation when my mother wore the two-piece munduneriyathu, with its simple band of colour running sharply along the border of the white fabric. As I walked down the village lane that led to the palaces of Padmanabhapuram, I felt a mild regret that my clothes were so carelessly chosen; to do justice to the palace before me, I ought to have dressed in spotless white myself.

Yet this knowledge of the Kerala aesthetic was not enough to prepare me for the shock that was Padmanabhapuram: the striking outlines of low, almost entirely blackened wooden buildings standing out in sharp silhouette against a hilly backdrop. Profusely but delicately carved, the walls of the palace complex were, in a word, humbling. Although the wood is greatly weather-beaten in some places, it cannot fail to impress the hardest of critics with its sublime elegance and its living truth as a symbol of the region's people and culture. The entrance to the complex, through which I passed unbecomingly in my jeans, was the padipura, the traditional gate of any old Kerala house. The doors were massive, and through them could be seen another doorway leading to the Poomukham—the building that housed the mantrasala, or council chamber, where the raja met with his ministers. This system of successive gateways belied the fact that Padmanabhapuram comprised a series of courtyards, enclosed either by walls or by the buildings themselves. I entered the Poomukham, noting with rising pleasure the wooden horsemen who stood there in welcome and the splendid woodwork, especially the ornamental carvings of lotus medallions. Ninety of these intricate pieces of work decorated the ceiling alone, and each was different from the other. Despite the original ornamentation in the building, the overriding impression was still one of simplicity, for the council room was comparatively small, with the ministers' wooden chairs set around a dignified wooden seat, more a gracious chair than an ostentatious throne. The arrangement suggested that this was a place for conversation rather than obsequies; in fact, the only real evidence of royalty in the complex was the massive oottupura, or dining room, nearby, which regularly seated two thousand Brahmins when they were summoned for free meals.

I lingered in the council room for a considerable length of time, examining the woodwork. The room felt cool, almost informal, and I felt extraordinarily comfortable there despite the raging heat and humidity outside. To achieve such an atmosphere of well-being in this southern coastal climate was an architectural feat in itself, for a sense of calm permeated every building in the complex. It was easy enough to associate the room with Marthanda Varma, as he once granted audience here to two ambassadors from a neighbouring state. One of them, it is said, began a lengthy harangue, and the other was prepared to continue, but the king put a quick and classic end to the proceedings.

'Be not tedious,' said he, 'for life is short.'[19]

The council chamber's design was brilliant: air and light entered the room through wooden louvres in such a way as to maintain constant temperature and perfect ventilation within. Strategically placed aromatic herbs and sandalwood sprinkled with water ensured that the room was fragrant on hot summer days. The shiny black surface on which I was standing was also soothing beneath my bare feet, and it took me a minute to realize that this was the original flooring, made from a combination of charred coconut shell, lime, egg white and vegetable extracts. I had read earlier that these ingredients had been used in the famous floor, but the quality of this workmanship was so superior and enduring that it looked like a more recent execution.

Although Padmanabhapuram appears at first glance to have been randomly designed, with each ruler having made his own contribution arbitrarily, the complex was actually built according to rules established at the very beginning. This remarkable discipline is first visible in the diminishing courtyards, which are carefully arranged to surround a fixed central point in the complex. The traditional building code is fascinating: it drew simultaneously from science, religion and the supernatural. Carpentry, as is evident in the marvellous woodwork, was extremely refined—building codes carefully specified the types of wood, the functions they served, their relative position to each other, and even who could use them, the latter depending on the person's position in traditional society.

Despite this rigid code, a distinct Chinese influence was visible in many aspects of the palace, from the quantity of wood to the tiered roofs, the Chinese throne and the thirteen beautiful martabans[20] once used by the women of the palace. This cross-cultural melding is seen all over Kerala, perhaps most famously in the Chinese fishing nets of Cochin, but more subtly in architecture. The roof of Padmanabhapuram's great dining room, for instance, is Chinese in design, built to suit a climate that involves periods of heavy rainfall as well as drought. To my eye, the style closely resembled that of both China and Indo-China. None of this was surprising, for Kerala had been engaged in trade with China, specifically for tea and spices, for centuries. It was, in fact, through Kerala that produce from China found its way to the West. Ibn Battuta encountered Chinese ambassadors in Kerala more than once in the fourteenth century:

> During my stay there [Kollam] the ambassadors from the king of China who had been with us arrived there also. They had embarked on one of the junks which was wrecked like the others [an incident that took place at Calicut while Batuta was there]. The Chinese merchants provided them with clothes and they returned to China, where I met them again later.[21]

Chinese trade was so well established that when Battuta halted at Calicut, he found no less than thirteen Chinese vessels in port. The larger ships carried a thousand men, six hundred of whom were sailors and the remainder of whom were men-at-arms. It was to Kollam, however, that most of the Chinese came, for the simple reason that it is closer to China.

As if to illustrate the local matrilineal instinct, the oldest building in the complex, the one that lies at its heart, is called the Thaikottaram.

This 'mother' palace is the original Darpakulangara Koyikkal, which translates simply to the Palace Near the Pond. Intricately carved wooden pillars support the Ekanthamandapam—the beautiful veranda that is really the pride of this particular structure—and looking along it, I felt a vague regret for the way of life long departed from this dwelling, though not, of course, from all of Kerala. The palace was built in the classic nalukettu style of a traditional house, with four sections facing an open courtyard, the nadumittam, in the middle; and even after centuries of use, it seemed to beg to be lived in again. This was really a functional house rather than a palace, for below its four bedrooms partitioned by wooden walls were a kitchen, a dining room of modest proportions, and a kulappura, or bathing room, near the pond. It was here that the Bhadrakali puja was held for a full forty-one days every winter, and I could well imagine the lively proceeding this must once have been. The image of the goddess was drawn on the ground using charcoal, rice flour and other processed ingredients, and ritual music—kalamezhuthum pattum—accompanied the worship.

Yet the oddest structure in the complex was not any of these: it was the Uppirikka Malika, which plainly translates to 'Building with Upper Stories'. In this structure, erected by Marthanda Varma, can be found more of the understated Padmanabhapuram style, but with a flight of fancy—an upward thrust that shoots out of the surrounding horizontal lines as if reaching to a higher world. And indeed it is, for the topmost floor of this tower-like pagoda is a sleeping chamber, not, as one might imagine, for the king, but for Sri Padmanabha, for it was believed that the great god reclined here every day. The pagoda rises four floors above the ground-level treasury, decorated in some places with beautifully executed murals and used by the king as living quarters. Successfully arguing my way past the caretaker to see the pagoda's upper floors, I admired the masterfully painted religious and cultural scenes and the sapramancham, the king's four-poster bed, made of sixty-seven different pieces of medicinal wood and believed to have been a gift of the Dutch East India Company. Through a window, another curious structure caught my eye—a pillar with a round stone on top. The king watched from here as young men who wanted to join the army tried their hand at raising the stone to the top of the pillar a hundred times. At a weight of thirty-eight kilogrammes, this must have been a difficult test, and the king, if he had a sense of humour, must have found it at least mildly entertaining. As I stood at the window, a stout, crinkly-haired Kerala matron entered, having brushed aside the caretaker as if he were evolutionarily inferior to a fly, herding her two daughters efficiently before her. I heard her explaining to them authoritatively that the order of floors in the pagoda was specially chosen: the top floor was for God, she said, her voice genuinely reverential, and the bottom floor was for money, which, of course, was worth nothing if one was irreligious.

'What were the middle floors used for, Amma?' asked one of the girls in all innocence. Her mother silenced her with a glare.

'The king lived there, you stupid!' supplied her sister. The girl subsided, peeved, but with the look of one who was going to satisfy her curiosity someday.

On investigating, I found to my satisfaction that a passage led from the first floor of the pagoda to the Anthapuram, or ladies' chamber. Here the queen and princesses lived, with all their attendants. The queen mother occupied a room in this chamber, in which a beautiful cane bed with ivory decoration still stands.

After the dimly lit, tranquil interior, coming out into the sunlight was like entering a brash technicolour world. I wandered about desultorily, taking a look at the large open hall called the Navathri Mandapam and returning disappointed; granite, however well carved, is simply no match for the wooden intricacies of the rest of the palace. It was perhaps time to leave, and in finding my way to the gate, I thought of Fra Bartolomeo, who had made a similar exit more than two centuries earlier. After halting at Padmanabhapuram for sixteen days—during which several knotty questions were discussed, including the shocking case of the Mapullians (Christian women) at 'Callurcada', who indulged in criminal intercourse with shudras and even lived with them as concubines—the priest prepared to depart. Evidently he had been well looked after, for he notes with admiration the simplicity with which the king's household was run, and records that the king sent him kopu every day, a dish prepared in the Malabar style.

> As soon as I had received the two letters . . . I departed from Padmanaburam. The minister paid me 100 Kalis, to defray the expenses of my journey; and gave orders that the coolies who carried my palanquin along the sea coast, from one place to another, should be paid from the royal treasury. When I arrived at Parur, the Mahometans there protested against the king's order, and would not carry me farther, under the pretence that, being a Tanguel or Christian priest, I was an enemy to their religion. I was obliged, therefore, to stop five whole hours till the king's Pravaticarer appeared, who caused the refractory coolies to be soundly beaten, and commanded them again to take up my palanquin.[22]

Emerging from the walled wooden palace, I found my driver quickly enough, and we drove back along the road that now replaced the 'Madacava' of Bartolomeo's day. This time, throwing caution to the winds, I returned the tentative smile that reached me by way of the rear-view mirror.

Notes

1. K.A. Nilakanta Sastri, *A History of South India from Prehistoric Times to the Fall of Vijayanagar* (1955; 4th ed., New Delhi: Oxford University Press, 1990), p. 107. Sastri goes on to explain that Sangam literature was 'the result of the meeting and fusion of two originally separate cultures, the Tamil and the Aryan. Its beginnings are no longer traceable, and the schematic anthologies that have been handed down doubtless represent a

relatively late phase in that epochal literary movement, and to this phase we have suggested the period AD 100–300' (pp. 330-31).
2. Ibid., p. 107.
3. Ibid., pp. 293-94.
4. Dried cinnamon leaf, or an extract thereof.
5. A fragrant ointment.
6. Quoted in Sastri, p. 126.
7. *The Travels of Ibn Battutah*, ed. Tim Mackintosh-Smith (London: Picador, 2003), p. 226.
8. Ibid., p. 320.
9. Sir Charles Fawcett, ed., *The Travels of the Abbé Carré in India and the Near East 1672 to 1674*, vol. I (1946; reprint, New Delhi: Asian Educational Services), p. 213.
10. *The Travels of Ibn Battutah*, pp. 219-20.
11. Ibid., p. 226.
12. When palm sap is allowed to ferment, it becomes a thick sweet alcoholic drink much favoured in Kerala.
13. P. Shungoonny Menon, *History of Travancore from the Earliest Times* (1878; reprint, New Delhi: Asian Educational Services, 1998), p. 184.
14. Quoted in Menon, p. 182. That the priest's description was fascinating was due in no small measure to the fact that he wrote this account during the reign of Martanda Varma's nephew, and was able to talk to the king's successor as well the generals of the previous reign, Martandapulla and M. d'Lanoy, all three of whom spoke personally with the priest (Menon, p. 183).
15. The patron deity of the Travancore rulers, an incarnation of Vishnu.
16. *The Travels of Ibn Battutah*, p. 220.
17. Quoted in Menon, p. 270.
18. Quoted in Menon, p. 185
19. Menon, p. 185.
20. Martabans, also called *pegu* jars, are vessels belonging to a particular type of large, glazed pottery. Pegu, interestingly, was the English name for Bago, a town in Myanmar that is reasonably close to the port of Martaban at the mouth of the Thanlwin (Salween) river, across the water from Moulmien (Mawlamyaing).
21. *The Travels of Ibn Battutah*, p. 227.
22. Menon, p. 275.

Devbagh
Beyond the Realm of Prose

The little harbour, ringed round with hills, is so secluded that it has nothing of the aspect of a port about it. Its crescent-shaped beach throws out its arms to the shoreless open sea, like the very image of an eager striving to embrace the infinite. The edge of the broad sandy beach is infringed with a forest of casuarinas, broken at one end by the Kalinadi river, which here flows into the sea after passing through a gorge flanked by rows of hills on either side.

—Rabindranath Tagore, *Reminiscences*

At the northern tip of coastal Karnataka, just south of the palm-fringed greenness of Goa, stands a tiny, unprepossessing port called Karwar. It is not much more than a feeble dot on an otherwise captivating state map, so for many years I cherished not the slightest wish to see it. Francis Buchanan had nursed a similar disenchantment; on 3 March 1801, he wrote with some distaste of the neighbouring towns of Sadashivgarh and Karwar:

> I remained at Sedasiva-ghur taking some account of the state of

> British Kankana,[1] and making preparations for my journey up the Ghats. The Petta, or town, here contains about twenty very wretched shops: all the other inhabitants live scattered on their farms. Cadawada, or as we usually pronounce it, Carwar, stood about three miles above Sedasiva-ghur, on the opposite bank of the river. It was formerly a noted seat of European commerce, but during the [Tipu] Sultan's reign has gone to total ruin.[2]

My image of the region changed only when I found, thanks to the investigations of my family, that Karwar, where the Kalinadi meets the Arabian Sea, is the port from which one sets sail to a number of islands just off the coast. The foremost of these is tiny Devbagh, on which a jungle camp offers a secluded retreat. All of a sudden Karwar became a more exciting proposition, and I found myself re-examining its position on the map. The town is accessible both from the coastal highway that links Malabar with Bombay, and from interior Karnataka by means of an intermittently wooded road between Hubli and the coast. Either way, it is a long day's drive from Bangalore, though in all fairness the two highways are very well maintained.

The first time I set out for Karwar was with family and friends, just after Christmas in 1999, as the new millennium approached. We took NH4, the great highway that connects Madras to Bangalore and then runs north-west to Bombay. The drive began in the shimmering greyness of a Bangalore dawn, its first leg an arduous effort to pass endless convoys of ponderous, top-heavy trucks. When the traffic eased after the town of Tumkur, we relaxed and began to enjoy the steady morning drive, interrupted only by a halt at a wayside restaurant in Chitradurga. Here, over tepid coffee and cumin-spiced samosas of dubious vintage, I remembered that this was the fortress town where my grandmother had spent some of her youth, as my great-grandfather Dunning, who was with the police, had been posted here. The town—which my grandmother and her sisters, like Buchanan before them, were more likely to have called 'Chitteldroog'—had caught my fancy when, as a child, I was told that a tiger had been captured there in my grandmother's youth and taken to the Mysore zoo. I thought a great deal about my grandmother that day, as we sat on foldable wooden chairs by the roadside. Buchanan had written,

> The plain of Chitteldroog is two cosses and a half from north to south, and one coss from east to west; the coss here being at least four miles. It is every where surrounded by low, rocky, bare hills, on one of which stands the Durga, or fort, formerly the residence of the polygars[3] of this country. By the natives it is called either Sitala-durga, that is to say, the spotted castle, or Chatrakal, which signifies the umbrella rock; for the Umbrella is one of the insignia of royalty.[4]

When the Vijayanagar empire fell into decline, the polygars gradually increased their territories to the extent that the Mughals at Sira began to covet this land. The nawab of Sira and Hyder Ali both attempted to conquer the fort town with no success; Hyder eventually resorted to bribing a Muslim officer to gain influence over the region. The fort walls, which extended near the foot of the rock, were strengthened both by Hyder and his son, Tipu Sultan, so by the time the British came to control the area, this was a very strong fortress.

I had visited the fortress before, with its winding stairs and lovely gates, its massive boulders and little temples, and its inhospitable scrub. The palace at the top was abandoned and picturesque, with the roots of trees hanging down among the ruined shrines and beetles scuttling among the grass and stones. From here, there were impressive views of the countryside that surrounded the congested little town below, and I thought of my grandmother then as well: she had learnt how to drive a car in Chitradurga, of all places, and during a maiden venture at the wheel had sent the district collector, who was bicycling placidly down a lane, into the nearest ditch. On my way up to the fort, I had noticed that the streets of the town bore ample evidence of the former

British presence, chiefly in the form of crumbling bungalows and government offices. Lingering at the top of the hill, I was tempted to stay longer, but it was very windy. After half an hour I made my way down again, stopping for a while at a pair of footprints sculpted into the stairs cut into the hillside, where a deity was said to have set foot. Further down, on the side of the hill, was a peculiar sunken stone pit with great grinding stones that had once been turned by beasts of burden. By this ponderous arrangement, the masters of the fort had ground not grain but gunpowder.

Buchanan, as usual, was not terribly impressed with the fort or its defences, for the subadar was absent upon his arrival and his inferiors were 'little disposed' to render 'any assistance, of which I was much in want'. He had a tendency to call a spade a spade, and rarely tried to look for any saving grace if he was displeased with a place he passed through. The surrounding country, though clear and rocky, was markedly unhealthy owing to a scarcity of water and the unfortunate tendency of the locals to 'wash their clothes, bodies, and cattle in the very tanks or wells from which they take their own drink', said our traveller, adding that wherever the water was scanty it became from this cause 'extremely disgusting to a European'. His people had been suffering from daily attacks of fever, and there was not much to do in this place, he wrote, for its agriculture seemed no different from that at Hari-hara and Davana-giri, and merited no further investigation.

As I sat at the wayside restaurant outside 'the inhospitable Chatrakal', eyeing the miserable grey dregs of coffee in my glass, there was nothing more to do but follow Buchanan's example and leave. Chitradurga was left quickly behind as we drove along a more open road, passing through fields of yellow sunflowers waving their brilliant heads in the breeze. At length, this Oz-like landscape took us to Hubli, where a diversion to the east continues to the coast.

Hubli, a dusty north Karnataka town, had its warts and pockmarks cruelly illuminated by an irritable afternoon sun. We were hungry enough to stop there for a late lunch, but glad to depart, for an apparently eternal traffic jam clogged the heart of its street system like a heavy black clot. When the town was finally behind us, its unattractive neighbourhoods were replaced by a strikingly pretty stretch of woodland where the air was clean and invigorating. It was not simply the deliverance from dull pollution that made the trees a welcome change; this was a princess among forests, not too dense or mature, but young and lively, transparently seductive. The road darted through patches of rust, yellow and green, showing the way through the woods like a length of silver, and it seemed to say with every bend and twist that a very special place lay beyond. Despite this delightful sense of anticipation, I drew in my breath sharply when, after we climbed and eventually came around a cliff, I had my first soul-lifting glimpse that year of the northern Karnataka coast. The road, now narrow and winding, as befitted a ghat, slipped and slid precariously through the tropical hills that shored up this part of the coast. Overflowing with giant green ears of elephant fern, the hills would have been arresting but for the more compelling distraction of the silver-blue Arabian, with its hypnotic vista of shifting water and sand. The surf rolled in far below, licking a cove like a great white tongue, and suddenly I couldn't wait to arrive, to feel the water touch my feet, and watch the froth settle time after time in lazy circles and vanish with a hiss and crackle into the sand.

Close to the mainland here is the beautiful island of Anjediv, which has a romantic history, and one that is sadly unknown today except perhaps by the Indian navy. During the Raj, it lay quite forgotten; *Hobson-Jobson* says, amusingly,

> It is a remarkable example of the slovenliness of English professional map-making that Keith Johnston's Royal Atlas map of India contains no indication of this famous island . . . It has, between land surveys and sea-charts, been omitted altogether by the compilers. But it is plain enough in the Admiralty charts; and the way Mr Birch speaks of it in his

translation of Alboquerque as an 'Indian seaport, no longer marked on the maps,' is odd.[5]

Long before the British omitted it from their maps, however, Ptolemy may have referred to Anjediv, and it was almost certainly the island of which Ibn Battuta wrote circa 1345, when he arrived at

> the island of Sandabur (Goa), in which there are thirty-six villages. It is surrounded by a gulf, the waters of which are sweet and agreeable at low tide but salt [sic] and bitter at high tide. On this occasion we did stop at this island when we passed by it, but anchored at a *smaller one* near the mainland, in which there was a temple, an orchard, and a water-tank, and on which we found one of the jugis . . . leaning on the wall of a budkhanah, that is an idol-temple; he was between two of its idols and showed the traces of continuous practice of religious austerities.[6]

It was quite like Battuta to add a story about this yogi, for his travels, steeped in medieval mysticism, are peppered with fantastic accounts of sages and ascetics. He also concluded on rather slim grounds that the yogi was a Muslim. That the island was home to another religion, Christianity, was evident well before the Portuguese built a church there—for in 1498, when an armed Portuguese boat was sent to investigate the island, one Nicolas Coello found 'a building, a church of great ashlar-work, which had been destroyed by the Moors, as the country people said, only the church had been covered with straw, and they used to make their prayers to three black stones in the midst of the body of the chapel.'[7]

It was here that the Portuguese commander Affonso de Albuquerque anchored during his attempts to capture Arab strongholds along the sea route to India from the Persian Gulf. In 1510, while girding his loins for another expedition to Socotra, Suez and Ormuz, he made his way up the coast from Cochin, planning to sail from Anjediva to Cape Guardafui, or present-day Somalia. Instead, hearing of the vulnerability of Muslim-ruled Goa from a Hindu conspirator, he made for the mouth of the Mandovi—and the rest, of course, is history. One minor offshoot of the imminent Portuguese empire was the fortification of the island they called 'Angediva', where settlers built the Forte Nossa Senhora das Brotas in 1682. Three centuries later, in 1961, Anjediv popped back on the map when, after fifteen years of post-Independence propaganda, India moved in to occupy Goa and 'liberate' it from the Portuguese. The Portuguese fired on an Indian vessel, the *Sabarmati*, from this, their old place of refuge. Indian forces, which were lining up to take over Goa, Daman and Diu, looked at the capture of Anjediv as a point of prestige, since Portuguese hostilities had originated there. On the other side, four ships were earmarked for the defence of Portugal's pride—the *Affonso de Albuquerque*, *Bartholomeu Dias*, *Gonsalves Zarco* and *João de Lisboa*—but at the critical moment of action, only the *Albuquerque* remained, the other three having left for Portugal. Anjediv was captured and the *Albuquerque*, ironically bearing the name of arguably the greatest Portuguese commander to have been associated with India, surrendered and beached herself at Dona Paula, south of Panjim. Looking out now at the deceptively calm Arabian, as still as a lake, it seemed hard to imagine any sort of hostility on its surface, yet it had seen plenty of naval conquest and commercial jealousy.

Karwar, at the bottom of the distracting ghat road overlooking the sea, is so tiny that its entire length can be crossed in ten minutes, from the matchbox harbour to the motorboat jetty. From here you can take a boat to Devbagh island, north of Anjediv, my destination for the eve of the new millennium. The island lies close to the mainland, suspended in the tiny estuary of the Kalinadi like an emerald at the end of a rippling chain. On the far side of the estuary, which is spanned by a bridge, is the border between Goa and Karnataka. A motorboat arrived as I stared up at the bridge and the trucks that slowly crossed it, continuing north to Panjim and Bombay. Along with several others, I heaved my bag into the boat and found a dry place to sit. A friend sat up on the prow, her back to me and her feet almost touching the water, with the confidence born of years of sailing small craft in the oily Madras harbour. As we set off at top speed, her thick black hair flying wildly in the wind, I could see the adrenaline flowing from her like a jet stream. It would have been good to see her face as well, for she was a busy and preoccupied software professional, not to mention a beleaguered mother of three. Her sons, aged seventeen, fifteen and six, chattered at the top of their voices, and the youngest enlivened the proceedings by threatening to fall out. She ignored them blandly and stared ahead at the water, taking in the rapidly closing distance between the boat and Devbagh's little jetty. Without knowing it, my friend defined the very quality of the island before us: for it possessed an insularity that enabled one to draw the blinds on the world and rest a while, not in the cool gloom of a darkened room but in the freshest air and sunshine, along a tranquil beach and in the warm, beckoning waters of the estuary.

The jetty was makeshift, built by hand with casuarina poles and branches lashed together unsteadily with thick, rough ropes of coir, the crude fibre taken from coconut husk. Climbing ashore, I knew I had come to a place of extraordinary serenity; it felt as though I had taken a long step off the Subcontinent, leaving the people, the garbage and the grime far behind. The only habitations were a well-hidden jungle camp on the riverbank and a small fishing village on the seaward shore. The presence of the latter was belied by a couple of ragged children who hid behind the trees and watched us alight, their eyes fixed brightly on our every move. A path led from the jetty to the clearing in the woods where the camp had been erected, and the children followed us, stopping to hide and stare from a distance and skipping through the trees to catch up when we walked ahead. On either side, long, needle-like casuarina leaves shaded us from the sun and trapped our sleeves and hair; arched branches towered overhead like an outdoor cathedral. When we came to the camp, a cluster of log cabins and canvas tents that seemed diminutive beneath the great trees, I looked around for the children but they had disappeared. Evidently the camp contained some cooks and attendants who would not have taken kindly to their meddling in such matters of state as the fish that was being gutted for dinner.

The tent I chose was a large and comfortable one, with nylon netting that kept the insects out while letting the sea breeze in—an ideal arrangement, for it was very warm here even in December. I surveyed my territory with great satisfaction and set off for the water, which shimmered most alluringly through the trees. It was safe to swim near the shore, though currents were strong further out, where the river muscled with the sea in a ceaseless philosophical battle. I sat down in the water and let the waves wash up over me and push me gently back along the sand. After the long drive, it took only twenty minutes of this to take away the stiffness.

When the sun began to sink, I got out of the water and walked heavily up the shore to the casuarina grove, where a hammock caught my eye. In it I lay blissfully suspended until sundown, disturbed by no one except a large brown cow that had strayed from the village. Pausing in its rumination, it stared at me with the air of an amateur naturalist surveying a strange and intriguing species. After a while it closed its mouth (which, despite being in mid-chew, had remained open thus far), then began to work on the cud again and went away, disappointed that I wasn't as remarkable as it had first imagined. I closed my eyes and rocked myself to sleep between the branches, one foot touching the sand below. As on Innisfree, the lake isle of which Yeats wrote with such tenderness, the water here lapped with 'low sounds by the shore', and here too did peace come 'dropping slow'. In all the time I spent on Devbagh, not a morning passed in the casuarina grove without the sound of Aunt Margaret reciting Yeats' lines in the back of my head.

I will arise and go now, and go to Innisfree,
And a small cabin build there, of clay and wattles made:
Nine bean-rows will I have there, a hive for the honey-bee,
And live alone in the bee-loud glade.

Nothing disturbed the tranquillity of this island; even the shouts of swimmers were softened by the sea breeze and floated across the beach harmlessly. The only time I awoke from one of my long naps in the hammock was when a butterfly decided—silly thing—that my toes were akin to flowers and settled on them determinedly, tickling me so violently that I half fell off in an effort to get rid of the visitor without hurting its delicate wings. It flew away indignantly and I righted myself with some difficulty, nursing a stubbed toe and reflecting that an alarm clock, while crassly contemporary, had a thing or two to be said for it.

Despite the intrusive wildlife, it was still poetry that was uppermost in my mind as I listened every day to the soft but urgent questioning of the leaves and the murmured response of sand and water. I was later delighted to discover that Rabindranath Tagore had visited Karwar long ago, and indeed had here written *Prakritir Pratishodha* (Nature's Revenge), a dramatic poem that he considered an introduction to his future work. Tagore had come here in the late nineteenth century to visit his brother Satyendranath, who, as the first Indian to join the Imperial Civil Service, was posted here as district judge. Then a young man, Rabindranath was fourteenth in a row of often illustrious siblings in an aristocratic Calcutta family. Two of his brothers were also of literary persuasion while a sister, Swarnakumari Devi, was the foremost woman novelist of her day. As a child, Tagore was refused promotion to the next grade at St. Xavier's School and summarily taken away, despite his clearly discernible talent for writing. In 1875, after the death of his mother, he was raised by his playwright brother Jyotirindranath and sister-in-law Kadambari Devi, both of whom wielded a considerable influence on his adolescent mind. The following year he accompanied Satyendranath to England, where he studied English literature at University College London, and wrote a series of rather indiscreet 'Letters from a Sojourner in Europe' on the London lifestyle. These letters alarmed his elders, and Rabindranath was recalled to India before he could experience said lifestyle any further.

Exploring the island was very pleasant, as it was just the right size for a whole day's expedition. I found that my favourite part of it was not its seaward side, where a fishing village somewhat ate into the serenity, but its eastern or landward tip: here was a modest tidal swamp that filled up in the afternoon, and at some times of the day actually allowed people to walk across the mud flats from the mainland to the island. So Devbagh was not really an island at all—it was a spit of land that was sometimes connected to the mainland. The point at which this charming indecision took place could be viewed satisfactorily from another tiny wooden jetty where a couple of boats were moored; I sat there and listened to the low, grumbling sounds of the swamp and the tiny liquid noise of the incoming tide. I loved rowing in the swamp when the tide rippled in, for it was gentle, and it rocked the boat slowly down a still little creek. Rowing back was a little more strenuous but hardly exhausting, as the swamp vegetation and wildlife all around distracted me. Birds flew low overhead and ducks swam lazily past, and in this season the whole tidal exercise was as benign as a bathtub being filled by a trickle of water and drained just as slowly. In the rains, of course, it was impossible to make the crossing to Devbagh on foot; it was dangerous even by boat, for the camp on the island was closed in July and August, when the south-west monsoon flung itself wildly against the west coast. By late afternoon, I made my way back to camp and found it alive with laughter as people ran an impromptu race through the casuarina avenues, hurting their feet on the thick roots protruding from the sand.

When night fell on Devbagh, it happened so suddenly that I was staring into the sunset one moment and into absolutely nothing the next. A strong torch barely lit the path before me, and it seemed as if the darkness was a living, predatory thing, moving in treacherous circles around the feeble pool of light. I was never quite comfortable in the dark until a few hours had passed and I had gotten used to it, so at nightfall I usually returned to my tent as soon as I could. Devbagh's night was thick and heavy, draping itself over the windows of the tents and cabins like an oversized quilt, and yet when I poked my head out of the canvas doorway and looked above the trees, the moon and the stars were unbelievably bright. They lay strewn across the night sky like bits of shattered glass, and shone so powerfully that I could not look at them for long stretches of time. It seemed as if a celestial broom had swept them into a thousand constellations, each random arrangement more complex and beautiful than the next. Night after night I looked out at the twinkling lights of Karwar across the water, bathing all the while in the brilliance of the stars above. In a few days the millennium would turn, but in relation to the unfathomable history of the universe, it seemed as if all we were about to celebrate was the passing of a nanosecond.

When Tagore was in Karwar, he once went up the Kalinadi in a sailboat with his brother's family. Returning, he got off the boat at the mouth of the river and walked home over the sand under the light of the moon. 'It was then far into the night,' he wrote, 'the sea was without a ripple, even the ever-troubled murmur of the casuarinas was at rest. The shadow of the fringe of trees along the vast expanse of sand hung motionless along its border, and the ring of the blue-grey hills around the horizon slept calmly beneath the sky. Through the deep silence of this illimitable whiteness we few human creatures walked along with our shadows, without a word. When we reached home my sleep had lost itself in something still deeper. The poem which I then wrote is inextricably mingled with that night on the distant sea shore.' The poem reads thus in English:

> Let me sink down, losing myself in the depths of midnight,
>> let the Earth leave her hold of me, let her free me from her obstacle of dust.
> Keep your watch from afar, O stars, drunk though you be with moonlight,
>> and let the horizon hold its wings still around me.
> Let there be no song, no word, no sound, no touch; nor sleep nor awakening,
>> but only the moonlight like a swoon of ecstacy over the sky and my being.
> The world seems to me like a ship with its countless pilgrims,
>> vanishing in the far-away blue of the sky,
>> its sailors' song becoming fainter and fainter in the air,
>> while I sink in the bosom of the endless night, fading away from myself, dwindling to a point.[8]

On a night of an ilk so magnificent that it once moved a great poet, the best thing to do other than stargaze was to ask some fishermen to take us out to a neighbouring uninhabited island. Such a journey by night was romantic in the extreme: the waves were strong, and they pitched the boat this way and that as we moved rapidly along the black water and through the dark, dark night, feeling uncomfortably close to Davy Jones' locker. Not even the strongest rum, consumed by the light of our precariously perched hurricane lamp, could dispel that feeling of danger; yet it was accompanied by a great excitement, for this was the stuff of storybooks.

Arriving at the island was a relief, for the ride had been unnerving. It was a pleasure to disembark in the still, inky waters of a tiny cove while the boat was some distance from the beach; there was no jetty, of course, so we had to jump over the side of the boat and wade ashore. I did so nonchalantly, concealing my considerable fright at undertaking this exercise in the pitch dark, but the water was shallow and comforting. There was a chilly wait before it was possible to dry off, for a driftwood fire had first to be lit on the pale moonlit beach. Behind me, on the very edge of the sand, rose a tall brooding cliff, on to which the fire soon sent giant, leaping black shadows.

Looking out at the black water, I shut out the conversation around me and thought of the many ships that must have sailed this way over the centuries. Even two thousand years ago, trading vessels had sailed to India in search of luxuries for Rome. There must also have been Arab dhows; heavy seafaring vessels built of rough-hewn planks held together with wooden nails and coir rope; and swift, long, single-masted native galleys known as foists, which often harrassed the larger, slower ships. Then there were the Portuguese caravels, round vessels with lateen sails that could carry large cargoes across the sea. A robust crew must have manned these early craft from Portugal, for five centuries ago, stepping off terra firma for a voyage of several months was no mean undertaking. The daily fare of those on board included meat, wine, biscuit, and sometimes cheese or onions. And what of the cargo they carried? Spices, of course, and pepper, and—less savoury— slaves captured to take home to Europe. Slavery was an ancient institution, but it was the Portuguese who systematically imported 'black ivory', eventually slipping into a terrible maltreatment of these people, whom they considered less than human, and to whom, hardened by an age that allowed the burning of heretics, they were sometimes inordinately cruel.[9] Further south along the Arabian coast, junks, zaws and kakams must have anchored in Calicut and Kollam, manned by the Chinese, who according to Ibn Battuta, were the wealthiest people in the world. The junk must have been a very impressive ship, for it carried a thousand men, six hundred sailors and four hundred men-at-arms. The factor of a Chinese ship came ashore like a great amir, wrote Battuta, 'preceded by archers and Abyssinians with javelins, swords, drums, bugles and trumpets'.[10]

Returning to Devbagh from the strange, lonely cove with its glassy water was akin to embracing civilization once more. Suddenly the safe, sturdy zip-up tent was the most sophisticated bedroom I could have wished for. Snuffing out my lamp and going to bed was a wonderful feeling; all around, the casuarina trees swished and sashayed in the breeze and birds called to each other tentatively. I could hear muffled giggles nearby, for the next capsule tent was occupied by my youngest sister and a friend, both of whom were contriving, for reasons best known to themselves, to sleep with their heads inside the zipped shelter and their feet sticking out. From a nearby log cabin came the muted but unmistakable sound of my father snoring. Smiling, I thought to myself that it was good to be in this lovely place surrounded by friends and family. If there was anything missing from this holiday it was the presence of my middle sister, then studying in Singapore. Images of that city came to me as I fell asleep, not of the bustling quays and the picture-perfect docks, but of the place as it must have been before the war, of bungalows set in impossibly lush gardens and of gracious old buildings on broad thoroughfares. It was warm on Devbagh, and a sudden stickiness descended as the sea breeze dropped, adding an air of verisimilitude to my dreams of equatorial Singapore. I rolled over, discarding my covers, and wondered sleepily if my sixteen-year-old sister, lost in a tropical, bougainvillea-drenched avenue in Bukit Timah, was thinking of us too.

Although I had believed that Devbagh was merely going to be a holiday, in fact an escape from the millennium celebrations that were sure to dominate the cities, there was no getting away from the fact that the turn of a thousand years was approaching. The island was, in fact, a deeply moving place to be at that much-awaited time, away from the fireworks and the wild street parties, yet thrilling, for it was close to the very womb of life. The emotions of that night defy accurate description, but they were such as I had never experienced before: a strange conflicting consciousness of mortality and immortality, of yesterday and tomorrow, of history and eternity, of nostalgia and anticipation. At midnight, time moved forward in a series of staccato moments so solid and tangible that they were frozen for all time in my memory. There were no clocks to watch or chimes to hear, but somewhere in the background I could hear the faint heartbeat of the cosmos and felt an insane, elemental rush of happiness that I was a part of it, however small. It took a while for this feeling to pass, and when it did, I realized I had been soothed, like an overexcited child, by the timeless motion of the waves on Devbagh's beach.

Notes

1. As opposed to Portuguese Canacona, which lay to the north, forming part of present-day Goa. *Konkan* refers to the area from the ghats to the sea, to the west of the Deccan Plateau, embracing northern coastal Karnataka and Goa. The word also historically refers to a people, and *Hobson-Jobson* suspects that the *Concondae* of Pliny (as far back as AD 70) are perhaps the *Konkanas*.
2. Francis Buchanan, *A Journey from Madras through the Countries of Mysore, Canara, and Malabar* (1807; reprint, New Delhi: Asian Educational Services, 1999), vol. III, p. 179.
3. Feudal chiefs of the Madras Presidency, usually in the southern districts of modern Tamil Nadu but also right up to the Maratha boundary. The word derives from the Telugu *palegadu* or the Marathi *palegar*, its Tamil equivalent being *palaiyakkaran* (holder of a feudal estate). See Henry Yule and A.C. Burnell, *Hobson-Jobson, The Anglo-Indian Dictionary* (1886; reprint: Ware, Hertfordshire, Wordsworth Editions Ltd, 1996), p. 718, for a detailed explanation.
4. Buchanan, p. 339.
5. *Hobson-Jobson,* p. 28.
6. *The Travels of Ibn Battutah*, ed. Tim Mackintosh-Smith (London: Picador, 2003), p. 217.
7. *Hobson-Jobson,* p. 28.
8. Rabindranath Tagore, *Reminiscences* (1917; reprint, New Delhi: Macmillan India, 2001), pp. 244-45.
9. K.G. Jayne, *Vasco da Gama and His Successors, 1400-1580* (1910; reprint, New Delhi: Asian Educational Services, 1997), pp. 22-23.
10. *The Travels of Ibn Battutah*, pp. 223-24.

Goa
Five Hundred Monsoons Now

The island abounds in corn and rice, and produces numerous fruits, as mangues, ananas, figues d'Adam, and cocos; but a good pippin is certainly worth more than all these fruits. All who have seen both Europe and Asia thoroughly agree with me that the port of Goa, that of Constantinople, and that of Toulon are the three finest ports in both the continents.

—*Travels in India*, Jean-Baptiste Tavernier

The first time I went to Goa, it was merely a drive up from Karwar for lunch on a late-December afternoon, a delightfully still-life undertaking. As my Aunt Margaret observed, the whole state appeared to be in the grip of a powerful siesta. Her Tibetan terrier, whose august descent had granted him access to our expedition, echoed this sentiment with a disdainful sniff and, removing his nose from the window, returned to the nether regions of the car. All along the road, blinds were pulled and shutters closed, pigs were shut up in their pens, and mongrels lay stretched in the shade with palm fronds and hedge leaves drooping listlessly over their forms. It seemed as if the very plants had given up trying to stand up straight, and as for people, there were simply none to be found: they were replaced in every village by life-sized effigies of old men stuffed into chairs by the roadside, tin cans placed hopefully on their laps to collect money for the season's revelries. These grotesque figures, sometimes bearing a painted coconut for a head, had, over time, in the general spirit of things, slouched forward in their seats in a disconcertingly realistic manner.

Given this restful state of affairs, we were taken aback to find on Colva beach a restaurant that was not only open, but employed a waiter who was awake. He detached himself slowly from the bar, surveyed us for a whole minute with something approaching interest, and finally offered us a table, since we did not seem to want to go away. The restaurant was only a thatched shack, with lizards lying drugged and immobile on the walls and cracked plastic menus on the sagging tables, but it had a certain charm that perhaps only the hungry and heat-struck could fully appreciate.

As we waited to be served, time inched its way forward at a pace that I have only ever borne witness to in Goa: the coconut feni[1] arrived after an eternity, followed an hour later by a dish of parboiled beef for the terrier, who had in the interim gone to sleep genteelly on my foot. I was half asleep myself by the time the lunch arrived, for the afternoon heat had caused me to consume—out of sheer thirst, of course—a larger quantity of the fabled feni than was strictly necessary. When at last the dishes arrived, they were placed before us with infuriatingly deliberate lethargy, and despite the appetite we had worked up while waiting, the food was rather less than the gourmet west-coast affair I had anticipated. The legendary Goan fish curry, of which I had been dreaming for a week, was a dismal little dish, decorated with a few slices of vintage tomato and complemented cleverly by under-cooked, indigestible rice and a wilted salad. Annoyed by this treachery, I collared the waiter—who, as it happened, was also the chef—as he shuffled past. He was, I thought, a poor representative of a community that had provided ships and hotels with famously skilled cooks for centuries.

'Your food is just terrible,' I said, after searching without success for a more civilized way to open conversation. 'And the fish curry doesn't taste at all like Goan fish curry. In fact, it's the worst fish curry I've ever eaten anywhere!'

'Yes,' said the man disinterestedly, flooring me with a single word as he investigated his ear with a splintered Cheetah-brand matchstick. Taken aback, and later much inspired by this novel rejoinder from one so enviably secure in his incompetence, I decided to abandon all things resembling the Protestant work ethic and return to Goa very soon— to stay, of course, for a lot longer than lunch. There was something irresistible about a place that had, despite commercial development, retained such a measure of old-fashioned lassitude and inefficiency.

As often happens with such resolutions, it was almost three years before I found time to return to the decadent former Portuguese colony. My interest in it, however, was nourished by both the delay and my sundry forays into its history, which had long preceded the British empire, indeed was an early marker of the age of European exploration. Goa was originally a Hindu seaport; the Muslims captured it in 1469 and made it, after Calicut, their chief sea base in western India. It was at Calicut that the Portuguese first arrived, led by Vasco da Gama, who, having found the sea route from Europe to India around the Cape of Good Hope, had unwittingly changed the course of world history. At this time merchandise from India, which included pepper, silk and slave girls, reached European markets only through the Persian Gulf and the Red Sea, from where it was taken by caravan to ships waiting at various ports to sail for west Asia and Italy. The immediate plan of the militantly Christian Portuguese was to hound the Muslims—Arabs, Turks, Egyptians and Persians—out of the waters that connected India's west coast with the Persian Gulf, 'to drive these infidels from the seas, to put Portuguese traders in their place, and to divert the Indian export-trade to the Cape route'.[2] Instead of pursuing a purely commercial rivalry, the newcomers adopted the most extreme measures to disrupt the long-standing, mutually beneficial trade between the Arabs and India. As Danvers wrote in 1894, in his classic history of the Portuguese in India,

> The destruction of defenceless towns, the indiscriminate murder of their opponents, and the wholesale piracy openly practised on the high seas in the name of a civilised nation, naturally enough raised a spirit of opposition and retaliation on the part of those whose interests and lives were so seriously menaced.[3]

All said and done, what the Portuguese embarked on was a daring, avaricious and bigoted scheme, which was to benefit Europe at large and return to it the trading glory that had faded with the rise of the Ottoman empire. In its early stages, however, it was little more than a hunt for 'Christians'—the Portuguese firmly believed they would find some—and spices, and gave little indication of the mingling of race and culture and the tremendous imperialist forces still to come. For following the sails of the Portuguese were those of the Dutch, the French and, most fatefully, the British, who proceeded to modify the map of the world on an unprecedented scale.

When I did return to Goa, it was not in December, the peak foreign-tourist season, or in the summer, when Indian families vacationed, but at the height of the south-west monsoon, when the beaches lie white and windswept, like a cluster of giant shells washed up on the Konkan coast. It is during this short, stormy period that the Goans have their state to themselves, while the land and the beaches recover from the stress of the holiday season. The long drive from Bangalore—on which my mother accompanied me to keep a kindly maternal eye on my doings—took us to the plateau's edge, then through the Western Ghats, and across the narrow coastal plain to the sea. It was a delightful drive through the living geography of the South, a drive that opened my eyes to the yearly rains in all their uninterrupted magnificence. On the Deccan, the road passed through a wide expanse of relatively treeless land, affording open views of the surrounding country. Rocks rose out of the plateau in stark, jagged eruptions, and over nature's dramatic stage hung the great purple curtains of the monsoon. Everywhere there was a sense of anticipation, until we passed the town of Hassan—with a few moments of sentimentality, for I had been born there—and the rain began to fall, gently but deliberately, almost in the manner of a benediction. The road then splashed through the lush, wet plantations of the lower ranges, before winding its way over the Western Ghats through the beautiful Shiradi pass. The mountains seemed supremely disconnected from the plateau, the other-worldly green of their upper ranges briefly visible through parting drifts of cloud. Here and there a stream rushed under a bridge, swollen to the status of a river by the monsoon's generosity; a railway tunnel sent a length of shiny black track shooting through the emerald-coloured grass. The mist lifted and fell, and the heavy drizzle came and went, giving us a series of rich images of the mountains and the brown, bubbling Netravati as it rushed mud-heavy to the sea. For tea and biscuits, we stopped briefly at a trucker's village where everything was soaking-wet, from the stray dogs hanging about at our feet and begging for crumbs to the great glistening tyres of the dozen lorries lined up on the road. Stepping over deep slushy tracks, we returned to the car and negotiated the last of the ghat, looking over our shoulders regretfully when we descended its last hairpin bend.

At the bottom of the ghat lay the palm-serrated Konkan coast, and on it lay Mangalore, another town of my early childhood. A thunderstorm had just cleared when we arrived, and from the eaves and porches of the town's brooding friaries and convents dripped myriad memories of the world when I was three. I remembered a kindergarten attached to the Roman Catholic college at which my mother had taught, and to which she had carried me on her shoulders every morning; I remembered the tiny house in which we had lived briefly, with millipedes dropping unpleasantly off the ceiling and lying in slick coils on the furniture. Above all I remembered the sound of the rain, the incessant thrumming on the roof tiles that had kept me awake night after night, listening intently until I could no longer resist sleep.

Mangalore was a trading town of old, but despite its coastal position it has very little historic architecture apart from the beautiful buildings of the college and church of St. Aloysius. Ibn Battuta, however, passing through during his journey down the west coast in the fourteenth century, found reason to halt here for three days, if only for the presence of a large Muslim population rather than any intrinsic charm. 'Manjarur,' he wrote, is 'a large town on the largest inlet in the land of Mulaibar.'

> This is the town at which most of the merchants from Fars and al-Yaman disembark, and pepper and ginger are exceedingly abundant there . . . There is a colony of about four thousand Muslims there, living in a suburb alongside the town. Warfare frequently breaks out between them and the townspeople, but the sultan makes peace between them on account of his need of the merchants.[4]

As we drove out the next morning, I reflected that it was a powerful destiny that had brought the Portuguese to India five hundred years earlier. In the fifteenth century, Portugal had been no more than a petty Iberian principality, yet by the early sixteenth it had become not only a Continental power to reckon with but also a large empire, with territories from Brazil to Malacca. The rival Iberian kingdom of Castilla–León almost completely severed Portugal's connections with markets beyond the Pyrenees, so it was natural enough that, with their three-hundred-mile coastline and profusion of sheltered harbours, the Portuguese looked seaward for commercial and exploratory opportunities. It was eventually to Portugal's credit that the terror darkening the Atlantic, the legends of watery doom, were dispelled once and for all. Though a few sailors from Italy, England and Normandy had tested the Green Sea of Darkness before, it was Prince Henry 'the

Navigator' of Portugal who catalysed the age of discovery—and indeed the age of empire—with his fifteenth-century studies and schemes of maritime exploration. The advantages of modernity were plenty: a revival of interest in learning, the voyages and discoveries of Columbus, Dias and Vasco da Gama, and Copernicus' new view of the world.[5] Science, however, was only the means to an end, for the real zeal that drove the Portuguese voyages forward came from a fanatic, crusading religiosity. It could never be forgotten, through all the colourful annals of the Portuguese empire, and of the international trade that flourished when the sea route to the East was opened around the Cape of Good Hope, that Prince Henry's primary goal had been the salvation of Christianity. His title, in fact, was 'Grand Master of the Order of Christ'.

As we drove through stirring fields of intense green, at times touching the sea, at times abandoning it to climb through a minor ghat, it was plain that Prince Henry had succeeded in his holy design to an unbelievable extent. Mangalore still has a large Roman Catholic population, and so of course has Goa. In every town we passed between the two, rain-washed Christian spires rose from among the palm trees. The monsoon gave us no rest, the rain beating down all the way, and the rivers we crossed—the Sharavati, the Tadri and the Gangavali— flowed full and mighty, with no boats except those rocking hard against their moorings by the bank. Later, reading Ibn Battuta's travels, I felt a happy stab of recognition when he described Honnavar, a town just after the Sharavati bridge, as being half a mile from the sea, on a large inlet into which ships could enter. 'During the bushkal, which is the rainy season,' he wrote, 'this bay is so stormy and boisterous that for four months it is impossible for anyone to sail on it except for fishing.'

My mother and I stood on the long bridge and looked out at the raging river. Not a craft was in sight, not even a fishing boat. Though I now associate Honnavar with this single image of the monsoon, it was interesting to read the rest of Battuta's comments, particularly about the women of the Shafi'ite community, who wore no sewn garments but only unsewn lengths of cloth, one end of which they gird around their waists, and drape the rest over their head and chest. They are beautiful and virtuous, and each wears a gold ring in her nose. One peculiarity amongst them is that they all know the Qu'ran by heart.

A few centuries later, Honnavar was home to Timoja, a prosperous Hindu pirate who encouraged the Portuguese to set their sights on Goa. With his squadron of foists—swift, undecked, one-mast galleys—Timoja regularly harassed Muslim traders in the Arabian; and his sovereign, the raja of Honnavar, paid allegiance to the Vijayanagar empire, 'the stronghold of fighting Hinduism'. The survival of the Portuguese in India owed much to their strategic friendship with this empire, for it shared their attitude towards the Muslims, and distracted the Islamic forces that might otherwise have united to push the Christian intruders back around the Cape.[6]

I surveyed Kumte, a small and otherwise uninspiring town near Honnavar, with great personal interest, for here in the nineteenth century, German Protestant missionaries had converted a Brahmin called Suwartappa to Christianity. As voluntary conversion was unpardonable in the orthodox community to which the man—my great-great-great-grandfather—belonged, he was compelled to leave Kumte and seek a new life in Mangalore. There his son Christanuja, 'Bearer of Christ', sought the hand of a woman named Magretha Furtado, who was half-Portuguese. Although the Brahmin conversion at Kumte was interesting, it was a chance event—a romance—on the Portuguese side that has always fascinated me, for this, amazingly, diverted my ancestry from the Roman Catholicism that was far more prevalent on the west coast. Magretha's father, Sebastian Furtado, was a Portuguese Catholic priest who, having come out to Mangalore and rashly fallen in love with an Indian girl, had converted to Protestantism in order to marry her. It was, of course, a good thing he had been born in relatively modern times; a few centuries earlier, the Goan Palace of the Inquisition had functioned with dreadful zeal. In what must have been yet another unusual marriage, the daughter of the former priest wed the son of the former Brahmin, and the two settled down happily at Balmatta, near Mangalore. They raised a large family, one branch of which was carried forward by my grandfather, and his cousin Manohar Watsa wrote a short autobiography with some interesting insights on the spirit of the times:

> The Lutheran missionaries had been given this land by a British officer named Belmont, and the land was named after him, but in order to accommodate the Indian tongue, the name was changed to Balmatta. And it was here that the missionaries had built a church, a girls' school, and the Basel Mission Theological Seminary. Nearby, in the heart of Mangalore, they also built a boys' school . . . many sons and daughters of local Christians were educated in those schools.[7]

So Christanuja, son of a Brahmin, relinquished his ancestral religion, but not the scholarly pursuits of his caste; apart from being proficient in Sanskrit, Marathi and Tulu, and learning Hebrew, Greek and Latin so he could read the Bible in the original, he wrote a much appreciated book, *The Anglo-Kanarese Pocket Dictionary*.

From Kumte we drove further north in the late afternoon. Karwar and its pretty ghat passed quickly enough, for we were eager to exit Karnataka before dark. Soon the narrow winding roads of Goa replaced the broad state highway, and up we drove through Canacona and Quepem, past Madgaon, Nuvem and Velha Goa, across the Zuari and the Mandovi, until at last we reached Bardez in the deep, liquid green of a monsoon evening. Our hotel was unimaginatively constructed within the boundary of Fort Aguada, built by the Portuguese in 1612 to protect the mouth of the Mandovi. One of the fort's solid bastions still juts stoically into the Arabian, part of a great fortification that once guarded the headland and contained as many as seventy-nine guns.

Although it is a bit of a walk up to the fort itself, the view is worth the effort, as is the aspect of the well-preserved fort itself. Aguada was thus christened because of the freshwater springs that bubbled within the fort walls; these were the main source of drinking water for ships that entered the Mandovi after a long spell at sea. This is not, of course, the only fort along the coast of Goa, for to the north—beyond the beaches of Sinquerim, Candolim, Calangute, Baga, Anjuna and Vagator—are Chapora, enclosing a bluff over the mouth of the Chapora river, and Tirakhol, guarding the northern boundary marked by the Tirakhol river. To the east of Aguada, protecting the narrowest point of the Mandovi, is Reis Magos (named for the Magi, the three kings who journeyed to Bethlehem to pay homage to the infant Jesus), while further south stands Cabo da Rama and finally the island fort of Anjadiv. However, Fort Aguada and its environs are a brilliant introduction to Goa, for the fort itself has magnificent, intact laterite walls[8] and a lighthouse with a commanding view of both the coastline and the city of Panjim. This is the only Goan fortification never to have been taken by force. Back at the hotel, the only reminder of the fort around us was the great seaward bastion, a vantage point from which to look out at the Arabian in its most magnificent mood, at the heaps of seaweed and other flotsam that had been washed up angrily ashore, and at the coconut trees bent over almost double in the wind. A shipwreck lies near the shore here, a sight made all the more lonesome and pathetic by the great waves that fling themselves against it in the monsoon.

Across the water from Reis Magos is Panjim, or Panaji, Goa's often-overlooked state capital. The city's diminutive proportions and relative orderliness set it apart from other Indian cities, and make it a pleasant place to spend a morning or two. After an hour, it becomes apparent that Panjim is not an Indian city at all, and only feebly attempts to masquerade as one; it is really a legacy of the Portuguese, from the quaint secretariat on the waterfront (built over a former Muslim palace) and the curious statue of the hypnotist Abbé Faria to the narrow streets of the historic districts of Fontainhas and São Tome. The first time I went to Fontainhas, it was in search of an old backpackers' haunt called the Venite, and it must be said that I walked past this modest establishment twice without noticing it, so taken was I by the dusty wrought-iron *balcãos* and the shadowy streetscapes of backstreet Panjim. When I did at length notice the sign for 'Hospedario Venite', I climbed a dingy staircase into a room that seemed to embody the city of the past, with its old wooden floor and wall advertisements for the Museum of Christian Art. Time had certainly stopped here; during the two hours I spent eating a surprisingly excellent meal, the frizzy-haired man at the next table apparently read the same page of a dog-eared magazine over and over again, playing happily with the fries on his plate. This mild eccentricity was far removed from the craziness of Goa's infamous raves and acid beach parties, much frowned-upon by the locals but accepted as an inevitable part of the tourist economy. It was a quiet and happy craziness, the sort that defined the real Goa; it was the *sussegado* that every deluxe hotel on the coast had tried unsuccessfully to emulate; in short, it was the real thing. With some regret, I relinquished my half-eaten plate of rich bebinca, gastronomically defeated, and made my way back down the stairs and into the slanting sunlight of a Fontainhas afternoon.

From this old district, close to which executions once took place, I wandered over to São Tome, which was as delightfully well-maintained and pretty as Fontainhas was seedy and suspect. Little chapels, overflowing pots of bougainvillea, pastel-coloured houses with large wrought-iron grills, signboards for quaint *pousadas*: in short, a lovely old residential neighbourhood. Though I went to other places in Panjim, from the imposing Church of Our Lady of the Immaculate Conception, with its massive bell and curious zigzag staircases, to the beach at Dona Paula and the riverfront at Miramar, my abiding memory of Panjim is the sound of someone playing the violin through an open window on a tranquil little street near a whitewashed chapel in São Tome.

One day my mother and I drove to Old Goa, the abandoned Portuguese capital a little inland, up the south bank of the Mandovi.

We skirted Panjim and then drove, in fierce rain, along a seventeenth-century causeway across a lowland, once a swamp, beside the engorged river.

'Holy Rama!' exclaimed my mother, somewhat oddly for a Protestant in Catholic country. 'Look at that water!' The river was so high that it had risen to the level of the causeway on either side, and the illusion of driving on water was precarious in the extreme.

'Um,' I replied, but the monosyllable was more than just a time-honoured form of communication with a parent; I was thoroughly distracted by both the monsoon splendour of the Mandovi and the sheer historicity of this stretch of it. With my head full of irresistible images of sixteenth-century ships sailing in from the Arabian, letting out crew and cargo at the landing stages upstream, it was only with the greatest difficulty that I kept my eyes on the road. It was up the Mandovi, in 1510, that a Portuguese fleet from Cochin had first approached Goa, led by the indefatigable Affonso de Albuquerque. It was this 'Governor of India' who had bound the Portuguese to a policy of territorial gain in the East, for their existing land bases at Calicut and Cannanore were far from secure; their might was confined to the seas. The Dom's plan was to conquer Malacca, Aden, Hormuz and Goa: Malacca because it occupied a strategic position on the trade route between the Middle and Far East, and Aden and Hormuz because they held the entrance to the Red Sea and the Persian Gulf.[9] Goa would provide a base from which Indian Ocean trade could be more closely controlled than from distant Lisbon. Built on Tisvadi island, which took its name from a triangular aspect—the rivers Zuari and Mandovi cut it off from the mainland on the south and north—the port of Goa offered a safe anchor for ships coming in from the sea. Here Albuquerque envisioned a naval base and prospective colony where shipbuilding, repairs and replenishment of stores would be controlled by the Portuguese, independent of the whims of local rulers.

On the eve of the Portuguese invasion of Goa that would later shape a culture distinct from the rest of the Subcontinent, the port belonged to Yusuf Adil Shah, king of Bijapur. The younger son of the Ottoman sultan Amurath II, Adil Shah had earlier fled to Persia to escape the dynastic violence of an elder brother who succeeded to the throne, and in the country of his refuge he was raised a Shia. When he came of age, he sailed to India as a warrior slave, and proved conclusively that the blood of royalty ran in his veins——for he ended his romantic career as king, and king of a dominion far from home at that. Learning from Timoja of Honnavar that Adil Shah was not in Goa at the time, Albuquerque entered the Mandovi and met with little resistance. Eight nobles knelt before the conqueror and gave him the keys to the city, and as he marched to Adil Shah's palace accompanied by bearers of a gilt cross, the local Hindus strewed gold and silver filigree flowers in his path to welcome their deliverance from Islamic rule.[10] So convinced was Albuquerque of the necessity of a base here that, quite apart from dismissing such early irritants as Timoja of Honnavar's request for the newly conquered territory in return for his services,[11] he eventually defended his new acquisition even against King Manoel of Portugal. In time, when Manoel began to doubt that the port was worth the cost of its occupation, suspecting it was more a feather in Albuquerque's cap than a jewel in the Portuguese crown, Albuquerque wrote to an influential friend in Portugal, saying, 'The King trusts you and takes your advice; bid him hold onto Goa until the day of Judgement.'[12]

Thus occupied, Goa would soon become a great and glorious capital, but Albuquerque's early hold on it was weak and short-lived. It was to the Mandovi again—at a time of the year much like this, 'a starless night of tropical rain'[13]—that he was forced to retreat when Yusuf Adil Shah's son and successor, Ismail Adil Khan, returned to Goa with sixty thousand troops and laid siege to his own city. Albuquerque knew that some of the local Muslims would aid Khan's attack, and so, wrote Danvers:

He at last, unwillingly, came to the conclusion that the only reasonable course for him now to adopt was to retire to his ships, but before doing so he ordered Gaspar de Paiva to proceed to the fortress and cut off the heads of Melique Cufecondal and of 150 of the principal Moors of the city, to hamstring all the horses that were in the stables, and to set fire to the arsenals.[14]

Despite its brutality, however, this was a feeble move. The south-west monsoon prevented the Portuguese from putting out to sea, so they rode at anchor in the Mandovi, running dangerously low on supplies as the damp spoiled Albuquerque's stores. At length, in August, the ships were able to leave, and their commander, nothing daunted, returned in November with reinforcements including twenty-eight ships, 1700 Portuguese troops and a large number of Hindu troops provided by Timoja,[15] ever willing to lend a hand against those whose presence he detested. The Portuguese took Goa yet again, and this time killed every Muslim in sight. In a report of this vengeful conquest for the glory of Portugal, Albuquerque wrote to King Manoel:

In the capture of Goa the Turks lost over 300 men, and the road between Banastery and Gomdaly was covered with the bodies of those who were wounded and died in their attempt to escape. Many were also drowned while crossing the river. I afterwards burnt the city in which for four days the carnage was fearful, as no quarter was given to anyone. The agricultural labourers and the Brahmins were spared, but of the Moors killed the number was at least 6,000. It was indeed a great deed and well carried out . . . the whole territory from Cintagola to Goa is now your Majesty's. I beg your Majesty to bear in mind that Goa is a grand place, and in the event of India being lost, it can easily be reconquered if we hold a key such as Goa.[16]

Suddenly the mile-long causeway was behind us, and the violent images recalled by the Mandovi in spate receded as we drove into Old Goa. My first view of the abandoned capital of the conquistadors was through curves of clear glass momentarily carved out by our windscreen wipers. The rain hammered in frenzied hope against magnificent old churches, but slipped harmlessly off their blackish-red walls in smooth silver sheets. I caught my breath, not at the splendour of the buildings or the driving rain, but in admiration of the resistance that one offered the other. Here, long after the conquistadors had departed, the empire had fallen and the powerful priests had learned their place in a more secular society, was indelible testimony to the once-flushed fever of the cross. Giant blocks of laterite still pinioned the tyrannical beliefs of an earlier day firmly to the soil; this was not a chapter of history that had been allowed to slide away with the oozing mud and rushing water of five hundred monsoons.

Flanked on one side by the Basilica of Bom Jesus and on the other by the Se Cathedral, I realized with a shiver that Goa Dourada (Golden Goa), the 'Rome of the Orient', capital of all possessions in east Africa and Asia—was an extremely determined vision. Although Albuquerque had dealt with priests unequivocally, making it clear that no inroads on his authority would be tolerated, the power of the colonial church later grew rapidly until it became a sort of Christian dictatorship. By 1552 the treasury was being emptied for alms, and whole Indian towns were deserted by the forcible conversion of their populations. As Jayne put it with classic irony: 'the nature of this propaganda may be inferred from the fact that, in Goa, every "Gentile" was driven to church once a fortnight and compelled to listen to a sermon of one hour's duration on the beauties of a Christian spirit.'[17] The guards of the old order were now gone, and the arches and towers of dozens of lesser structures were crumbling or had sunk, forgotten, into the thick undergrowth, but the great churches of Old Goa were still alive with a gentler, more mellowed incarnation of the old spirit.

The massive Basilica of Bom Jesus that stood brooding before us was a Jesuit stronghold. Apart from the sheer size of the building, the first thing that struck me when I entered was the giant, gold-leaf statue of Ignatius Loyola, founder of the Jesuit order. The Jesuits had been foremost among the three fraternities that established missions in the colony; the other two were the Franciscans, who appealed directly to the poor, interpreting their suffering in terms of joy, and the Dominicans, who came to instruct their perceived inferiors yet absorbed much local flavour in their activities.[18] The Jesuits, despite an arrogance that made them unpopular with the government and the other fraternities, brought a spirit of service and sacrifice, using medical work and education as the tools of their creed. While on the one hand they pompously built a college on an elevated piece of ground that 'shut the air' out of the house of the Augustinians, they also rebuilt a hospital that had been started by Albuquerque, and made it better than the best hospitals in Europe at the time. The many schools they ran met the educational needs of all Goan youngsters, and it was therefore not surprising that the Portuguese colonial government eventually grew jealous and suspicious of their influence and suppressed them altogether in 1773.

Facing the altar in the basilica, I saw to my right an elevated casket containing the 'miraculous'—relatively undecayed—body of St. Francis Xavier, the greatest Jesuit in Goa. The cadaver was not a sight destined to be forgotten in a hurry; it returned to haunt me for several nights until I forcibly diverted my thoughts to the saint's life and times instead of his unfortunate remains. He had come out in 1542, when Goa Dourada was firmly established as the capital of the Portuguese colony, its military headquarters and naval base, and the main trading point for all produce from the East. Xavier was impressed at first sight, and wrote to the Society of Jesus in Rome: 'It has a college of Franciscans, really very numerous, a magnificent cathedral with a large number of canons, and several other churches. There is a good reason for thanking God that the Christian religion flourishes so much in this distant land in the midst of heathen.'[19]

Xavier's 'good reason', however, rapidly faded, for he was soon to see that the young colony had already begun to sink into immorality. Among the facets of Goan life that he later most strongly criticized were the corruption of merchants and government officials and the popular pastimes of Goa's colourful society, which included drinking, idling and stealing when money ran out. I wondered several times during that trip what the good saint would have thought of the colour photographs of his hideously blistered feet and claw-like hands that are still lovingly on display in the most unlikely places, most startlingly under the glass of a welcome desk at a small hotel in Anjuna. When I asked the owner why he kept such gory images there, he explained without taking offence: 'That's St. Francis' body. That's the miracle of God.' Perhaps the saint would have approved after all, as the man's faith was touchingly genuine.

For all its latter-day faith in the Catholic saints, Goa's early corruption was, unfortunately, one of the main reasons for the brevity of the colony's success. As early as 1539, Dom João de Castro, one of the more upstanding servants of Portugal, reported home to the king that out of sixteen thousand men on the payroll, only two thousand, apart from the garrisons of the fortresses, were actually in evidence.[20] The others were fictitious, created to supply officials with greater incomes than they had earned. How deeply the administration was diseased is evident from the fact that the viceroy himself—in Castro's time a Dom Garcia de Noronha, ironically a nephew of Albuquerque—made no attempt to conceal his desire to bleed the colony for personal gain, initially by selling every vacant civil and military office to the highest bidder and paying no salaries except, naturally, to himself.[21] While the officials in Goa grew fat upon the spoils of such malpractice, the common soldiers practically starved. They received payment only erratically and were often forced to fend for themselves, foraging through the colony for subsistence work and charity. Many of these men came from the lowest classes of Portuguese society; often they were convicted criminals who had been allowed to serve their terms by working in the colonies, or who were granted amnesty if they chose to enlist. Eventually, matters came to such a sorry pass that

> the Governors of India had ceased to trouble themselves with governing . . . the soldiers, being subject to no discipline, became insolent and devoted themselves to amusement . . . [and] the officials generally endeavoured to enrich themselvs by extortion and injustice, by which means they also entirely alienated the natives from Portuguese rule.[22]

Gone was Albuquerque's dream of a colony populated by a sounder breed. He had encouraged Portuguese men to marry Indian women, Brahmins and Muslims who were baptized, with the intention that the married men would become 'colonists' rather than mere soldiers. This policy might have worked had Albuquerque been succeeded by men such as himself, but the system fast deteriorated. The men he had intended to be craftsmen, gunsmiths and so on found native slaves to attend to business while they lounged about and drank to celebrate their profits. The women, too, grew rich on the dubious earnings of slave girls. In short, a large section of Goan society was decadent and indolent in the extreme, and instead of a class of colonists was bred a colony of idlers, of whom the French traveller Jean-Baptiste Tavernier was moved to observe:

> The Portuguese who go to India have no sooner passed the Cape of Good Hope than they all become Fidalgos or gentlemen, and add Dom to the simple name of Pedro or Jeronimo by which they were known when they embarked; this is the reason why they are commonly called in derision 'Fidalgos of the Cape of Good Hope.'[23]

Outside the basilica, the rain had stopped for a few minutes and I was able to look around more clearly, though the leaden sky cast a gloomy pall over the abandoned city. Old Goa felt like a tomb, yet like all tombs it brought back fleeting sensations of the life gone by. In the absence of people, indeed of any link to the present beyond the macadamized road surface, it was easy to picture the scene in the square and the *ruas* of an earlier time, when the monsoon had passed and the setting sun shone brilliantly on baroque buildings the colour of dry, darkened roses. In an evocative description of a typical Goan evening, Jayne wrote,

> In the hothouse atmosphere of Goa an exotic taste for display soon took root and flourished. When the sun was low each fidalgo who could afford a horse and jewelled harness hung with bells and trinkets of gold and silver, would ride forth in state to be admired from discreetly curtained lattices . . . A retinue of liveried slaves would accompany the cavalier, to carry his indispensable armoury of umbrellas and inlaid weapons. So, stiff and splendid in silk, brocade and armour, he would prance through the city. The lesser nobility of the boarding-houses, unable to singly purchase this attractive outfit, would share the glory and the cost, so that each subscriber in turn could take the air in gorgeous attire, under the shade of an umbrella carried by his attendant ad hoc.[24]

This glory, however, was ill fated, and came to a rather quick end. The Abbé Carré, who visited Goa in the mid-seventeenth century, wrote a heartfelt description of its ruinous condition:

> [I]t seems that this grand town, once so rich and called the Treasury and Queen of the East, is now at its last gasp. One sees no longer the splendour, magnificence, and those fetes, which drew all the Eastern people here to seek the friendship and goodwill of the Portuguese. Indian ambassadors, laden with rich presents, no longer come to Goa: nor do kings and princes

send their daughters to serve as slaves to the wives of its Viceroys. The Portuguese ladies now can no longer go out in carriages or palanquins of gold, enriched with precious stones and other valuable ornaments. They are no longer worshipped by troops of slaves, who bowing to the earth present them with incense and perfumes in golden vases, as if they were little human goddesses. No, they have brought the just anger of the Almighty on themselves by this luxury, these honours, and the idolatry, which they extracted with such overweening pride. Yet they still keep this pride in their misery and degradation.[25]

Away from the basilica and the intact structures around it are the ruins of the rest of the old capital. As we passed the half-fallen tower of the church of the Augustinian monastery, I thought about the other side of the coin: as great as the early dream had been, it had suffered from classically poor execution. Although Albuquerque—who, as a creature of his time, could be as barbaric as the occasion demanded—had refrained from interfering with local custom except to ban sati, this early tolerance was snuffed out by the altar boys who followed him. The Portuguese soon gained a name for an unsurpassed breed of intolerance, climaxing in the Inquisition. All 'heathen' temples in Portuguese territory were destroyed by viceregal decree, and non-Christian priests and teachers driven away. Although the law required conversions to be carried out by persuasion, it was a trifle farcical, as the means of 'persuasion' it allowed were not clearly distinguishable from force.[26] Close to the Se Cathedral across the road from the basilica was once a large square called the Terreiro de Sabaio, along whose boundary once stood a number of great buildings including the Senate, the Royal Tobacco Warehouse and the dreaded Palace of the Inquisition. When the colony's government lost control over the religious orders that had taken over Goa, a large-scale persecution began, with even the long-faithful Syrian Christians treated as heretics. The Inquisition descended on Goa for two centuries, and many an unfortunate prisoner met his end at the whim of an uncompromising body of judges. From the prison cells of the palace, captives were led to face the dreaded *auto-da-fe* (trial of faith) in the public square, grimly announced by the tolling of the cathedral bell. Those convicted of heresy were burnt at the military parade ground at the edge of the capital, while those who 'admitted' they were heretics were kindly strangled before being burnt.

The Abbé Carré devoted several pages to the expression of his low opinion of the Goan clergy, and in questioning their poor treatment of other European ecclesiastics, he concluded that

> they do not want people of honour or decency, or any one of probity and virtue like our French priests. They cannot endure . . . that these enlightened persons should learn of their ignorance, manner of living, indulgence in trading, and the abuses and impieties they commit in this country, far from the bright light of our doctrines.[27]

When Jean-Baptiste Tavernier visited the colony in 1648, he found a sad example of its overall decay in the decline of Goa's great hospital. Although it once possessed a 'considerable income' and sick persons were 'very well attended to', things had changed quickly, and in the late 1640s many Europeans who entered apparently did 'not leave it save to be carried to the tomb'. With his characteristic relish for medical peculiarities, Tavernier went on to describe the methods of treatment:

> I forgot to make a remark upon the frequent bleedings in reference to Europeans—namely, that in order to recover their colour and get themselves into perfect health, it is prescribed for them to drink for twelve days three glasses of 'pissat de vache' [cow's urine] . . . but, as this drink cannot but be very disagreeable, the convalescent swallows as little of it as possible, however much he may desire to recover his health.[28]

Eventually, the capital of the colony grew so diseased that it had to be abandoned. The island had never been healthy; cholera had appeared in 1543, and epidemics had become frequent. When the population began to thin, abandoned pools and tanks became breeding grounds for mosquitoes, and malaria joined the ranks of local ailments. Finally, the grand city was deserted by its upper class for the suburb of Panelim, first the viceroy in 1695, and then the archbishop and nobility. In 1712 a scheme for a new capital at Marmagoa was dropped, and in 1777 the government decided to reconstruct the old city on the same plan, cleaning its drains and aqueducts. Over the next five years, however, many reconstruction workers died of cholera and malaria, and few families could be persuaded to move into the old city. By 1843 the civil administration had moved to Panjim, and it was declared the new capital by royal decree;[29] but with its handful of modest buildings and cramped town design, it was a poor successor to the capital of old. Tragically, by 1846 only one building in Goa Dourada, the Convent of St. Monica, was still inhabited, and thus the ghost capital gave up its spirit more than 150 years ago.

In all the times I have visited Goa since then, I have not been able to bring myself to return to Old Goa. That first visit was poignant and disturbing, and I had little desire to reacquaint myself with the waning wonder of the St. Francis miracle. I usually spend my time exploring the smaller villages and the more remote monasteries and temples, wandering through the backstreets of Panjim, cycling through the lovely paddy fields with the sea breeze full in my face, stopping to eat in old-fashioned restaurants such as Fernando's at Raia, and inspecting old mansions and country houses, a few of which, with their translucent oyster-shell windows and collections of antiques, are open to the public. Particularly in the off-season, one can enjoy much of Goa without distraction, though the tourist months do bring such pleasant peculiarities as the Anjuna flea market—founded by hippies who sold their belongings to extend their stay, and now a large and colourful undertaking dominated by tribal craftspeople. More is visible when

Goa is free of visitors: apart from the handful of shop signs in Portuguese, with the occasional 'Apotheek' and 'Barberia', there is plentiful evidence of a hybrid culture. Christian emblems are everywhere, with even some small garden patches bearing a stone or plaster cross. The women wear Western dress, though their features are usually distinctly Indian, and the popularity of meat and alcohol consumption is quite marvellous. Although Goa is technically part of India, it remains different at heart, with many of its people referring to those in the rest of the country as 'Indians'. Much has changed in the four decades since Goa was absorbed into India, with the world—first hippies and now the monied classes—having rediscovered it, but the little state always manages to find itself again, to catch its breath between the annual influxes.

One night, on the monsoon trip I made to Goa with my mother, I drove out in search of a telephone booth and found more than I was looking for. Passing a tiny shack with the appropriate yellow sign, I turned back to investigate. The rain had not abated and I was not in a sweet temper, having just taken a wrong turn into a pig farm, out of which unhappy place I extricated myself and the car with the greatest difficulty. There was, I thought at the time, no worse corner to be boxed into than a dead end that appeared to be thigh-deep in grunting, rooting pigs as far as the eye could see, which admittedly was not a great distance in the dark and the storm. As I entered the dripping shack, it was heartening to see signs of human life—two 'girls' well over fifty lounging over the counter, listening to the radio and reading dog-eared women's magazines. While mopping my face with my sleeves and trying to dial my number, I listened to them talk, for evidently they were having a great deal more fun than I was. I couldn't quite catch the conversation, but the rising excitement was palpable when a young man came into sight outside, his motorbike spluttering to a halt. They hastily smoothed their hair and flattened down their patched and darned blouses, and then pretended they hadn't seen him until he walked in.

'Gimme a peg, aunty,' said the fellow to the elder of the two, who blushed and fluttered. Miraculously, a folding table was pulled out from under a dirty desk and a chair set beside it, close to where I was standing. From a cupboard emerged a plastic lace tablecloth of indeterminate age, a grimy glass and some rum, and a bottle containing a now-flat aerated drink. The young man was invited to sit down and a generous drink poured. The telephone booth had, in less than a minute, become a bar, and, to my embarrassment, I was now the chief topic of conversation.

'Still she's trying,' whispered one woman to the other.

'Tell her now,' was the laconic reply.

By then the young man was staring at me unabashedly, unsure whether to condescend to be amused by an 'Indian'.

'Out of order!' they chorused suddenly, turning towards me and giggling, their lank grey hair falling round their faces. There was a sudden burst of laughter from the neighbourhood dom.

Notes

1. Feni is a strong local liquor in Goa, distilled either from the juice of the cashew fruit that is grown widely in the area or from coconut milk. Cashew feni is by far the harder to stomach.
2. K.G. Jayne, *Vasco da Gama and his Successors 1400-1580* (1910; reprint, New Delhi: Asian Educational Services, 1997), p. 73.
3. Frederick Charles Danvers, *The Portuguese in India* (1894; reprint, New Delhi: Asian Educational Services, 2003) p. xxxv.
4. *The Travels of Ibn Batuttah*, ed. Tim Mackintosh-Smith (London: Picador, 2003), p. 221.
5. Jayne, pp. 2, 6, 9.
6. Ibid., pp. 73-74.

7. Manohar C. Watsa, *Never Say Die: An Autobiography* (Toronto, 1994), pp. 3-6.
8. The laterite blocks were of a striking and regal shade of blackish-red, and on closer examination appeared to be pitted and many-textured, with rainwater collecting in every available nook. Of this unusually strong and beautiful building material, found all along the west coast, Buchanan had observed:

> What I have called indurated clay . . . is one of the most valuable materials for building . . . It is full of cavities and pores, and contains a very large quantity of iron in the form of red and yellow ochres. As it is usually cut into the form of bricks for building, in several of the native dialects it is called the brick stone (Itica cullu). Where, however, by the washing away of the soil, part of it has been exposed to the air, and has hardened into a rock, its colour becomes black, and its pores and inequalities give it a kind of resemblance to the skin of a person affected with cutaneous disorders; hence in the Tamul language it is called Shuri-cull, or itch-stone. The most proper English name would be Laterite, from Lateris, the appellation that may be given to it in science.

9. Jayne, p. 80.
10. Ibid., p. 82.
11. Danvers, pp. 189-90.
12. Jayne, p. 104.
13. Ibid., p. 82.
14. Danvers, p. 199.
15. Jayne, p. 84.
16. Danvers, pp. 211-12.
17. Jayne, p. 183.
18. Ibid., p. 184.
19. Ibid., p. 188.
20. Ibid., p. 291.
21. Ibid., pp. 290-91.
22. Attrib. Diogo do Conto, *Observaçoes sobre as Principaes de Decadencia dos Portuguezes na Asia*, quoted in Danvers, p. xxxviii.

23. Jean-Baptiste Tavernier, *Travels in India*, ed. William Crooke, trans. V. Ball (1925; reprint, New Delhi: Asian Educational Services, 2001), vol. I, p. 150.
24. Jayne, pp. 189-90.
25. Sir Charles Fawcett, ed., *Travels of the Abbé Carré in India and the Near East, 1672 to 1674* (1946; reprint, New Delhi: Asian Educational Services, 1990), p. 216.
26. J.M. Richards, *Goa* (New Delhi: Vikas, 1982), pp. 25-26.
27. *Travels of the Abbé Carré*, p. 211.
28. Tavernier, p. 160.
29. Richards, pp. 37-40.

Coromandel Colonies

Madras
The Forgotten Fort

Changes of time are fickle, and if you suffer this opportunity to pass over, you shall perhaps in vain afterwards pursue the same when it is fled and gone.

—Francis Day to his superior Andrew Cogan,
after having negotiated with a local ruler
for a strip of land south of Machilipatnam[1]

I had lived in Madras, that little-praised metropolis on the Coromandel, for six years before it occurred to me that it might be vaguely in order to visit Fort St. George. This was where today's six-million-strong city and its steaming suburbs had taken root four hundred years earlier, in the shape of a fortified English 'factory' built by a fistful of traders and mercenaries. In retrospect, it seems unthinkable to have so carelessly overlooked this orchid among the weeds in my backyard. I had been dimly aware of the fort's existence, of course, but perhaps it was the ungainly bulge of the present-day secretariat of Tamil Nadu in the very womb of the defences, and all the hangers-on thereof, that had diminished its approachability. Despite living on the edge of Egmore,

I had been unmoved by the fact that this neighbourhood was once part of the fort's generous social hinterland; in fact, my apartment block possibly stood on the site where an English garden house had once nestled among trees on sprawling grounds. Facing the Bay of Bengal a few miles to the east, the fort remained on the periphery of my consciousness.

I never think of those six years without an odd feeling of guilt, for Fort St. George has few enough admirers in the great unruly city, and has come to accept its own abandonment with a meekness that is hard to countenance. The fort's ghosts are content to slumber, unsought and undisturbed, behind the solid ramparts that have protected them for centuries from the incursions of the world. It is as if they are lost in a deep, shadowy contemplation of romances past; of assaults thwarted and sieges held; of tragedies from which the pain has long since seeped away; of bales of chintz and muslin that built many a quick fortune; of pink and brown seashells lying scattered on the shore, and catamarans bleached ivory in the sun; and, incessantly, of the shifting sands upon which began and ended a thousand voyages. Now, when I think about their world more intimately, I reflect that it must take a special night to awaken these men and women, to persuade them to surface briefly from under the dark folds of their buried layer of time. A summer night, perhaps, when the sea breeze grows irresistibly sweet and altogether too reminiscent of life; a night when souls might return despite themselves to pace the edge of the moat and await the appearance of a ship on the horizon or a horseman in the distance, to listen once more to the strains of song drifting across from the barracks, or merely to rejoice once again in the sentiments of a letter written lately from home in a familiar and beloved hand.

It was only when my father came across for a short vacation one year that I went over to the fort and took a look, for my love of history was yet nascent compared with his.

'What's there in this city that we can go and *see*?' he asked hopefully one Sunday afternoon. He was, I suspect, a little tired of sitting around all morning in his pyjamas drinking beer and making fatherly conversation with me, touching as this parent–child ritual was. 'You know, some old cemetery or something.'

'We could go across and see Fort St. George,' I said, a little reluctantly. The day was hot and the beer was cool and frothy, at least if one drank very quickly. 'I've always meant to go.'

We abandoned our heavy stone mugs and set off in a humid, sweaty silence. The romance of the past was about the last thing on my mind as perspiration ran in rivulets through my hair and trickled wantonly down my spine. I shifted and leaned hard against the back of my seat, taking an inconsequential satisfaction in interrupting this rude descent.

'I have never understood,' declared my father, looking out of the car window and taking in a hundred hot, hurrying pedestrians with an imperious wave of his hand, 'why in a *free country* all of these people choose to live in Madras of their *own volition*.' This being a familiar question, I acknowledged it with a gloomy nod, ignoring the aspersions it cast upon my own intelligence and inclinations.

With this brief, unromantic visit on a disgustingly hot day, however, was born my enduring love affair with Madras's forgotten fort—an affection that has returned me time and again to the corridors of Clive and Wellesley, and the streets of Streynsham Master and Elihu Yale. For it was here that the seeds of the eastern British empire were first sown and the bulb of modern India planted, here within the ramparts of a small fort built in 1640 and named after England's patron saint. Some dismiss Fort St. George as a mere emblem of colonialism, an early stronghold of the pernicious East India Company, but it is infinitely more than that. Within the fort were carefully moulded the prototypes of every system greater India would later adopt, from surveys, communication and administration to education, medicine and the military. It is both strange and sorry that, despite the best efforts of the city's tiny communities of storytellers and heritage enthusiasts, this immense significance is overlooked.

In all honesty, there is not, at first sight, anything of earth-shaking interest in the fort. The facade is plain and unremarkable: a cluster of warehouse-like buildings separated by narrow streets that host what appears to be an interminable employees' tea break, from which the participants occasionally stray back indoors in a brave attempt to perform some official duties. Unlike many such historic sites, the premises do not cry out for attention—and herein lies their greatest tragedy. A judicious fraction of the historic buildings has been maintained just well enough to keep both vociferous complaint and enthusiastic exploration at bay. Half a dozen signboards, erected no doubt out of a grim sense of duty by the ASI, blandly draw one's attention to the fact that this building or that is a national heritage monument, following which they list the number and variety of ways in which one might be prosecuted should one presume to tamper with the structure. The name of the building, the date and method of its construction, or—heaven forbid—the purpose it might once have served are almost always withheld.

Should one manage to read to the end of one of these signboards without interruption, any further loitering with map in hand causes the fort's military personnel to nip in the bud any interest in a subject as wickedly intellectual as history. More than once have I been abruptly asked to turn about and march away from such state secrets and chests of buried treasure as these dilapidated old structures might contain.

'Yes?' an armed guard once asked in belligerent challenge as I pottered about the premises, looking vapid, benign and, I would imagine, incapable of any sort of subversion.

'Hmm?' I responded absently, still investigating the southern face of St. Mary's Church.

'*Hmm?* Ha! Yes? What?' he persisted indignantly, getting louder and ruder with each syllable, obviously irked at being mumbled at by a map-toting woman.

I looked at my diagram of the fort circa 1653 and decided it would be pointless trying to explain my mission. Already a bristling bevy of guards had turned around to regard me with deep suspicion. Resisting the urge to tell the youngest and pimpliest of them to do up his shoelaces, I concluded that the only living thing that could safely display an interest in these buildings for more than a minute was the audacious species of weed that flourished in the plentiful fissures in their walls. This hardy, annoying plant seemed an appropriate symbol of the authorities' indisputable right to stand petty guard over monuments until they fall down all by themselves, should no one possess the impertinence to assist them to a quicker, less painful demise.

If citizens are not allowed to study the fort and its possessions freely, I reflected when I visited with my father, they might at least be permitted to pay some sort of homage, however perfunctory, to its founders. It is tragic that not even one tiny, humble corner of Madras carries a reminder of Francis Day, Member of Council at Machilipatnam, who searched the Coromandel for land on which to build a fortified factory for the English; or of his superior Andrew Cogan, Chief Factor, who gave Day his full support for the erection of the said factory, or of the dubash (literally, speaker of two languages) Beri Thimappa, who helped the East India Company negotiate with local governor Damarla Venkatadri for land. Without the enterprising Day and Cogan, and the fort they founded north of the Portuguese settlement at San Thome, the city of Madras would not stand in its present location.

Yet the pair was much criticized even by their contemporaries. The great oil-soaked, soot-encrusted harbour of today, and the marina, with its long display of splendid Indo-Saracenic buildings and memorials to latter-day popular leaders, might still be a desolate strip of bare yellow sand. As S. Muthiah, a veteran chronicler of Madras, writes,

> Day and his superior at Machilipatnam, Cogan, together with their Indian assistants and a few writers (clerks), 25 European soldiers, led by Lt Jermyn and Sgt Jeffery Bradford, and local artificers eventually arrived at Madraspatnam in the *Eagle, Unity* and a third ship on February 20, 1640, to start work on their settlement, despite getting little or no encouragement from

their superiors either in Surat or Bantam (Java). Yet, for all their inestimable contribution to the founding of this metropolis, Day and Cogan were hounded into oblivion by John Company.[2]

And there, needless to say, Day and Cogan have remained. Day returned to England and was never heard from again. Cogan, after being cleared of the charges the Company had brought against him, actually offered his services again but was refused. He settled down in Greenwich, but rural tranquillity was not to be his for long; his fortune was sequestered by a parliamentary committee, and he was soon swept up in the events of the civil war and had to flee to the Continent. He returned to England eventually, but died soon after his daughter petitioned the king for compensation.[3]

As for the fort, what could have been a marvellous historical district is an unhappy mixture of gracious but largely unnamed buildings, some well kept and some falling apart. The fort's congested, disorganized streets are today monopolized by smoke-belching Ambassadors belonging to the secretariat of Tamil Nadu, whose original building occupies the very site of Day's first fort.[4] This establishment intends to move to a new state-of-the-art complex in another neighbourhood, and one wonders what will become of the fort after the wheels of government have rolled away. The military presence will probably remain, but one hopes that more attention will finally be given to conservation. There are rich possibilities: old streets can be brought to life once more, historical tours permitted with knowledgeable guides, the tombstones in the churchyard restored, and the cobwebs blown off the treasures in the Fort Museum. Until such time as the authorities are possessed by some enterprise and imagination, however, the fort is doomed to its present state, and its story will have to be told to the accompaniment of car horns and grinding gears, from beneath a shroud of dust and grime.

By the time Fort St. George was built, in the mid-seventeenth century, the East India Company had been in operation for forty years.

It was Queen Elizabeth I who had signed the royal charter creating the 'Governor and Company of Merchants of London trading into the East Indies', and the body so formed was no ordinary trading company—it was the product of a new England, a country that had recently undergone a heady transition from uncivilized and relatively unimportant to civilized and remarkable. Like a splendid new ship with billowing sails, Elizabethan England was propelled into an age of physical and cultural exploration by generous patriotism and 'a new English pride linked to the Protestant faith',[5] not to mention a blossoming of the arts. This gave the country a certain adolescent boldness, the confidence to blithely defy the exclusive eastern trading rights claimed by the Roman Catholic states of Spain and Portugal, who had begun their explorations much earlier. Fortuitously, the mood at the English court was one of patronage, particularly of such figures as John Dee, a cartographer and philosopher who had both a 'mystical vision of a new European Golden Age with England in the lead' and a 'highly practical understanding of navigation, trade and commerce'.[6]

The time was thus right for an enterprise that would drive the English eastward in search of more challenging opportunities to flex their new-found musculature. The original subscribers to the Company were 218 London merchants, and Antony Wild, in his delightful book *The East India Company*, examines what they were granted:

> The expansion of European trade eastwards had led to the formation of various national incorporated companies, all including the local version of the word 'Indies' in their names. The Charter of the English East India Company, granted in 1600, gave it a monopoly on all English trade to the east of the Cape of Good Hope. That such a definition could be stretched to encompass the entire globe—the Cape of Good Hope is, after all, but a long voyage east of the Cape of Good Hope—did not occur to those who drafted the Charter. One hundred and eighty years later the Company could be found trading as

far east as Vancouver in the American Northwest, buying furs (with, one hopes, a due sense of the linguistic irony) from the Indians there.[7]

Between 1600 and 1640, the Company shadowed the sails of other European powers like the Dutch and Portuguese, voyaging east in a late bid to join the spice race. Its endeavours ranged from legitimate attempts at trade to downright piracy, a significant instance of the latter being the seizure of a Portuguese ship carrying pepper and Indian cotton cloth. The ill-gotten cloth was subsequently sold in Java and Sumatra—and thus was shaped the future of the Company's activities.

For, having failed to establish a proper trade link with the Spice Islands, where the Dutch were already well entrenched, the English turned their attention to India and its easily marketable textiles. With the permission of the emperor Jahangir, the Company established a factory at Surat, a large Mughal port 150 miles north of Bombay. This was followed by Machilipatnam, on the coast of present-day Andhra Pradesh, and then by Madras and Bombay. In Bengal, factories were founded at Hooghly, Cassim Bazar and English Bazar. Indian textiles became quite the thing in England, and the result of this popularity was the 'piece' trade, as opposed to the spice trade upon which the Company had originally set its sights. Without the large and profitable cargoes of calico, muslin, silk and chintz that were shipped home to a willing market, the Company might have floundered and sunk at a very early stage. As Wild puts it, 'whilst the Company's long-held dream of exporting fine woollen English broadcloth to the East was never realised, it was as cloth merchants that they survived.'[8]

The Company eventually burgeoned into the largest commercial enterprise the world had ever seen, conducting not only trade but also war and politics—indeed, the entire affairs of state of large parts of the Subcontinent, with an army far larger than that of Britain itself. Three 'presidencies' grew out of its main trading posts, Madras, Bombay and Calcutta. After the Mutiny of 1857, it was inevitable that the British

Crown take over the Company's possessions, which it did with great pomp on 1 November 1858. However, 'it is doubtful,' says Wild, 'whether many understood the difference. John Company had always been an elusive character, and the loyalties he had engendered were a measure of the vigour of his actions and the depth of his purse, not of personal merit.'[9]

When the Crown took over, it continued, as the Company had done, to 'impose its rule through tiny, isolated cantonments of English traders, soldiers and administrators'. Though some British settled in India, the majority did not sink roots, and this was the pattern established throughout the East. Neither India nor any eastern possession became a real Crown colony such as Australia, Canada, Kenya or Rhodesia, where permanent settlers took over the land.[10]

Not much of this was evident in 1640, but in the light of things to come, it is not altogether fantastic that a rude structure in south India by the unimaginative name of Fort House, and the dozen thatched huts around it, grew so quickly into a place of importance. In 1641, a year after Fort St. George was founded, Andrew Cogan shifted his base from Machilipatnam to Madras, and with this move, the little fort spearheaded by Francis Day became the centre of British power on the Coromandel. The Company's servants being well aware that political strength and English representatives in local courts paved the way to prosperous trade, the fort was destined to widen its influence rapidly: less than two decades after it was built, Fort St. George became the locus from which the Company 'ruled' its possessions, including Bengal in the north-east and Bantam in present-day Java. All Company settlements in India were brought under Fort St. George in 1658—ironically, the same year in which Aurangzeb ascended the Mughal throne. From then, for a whole hundred years, the fort and Madras—the settlement that steadily grew around it—reigned supreme, until the wheel of fortune came to a halt on the banks of a great tidal river in Bengal.

By the 1650s Fort St. George had assumed more complete, if still diminutive, dimensions, much of the construction having been financed by Day himself. Around the fort (which was also known as the Castle) were built the houses of European settlers, chiefly Portuguese from nearby San Thome, a Catholic settlement in the area where it is believed that Thomas Didymus, the 'doubting' apostle himself, was martyred. Day and his immediate successors had invited these settlers (as 'the first thing that was required was a population') and even lent them money to build their houses, but the size of this settlement never exceeded fifty houses in the century that followed. J. Talboys Wheeler, in his invaluable history of the Madras Presidency, describes the 'strange old fort' of the 1670s during the reign of merry King Charles: in the fort, which was synonymous with White Town,

> There was the Warehouse piled high with goods of all descriptions; some which seemed fresh from Aldersgate Street or the Cheap . . . the little Chapel, where every man in the Agency, from the youngest Apprentice up to the Honorable Governor himself, was compelled to attend the daily reading of Morning and Evening Prayers, besides two sermons on Sundays, and something extra on Wednesdays. There was the Refection Room, where all the members of the Agency took their dinners and suppers . . . There was the School room where all the children of all the soldiers, and others were taught to read and cypher . . . the Council Chamber, where all the members of Council were summoned to attend on every Monday and Thursday morning, at eight o'clock, either by the Secretary himself, or by one of the Writers and Factors under him.[11]

To the north of White Town thrived an ever-growing commercial colony of Indian and other settlers, known rather inelegantly as Black Town. Wheeler refers to this town as well:

Here the houses and population had rapidly increased in

numbers; and the streets bore a very different appearance from the collection of bamboo huts which rose up during the earlier days of the colony. In the Choultry Plain to the southward of the Fort, the weavers and painters in the employment of the Factory appear to have erected a little village for themselves; whilst the fishermen at the mouth of the Triplicane River were living, marrying, and dying—catching fish, making nets, and celebrating their own peculiar festivals—just as they had done in the old days of the kings of Chola and Pandya, and in all probability just as they will still be doing some thousand years hence, when Lord Macaulay's New Zealander comes poking about our tombs, and wondering what manner of people we have been. Two or three miles off were the little Native villages of Nungumbaukum, Egmore, Persewaukum, and Perambore, which were too far off to be visited by the Europeans of that day.[12]

It is hard to imagine how, over the course of a few hundred years, these and other remote and ancient villages, and the Portuguese settlement at San Thome, together became the fourth-largest city in India.

Into this fledgling colonial world on the Coromandel arrived in 1672 a Boston-born, England-bred youth by the name of Elihu Yale. Having obtained employment with the Company, he reported to the fort during the governorship of the independent-minded Streynsham Master, among whose enterprises was the building (without the Company's permission) of St. Mary's Church in Fort St. George. The Company was not predisposed towards missionary activity, but in the fort, as eventually across India, the Christian community began to make its own arrangements for worship. The young Yale contributed three-fifths of his annual salary in pagodas to the subscription for the church, which was designed and constructed by the fort's master gunner (the gunners were also engineers). This donation was, of course, neither the last nor the most famous one Yale was to make.

Yale had a successful career at the fort: he rose to the position of governor by the age of thirty-nine and amassed a vast fortune, presumably by engaging in the kind of independent business not uncommon among Company servants. During his Fort St. George years Yale made some important contributions to the development of Madras, adding to the Company's territories and, further afield, building Fort St. David near Cuddalore 'to ensure the Company's toe-hold in India when the French threw the English out of Fort St. George'. It was also during his time that the Corporation of Madras was established. However, he is remembered not for any of this, but for a modest contribution that he made in later years to the Collegiate School in Connecticut, later to become a famous Ivy League university. It is recorded that Yale contributed 'textiles, books and pictures', of which 'the textiles realised £562 12s' and the 'books and paintings were valued at £600'.[13] It was not so much the nature but the timing of the gift that caused the university to be named after Yale, for at the time it was a struggling institution.

Thus was he immortalized in America, far from the south Indian port where he had built his fortune, and from where he departed under somewhat unhappy circumstances, charged by his colleagues with greed and bad management. The controversial end of Yale's tenure as governor is evident from this extract from a letter sent by the Court of Directors of the Company:

> Mr Yale, our late President, we would have continue at Madras until the arrival of our supervisor, Captain Goldsborough; that all differences may be fairly adjusted there by the wisdom and moderation of Captain Goldsborough; and that upon Mr Yale's return hither, we may have nothing to say to him but to bid him welcome home.[14]

St. Mary's Church, at which Yale worshipped during his days at the fort, and where he was wedded to Catherine Hynmers—the first marriage to be consecrated in the church—is the oldest church built by the Anglicans east of Suez. In 1948 it was given over to the Church of India, now the Church of South India. That the 1680 building still survives is largely due to the fantastic four-foot breadth of its walls, not to mention its two-foot-thick roof comprising three semicircular masses of solidly laid bricks. As the church was built close to the sea, it had to be strong enough to withstand both cyclones and sieges, including cannonballs fired from French ships.

What fascinates me most about the building is not so much its architecture or anything it contains, but the gravestones with which its compound is paved. The first time I visited the fort, my father and I looked about for the old English tombstones that, according to Colonel Reid in his lovely little guidebook *The Story of Fort St. George*—not available, of course, in the fort—had been shifted here two centuries earlier from a nearby cemetery after the French, during their seiges of the fort in 1746 and 1758, had used them as gun platforms and shields. Imagining that the stones stood somewhere in the churchyard, we looked about for a few minutes only to discover, to our dismay, that we were actually *walking* on them.

Treading gingerly on these weathered slabs, we found that many were broken and had been patched together roughly. Damage was sustained not only during the French sieges but also later, when the British themselves took the ill-fated stones up to the ramparts to use as gun platforms. In fact, according to Col. Reid, they were returned to their present position only in 1807.[15] Now laid head-to-foot around the old church like bizarre paving stones—as if all that is English must be contained within this compound—the stones are left to the mercies of the elements and of those who tread on them. Among other remarkable engravings, the oldest English tombstone and inscription in India lies here. Dated 1652, it bears the words:

Memoriae Sacrvm
Dominae Elizabethae Baker,

Domini Aaronis Baker
(Anglorvm, hisce locis)

—the last line of which translates loosely to 'English, buried here'.

Elizabeth was the wife of Aaron Baker, the first president of Madras. She died at sea after childbirth, her ship still three weeks from Madras, and was brought to the fort to be buried. I winced involuntarily as I watched a motorcycle being wheeled casually across her epitaph and out of the church gate. My father had not noticed; he was gloomily inspecting the damage done to other stones by a line of flowerpots, which, by generously leaking water and spreading the prodigious quantities of guano already spattered across the stones, were doing their bit to make some of the historic inscriptions virtually unreadable.

St. Mary's was once the stage for the courtly splendour encouraged by such men as Streynsham Master, who founded the tradition of the governor attending services with much ceremony:

> Master, and the first congregation, set conventions that were to be followed for many years—full wigs, the most constricting of European clothes, the Governor in periwig and laced coat walking in state from 'Fort House' to the church between 200 soldiers drawn up in two lines all along the short walk, the residents awaiting his arrival then following him into church while the organ pealed the voluntary . . .[16]

Not surprisingly, such elaborate practices wilted in the sultry Madras climate, but other traditions nurtured by this early church acquired a significance their early patrons could hardly have envisioned. The fort's first hospital, for instance, began in 1664 as a tiny place to treat sick Company soldiers, in a house rented by Governor Edward Winter from Andrew Cogan. A subscription was then raised and a two-storey hospital building constructed near St. Mary's, to be administered by the church.[17] Several times did this first proper Western-style hospital relocate, growing all the while into what is now the massive government health system. Apart from medicine, the fort's Christian community supported charity, and its early poor-relief activities developed into the Friend-in-Need Society, a large institution that runs old-age homes across the country even today.[18] Today, few who pass St. Mary's on a Sunday and hear the congregation singing lustily over the sounds of traffic associate the church with any such illustrious past.

Also born within the fort, closely affiliated to the church, was the institution of English education in India, arguably a factor in the country's present success in international business environments. Strangely, it was not an Anglican but a Capuchin missionary, Ephraim de Nevers, who first conducted an English class in his own house, even before St. Mary's was built. In his description of the fort circa 1670, however, Wheeler mentions the practice of sending out a schoolmaster from England:

> There was the 'Schoolmaster', at a salary of fifty pounds a year, who had been sent out to teach all the children of English parents to read, write, cypher, and hate the Roman Catholics. Any parents whatever,—Portuguese, Hindoo, or Mussulman,—might likewise send their children to be similarly taught; but only on the condition that they should also be instructed in the principles of the Protestant religion.[19]

India's first Western-style school was the work of the Anglicans: St. Mary's Charity School, founded in 1715 by fort chaplain William Stevenson. The 'Rules for the better establishing and management' of this school, 'erected by the unanimous consent of the Vestry of St. Mary's parish' laid down

> That in some convenient place within the English town, there be proper accommodation made at first for 30 poor Protestant

Children, diet and education gratis . . . That the children, whether boys or girls, shall be taken into the school house at five years of age or thereabout; and be put out to service or apprenticeships when they are about 12 years old. And while they are entertained in the school, the boys shall be taught to read, write, cast accounts, or what they may be further capable of, and the girls shall be instructed in reading and the necessary parts of housewifery.[20]

The Charity School shifted location and changed names a few times before coming to its present site in Kilpauk as St. George's School and Orphanage. The choir of this school has sung at St. Mary's for close to three centuries. Although St. George's is only one among the city's dozens of English-medium schools, therein lies its significance: there are now countless such schools all over India. Whatever its accent and grammar, whatever the peculiarities of its idiom, English still approaches the status of an Indian lingua franca, at least in the cities and in corporate dealings. There are, in fact, more English-speaking Indians in India today than there were when the British left in 1947.

The fort's original white settlement, in which all these systems and more germinated rapidly in the semi-tropical warmth, was a busy enough place with the work of trade and administration being carried on within. Equally interesting, however, was the bustling, cosmopolitan commercial colony next door. The first settlers in Black Town were weavers, bleachers and dyers from Andhra, followed by the merchants, traders and financiers who did business with them. The latter were Gujaratis and Marwaris—foreigners in the South, yet hardly the most exotic of the settlers around the fort. Armenian Street was named after the community of Armenians who lived there (and left their church for posterity), and a small settlement of Jews thrived on Coral Merchant Street. Wheeler recorded the Armenians' first appearance in India, during Elihu Yale's governorship, as a 'great event' in the history of Madras. A contract had been signed between Sir Josiah Child, on behalf of the Company, and Coja Panous and Sir John Chardin on behalf of the Armenian nation, granting the Armenians 'equal share and benefit of all indulgences' that the Company had granted or should grant to any of their own 'Adventurers' or other English merchants. They were also to be permitted 'to live in any of the Company's cities, garrisons, or towns in India, and to buy, sell, and purchase land or houses, and be capable of all civil offices and preferments in the same manner as if they were Englishmen born . . .'[21]

The Jews were treated well, too: the charter of the first Corporation of Madras awarded them equal representation with the English, Portuguese and Hindus.[22] Their chief business was the export of diamonds to London and the import of silver and coral. Sadly, all that survives of their once prosperous presence are their tombstones, shifted from their original location to the Lloyd's Road cemetery. Though the Jews and Armenians are long gone, the colony they shared with Indian traders survives 350 years later as Georgetown——still the heart of commercial activity in Madras, with its narrow streets and old merchant houses.

Antony Wild describes a typical landing in Madras during the Company's rule, before the Crown took over and built a harbour:

> East Indiaman moors out to sea; passengers prepare to board native outriggers which have rowed out through the rollers; ladies modestly avert eyes from eight near-naked boatmen; price renegotiated for landing; passengers and luggage loaded; boat thrown around in waves; price renegotiated upwards; hair-raising final surge through surf; passengers and luggage deposited damply on beach; first unbelieving glimpse of the classical buildings of the city, glistening white with a stucco made from burnt seashells.[23]

Perhaps the more distinguished travellers made their way to the fort's 'Snob's Alley', St. Thomas Street, close to St. Mary's Church. This street is now closed to the public, but even a glimpse gives a sufficient taste of the old days. On one of my visits, I managed to get a little way down the street without anyone noticing, and I was enthralled by the old houses on either side, the lower parts of which probably predate the French sieges of 1746 and 1758 and the higher storeys having been reconstructed between 1760 and 1780.[24] A record of the rent roll of 1688 shows that the houses were owned by British and Portuguese alike, some of them women; and about half the properties were rented, mostly to British tenants. Sanitary conditions in the fort could not have been very impressive, for Wheeler points out that there were eleven christenings, thirteen marriages and 101 burials that year.[25] Hygiene aside, what a place the fort must have been in its heyday. Looking down Snob's Alley, one can easily picture the lower floor of each house storing all manner of interesting goods for private trade, the narrow street crowded with traders, servants and visitors, and the bustle parting for a minute now and again when a lady passed in a palanquin or a merchant returned home at the end of the day. Reid, whose book contains a delightful aside to this effect, says, 'Perhaps a more peaceful touch might come from the balcony down the street where the light caught the fair ringlets of a young lady sitting in a long chair waiting hopefully for the sea breeze.'[26]

The fort was initially guarded by walls on three sides, with the Elambore River offering modest natural protection on the western boundary. In the early days this sufficed, as the fort faced no significant threat; sieges were minor.[27] The Company first recruited just fifty men to form the core of the Madras European Regiment, and the group grew gradually, a battalion at a time.[28] In 1670 there were two companies of roughly a hundred men each, and a number of native 'peons'; the latter were 'armed with swords and bucklers, bows and arrows, and other primitive weapons of the country'.[29] The board of directors in London was not convinced of the need to spend large amounts of money on troops, fortification and ammunition; the profit-and-loss account and the Company's ability to pay dividends were all that mattered. In the middle of the eighteenth century, however, when the fort had been in existence for a century, a more potent political stew began to bubble and hiss, with disastrous consequences for the little settlement on the Coromandel. It was in 1754 that the first King's Regiments came to India, with a squadron of the Royal Navy under Rear-Admiral Watson and a detachment of the Royal Artillery. This was the first instance of military assistance from Parliament.[30]

It was inevitable that, with its large territorial and monetary control and alliances with local rulers, the Company would become entrammelled in the shifting politics of the South. In Europe, starting in the 1740s, France and Britain were involved in the War of Austrian Succession, the beginning of a struggle for empire that would last three-quarters of a century. In India, represented by their 'companies', the two countries aligned themselves with rival contenders for the throne of the Carnatic. The French, in alarming proximity at Pondicherry, thus constituted a very real threat to the English, and one way or the other—by accident or design—Madras and Pondicherry found themselves at war, officially or unofficially. Fort St. George was at the heart of the action in this complex age.

Such was the state of affairs when an eighteen-year-old bookkeeper from Shropshire by the name of Robert Clive was sent out to India to be a Company writer, drawing a modest £5 as annual salary. His unlikely ambition to join the military was not realized until the French, on the order of Dupleix, attacked Madras from the sea and took the fort in 1746. Fort St. George was held by the French for three whole years, during which time Clive contrived to escape his captors and joined the English forces on the outside as a volunteer, distinguishing himself enough to be granted his commission as an ensign. This event was recorded in a dispatch from the deputy governor of Fort St. David near Cuddalore, south of Pondicherry:

Mr Robert Clive, writer in the service, being of martial disposition, and having acted as a volunteer in our late engagements, we have granted him an Ensign's Commission upon his application for the same.

The same dispatch spoke of the miserable situation in which the British had now found themselves, and of the excesses of the French:

> The proceedings of the French . . . have in general been so cruel and inhumane, that they seem rather to imitate a persecution than a war. They have refused the Commodore to exchange a single prisoner, notwithstanding the several they owe us, and we have some of theirs; and on a sudden drove away all the women and children that had liberty to stay at the Mount: plundering them of everything they had, and afterwards set fire to their houses . . . They have been very busy fortifying the White Town in Madras and have nearly destroyed the Black Town.[31]

In 1749, the fort came back to the English after peace was negotiated in Europe by the Treaty of Aix-la-Chapelle, and Clive resumed his civil duties. But as fate would have it, he had a second shot at the military when war broke out again in the Carnatic, and he brought great honour upon himself by his exemplary leadership in the defence of Arcot and his support of Stringer Lawrence during the relief of Trichinopoly. Although he returned to England due to ill health, his deeds were not forgotten, for, when he returned in 1755, it was as deputy governor of Fort St. David.

A year later, after Nawab Siraj-ud-daulah had captured the Company's settlements in Bengal and the infamous Black Hole of Calcutta episode had taken place, Clive was summoned to Madras and dispatched to Bengal in charge of the Company's land forces. He took Calcutta in January 1757, and six months later inflicted a crushing defeat on the nawab and his huge army at the Battle of Plassey.

Clive had left the South for good, and the rest of his story is well known; but what he left behind him was a still-burning, yet-unquenched French ambition. In 1758, the French once again besieged Fort St. George, this time so severely that every building except St. Mary's was wrecked. For the next two decades, reconstruction dominated the scene, and thus the map of the fort circa 1781 is more or less the present layout. The French were subsequently defeated at Wandiwash, and Pondicherry, that seafront town that harboured Dupleix's dream, was taken in 1761. When the French threat eventually petered out, the English became the uncontested white power in India, and no European threat would ever reappear with the same strength. In the eighteenth century, considerable danger was posed by Hyder Ali and Tipu Sultan of Srirangapattana, but the latter was silenced when his river fortress was breached and taken in 1799. With Pondicherry and Srirangapattana both subjugated, the era of British militarism in the South came to an end. Less than twenty years after Clive's historic victory at Plassey, it was Bengal that became the centre of British activity in India, as Calcutta became the 'capital' of the Company's territories in 1772. Sadly for the South, Fort St. George lost its great status to Fort William, by then a massive and impenetrable fortress by the Hooghly.

Although Madras had been thus, in a way, abandoned, and Kipling was moved to describe it in the nineteenth century as a 'withered beldame brooding on ancient fame', the wheels that had been set in motion continued to roll. Immigrants had not flocked to the periphery of the fort for nothing in the early days; their descendants carried on the same activities, and commerce continued to flourish. The city itself grew rapidly, as the white settlement had long since burst its fortified seams and spilled out into garden houses in new residential areas. The English acquired village after village until, by 1800, the city had expanded so far that it was bounded by the Adyar River in the south and Kilpauk and Perambur in the west, areas not considered central even today. It was at this time that the Great Indian Trigonometrical Survey was launched, with its original baseline a seven-mile stretch of

Mount Road, the thoroughfare that ran between Fort St. George and St. Thomas Mount and is still an arterial road. It is hard to see any such glorious history in the dreadfully crowded road of today, but here and there an old building from a more gracious time is still visible, weeds sprouting from its forlorn towers and balconies, struggling to hold its own in a ragged, untidy skyline.

On a fine summer afternoon not long ago, I accompanied a visiting cousin from Wales on a somewhat rushed tour around the city. We paused to admire the four-hundred-year-old Portuguese Catholic church on St. Thomas Mount, drove past as much heritage architecture as we could squeeze in, and eventually wound up at Fort St. George. There, as I had expected, my cousin was particularly fascinated by St. Mary's, and spent a great deal of time exploring its interior and poring over the pamphlets at the door. Nothing, however, gripped his attention as firmly as a signboard outside the Fort Museum, although we had reached its doors too late to be admitted.

> The Fort Museum was organised in February 1948 in view of the entire protection of Fort St George as a monument of National Importance by the Archaeological Survey of India. The Museum houses antiquities of colonial [sic] period and its contemporary period of India, throwing light on the various antiquities of the last three centuries reflecting the south Indian history.

We grinned for a while over the peculiarities of this notice, but as the afternoon turned to evening I decided I had had quite enough of feeling ashamed of the way so many historical districts were allowed to fall into ruin in India. My cousin had lapsed into silence, which was unusual, and I wondered what he was thinking about so seriously as we walked to the car, parked near the church. Then I realized he was staring meditatively at something as we strolled along: ahead of us, in a disused garage space, was—of all the unfortunate objects—a large white commode, complete with broken flush tank, lying stricken on its side. Horrified, I tried to direct his attention to the fort's less disgraceful features, but it was too late: he was nodding to himself in an all too understanding manner.

'Evidently', he remarked, caressing his moustache gravely and delivering the judgement I was dreading, 'we are still in the *colonial* period.'

Notes

1. Col. D.M. Reid, *The Story of Fort St. George* (1945; reprint, New Delhi: Asian Educational Services, 1999), p. 1.
2. S. Muthiah, *Madras Rediscovered* (Chennai: East West Books, 1999), pp. 10-11.
3. Sir Charles Lawson, *Memories of Madras* (1905; reprint, New Delhi: Asian Educational Services, 2002), pp. 9-11.
4. Reid, p. 5.
5. Antony Wild, *The East India Company: Trade and Conquest from 1600* (New Delhi: HarperCollins, 1999), p. 11.
6. Ibid.
7. Ibid., pp. 9-10.
8. Ibid., p. 24.
9. Ibid., p. 180.
10. Ibid., p. 180.
11. J. Talboys Wheeler, *Madras in the Olden Time: A History of the Presidency from the First Foundation of Fort St. George to the Occupation of Madras by the French (1639-1748)* (1861; reprint, New Delhi: Asian Educational Services, 1993), pp. 26-27.
12. Ibid., pp. 31-32.
13. Muthiah, p. 43.
14. Wheeler, p. 134.
15. Reid, pp. 43-44.
16. Muthiah, p. 32.

17. Ibid., p. 309.
18. Ibid., p. 37.
19. Wheeler, p. 29.
20. Ibid., pp. 339-40.
21. Ibid., pp. 118-19.
22. Muthiah, p. 123.
23. Wild, pp. 50-51.
24. Reid, p. 52.
25. Wheeler, pp. 139-40.
26. Reid, p. 53.
27. Ibid., p. 13.
28. By 1700, this regiment had become the 102nd Royal Madras Fusiliers, who would much later merge with the Bombay Corps to form the famous Royal Dublin Fusiliers.
29. Wheeler, p. 29.
30. Reid, p. 24.
31. Wheeler, pp. 667-68.

Pondicherry
The Empire That Never Was

As we contemplate, indeed, the great achievements of France on the soil of Hindustan; as we read the numerous examples of the mighty conceptions, the heroic actions, the mental vigour, and the indomitable energy displayed there by her children, we cannot but marvel at the sudden destruction of hopes so great, of plans so vast and deep-laid.
—G.B. Malleson, *History of the French in India*, 1867

On a rough and windy morning in October, I boarded a seemingly saturated bus at the state transport corporation's bus stand near the Madras High Court. A penurious eighteen-year-old at the time, I could afford only this mode of transport, with a high degree of planning and forethought. Those were the days when the occasional 'middle' piece for the *Deccan Herald* had been the sole supplement to my college allowance, not much help (generous though the paper was) in supporting such frivolous pastimes as travel. I shoved my way resignedly into the vehicle's innards and realized that I would probably have to stand for the entire journey, sandwiched between two overweight men of indeterminate motive and moral. As the bus started up with a roar and lurched its side-heavy way towards the southbound highway, I consoled myself with the thought that in a few hours I would be in Pondicherry, a town I had longed to visit ever since my head had been filled with accounts of its charms from college seniors who had taken advantage of its cheap accommodation, plentiful alcohol and distance from Madras to indulge in such pleasures as were forbidden in our convent-like hostel.

The drive was long, hot and decidedly boring, despite the monsoon clouds and the pleasant contemplation of escape. The bus had taken the inland route via Chinglepet, and the lorry traffic was devilish enough to distract me from the countryside. After five hours, I was propelled along the aisle and out of the bus, and found that we had pulled up at the corner of a hideously crowded intersection. 'Paandicheri!' shouted the conductor, gesticulating in annoyance at my reluctance to clear the way for boarding passengers. I looked around and tried to find my bearings, but simply could not believe that this was the place of which I had been so enamoured in my imaginings. The streets were narrow and uninspiring, indeed downright squalid; the usual lunatic cyclists wove slow, lazy semicircles from one side of the road to the other; and people spilled almost continuously into the face of oncoming traffic from dozens of tiny shops and stalls. Over everything was a thick coating of unlovely grey, no doubt a combination of dust and oily exhaust. In short, there was no evidence of any difference, spectacular or otherwise, from your average dismal small town in the South.

Disappointed and lost, I pushed my way down an incredibly congested street leading eastward across a canal, in the hope that I was heading towards food and lodging. A few minutes after crossing I caught my breath, for it was as if an entirely new town had mushroomed at my feet, with the people and the traffic dying instantly into an unpleasant memory. The streets were still narrow, to be sure, but here boughs of burgeoning bougainvillea spilled on to clean, regular pavements, on either side of which loomed tall doorways and brilliantly whitewashed facades. Brass door knockers caught the sun and gleamed, as did polished and painted woodwork; parallel iron bars sprang from massive window frames like the stretched strings of a giant harp that had frozen while in play; leaves blew down the street to collect in carelessly artistic heaps at the street corners. There was a Pondicherry after all, and I marvelled at the contrast between one side of the canal and the other. On the east side, into which I had strayed, one instantly wanted to belong, to ring one of the great knockers and be received into the cool inner courtyard of an unknown home. Of course, one could do no such thing, for every building was tantalizingly high-walled, aloof and self-contained, immersed in its private thoughts. You could not tell from passing a home whether it housed six people or twelve, whether there were children, or (this was what really set it apart from the rest of India) what was being cooked for lunch. This was the curious three-hundred-year-old French quarter, a small rectangular area so distinct and so elevated from the run-of-the-mill that even in a land known for its casteism and division, it was remarkable as a town within a town, or even, perhaps, the remains of a country within a country. I did not know it then, but I would visit this far-flung fragment of the Mediterranean time and again over the next decade; it would turn into my habitual point of escape from Madras, as close to the south of France as I was likely to get on a journalist's income.

The miraculously preserved streets and buildings, though very much part of the living townscape, are deeply evocative of days of the past and of the 'other' power that contested and, fascinatingly, almost won India. In the sixteenth and seventeenth centuries, four major maritime powers in Europe—Portugal, Britain, France, and Holland opened serious trade with the East, creating loops of continuous commerce around the cape and into Asia. France was the last to enter the race, after the other three had already taken home considerable wealth; but as the sympathetic historian G.B. Malleson wrote in 1867, 'their natural genius asserted itself in a manner that speedily brought them on a level with the most securely planted of their European rivals.' France at this time, he continued, was a restless nation, 'the fomenter of disturbances in Europe' that soon found in India a 'wide field for its display'.[1] What made this restlessness doubly original was that it preceded British imperialism by a long mile. The ambition that spiced French dreams of a universal dominion in the West began, before long, to whisper of a French empire in the East. That such an empire was lost before it could be built was but a quirk of fate, that India fell to the isle and not to the Continent a mere flick of the fingers of history.

It is to this bitterly coveted empire that Pondicherry remains a living memorial—the influence of her former government remains in every stone of the formerly 'white' part of town. Though the settlement was wrested several times by the British, it was always returned to the French and continued under their rule until 1954, when it became a union territory of India. Half a dozen distinctive streets, a cluster of heritage buildings and the odd French-speaking person are all that remain of almost three hundred years of French occupation, barring one major intangible: a sense of identification with a Western nation, and in this case an eccentric pride in its Continental flavour. The very names of the streets reflect this: I cut across Suffren Street, the Rue Romain Roland, and the Rue Dumas until the street I was following fetched up on the waterfront. Having reached the sea-skirting Goubert Avenue, with its broad promenade and pretty street lamps, I had just drawn a line through the heart of what was locally known as the French quarter. Affinity for the mother country can be seen all over this quarter, from the French *tricolore* flying over the impressive consulate on Compagnie Street to the red *kepi* hats still worn by local police. It seems as if nothing will ever completely take away Pondicherry's Frenchness—not the succession of English and Tamil as far more widely spoken languages, nor the west-side crowds drifting democratically into the French quarter in the evening to take the air on the waterfront, bringing in their wake hydrogen-balloon carts, vadai stalls and baskets of jasmine. The solid old *douane* (customs) building looks out over all the mayhem with tolerance, almost as if it knows that this time of day will pass and another peaceful morning in the sun lies ahead, with an uninterrupted view of the rocky waterfront and the moody, changing colours of the bay.

Perhaps the best way to understand the soul of Pondicherry is to wander in the French quarter at night, when the streets are almost deserted and the past seems even closer than it does during the day. There are dim lights in the windows then, and half-drawn curtains, and the lines between the centuries separate like the surreal layers of a dream. One of the most shadowy streets is the Rue François Martin, a quiet lane that runs parallel to the waterfront from North Boulevard, the northern boundary of the grid of streets that constitutes the French quarter, to green old Government Square at its heart. Though not as impressive a street as some of the others in the grid, the rue evokes the settlement's infancy—the late seventeenth century, when Pondicherry was ruled by François Martin of the French Compagnie des Indes, one of the most far-sighted Frenchmen ever to have served his country in the East. Originally in the service of the Dutch East India Company, Martin joined that of his compatriots at an early age and, during the French occupation of San Thome in 1672 (their first attempt to establish themselves on the Coromandel),[2] was ordered by his directors to negotiate with Sher Khan Lodi, representative of the king of Bijapur[3] in his Carnatic and Tanjore territories, for the grant of a piece of land to the French. After doing so, he was allowed to buy a small area on the coast near the mouth of the Ginjee river. When the French surrendered to the combined forces of the Dutch and Golconda[4] at San Thome in 1674, Martin found himself in charge of sixty Europeans, a frigate and some ready money, and with these assets he proceeded to the place called Puthucheri or New Town by the locals and Pondicherry by the foreigners. Here he built sketchy defences, within which a number of houses were erected, and a trading factory, which attracted Indians to settle in the town that grew around it. Martin was much impressed with the settlement's possibilities: in letters home, he praised the roadstead before it, which prevented men-of-war from coming too close, and observed that the site was sheltered from the monsoon.[5] The fledgling town soon prospered, and eventually attracted some Roman Catholic zeal—in 1692, on the other side of the present canal, the Jesuits built the peaceful Eglise de Notre Dame de la Conception Immaculée, a medieval-style building that still stands, renovated two centuries ago, on Mission Street.

Just a year after this church was built, however, neither the advantages of Pondicherry's situation nor, perhaps, the prayers of the Jesuits were strong enough to save the little settlement. The Dutch, tired of the French thorn in their side, took a page out of the War of Grand Alliance[6] that was then being fought in Europe and appeared triumphantly in 1693 with a fleet of nineteen vessels carrying two thousand European sailors, fifteen hundred European troops, several brass guns, cannons and heavy artillery. François Martin was virtually defenceless against such a monstrous attack, so it was left to him to watch the ruin of all he had built in two decades—a fortified town, a thriving trade, and the foundations of wealth and social harmony. Leaving all this to the mercies of the Dutch, he returned to France with nothing to show for his trouble. Or, as Malleson wrote in 1867,

> Was there indeed nothing? Aye, if experience of a distant country, if successful management of mankind, if the ability to make for oneself resources—if these be nothing, Martin returned to his country destitute indeed. But in that age such acquirements were more highly considered than they sometimes are now; and no long time elapsed before Martin was to feel that they had gained for him the confidence of his country to an extent that enabled him to repair the losses of 1693, and to rebuild on the old foundation a power whose reputation was to endure.[7]

When Martin made the long voyage back around the Cape after

the Dutch had returned Pondicherry to the French following the end of the war in Europe, he found the place changed, and not for the worse. Having recognized Pondicherry's worth, the Dutch had begun to lay foundations there for their own Indian capital: they had strengthened the settlement's defences, making it the strongest European fortress in India, and continued Martin's cordiality with the local people. One of the terms upon which Pondicherry was handed back was that all this development should be left untouched—and the French even reimbursed the Dutch for the cost of construction. Martin furthered the work of fortification, and laid a town plan providing for the construction of more than a hundred houses in less than a year.[8] By 1701, the French factory at Surat—where the supreme French authority in the East had been centred since the abandonment of Madagascar in 1672[9]—was closed, and the seat of power shifted across the country to Pondicherry in the South. In recognition of all he had done for France, Martin was appointed president of the Superior Council of the Indies and Director-General of French affairs in India. Yet despite all his efforts, the Compagnie des Indes did not prosper as it should have done, for its affairs in France were poorly managed, and by the close of the seventeenth century its funds were almost exhausted. It is ironic that the company should have floundered at a time when its governance in India was in the hands of a man of such integrity. Yet it seemed inevitable that, like Madagascar and Surat, Pondicherry too would teeter and fall—and at this critical juncture, Martin died.

Needless to say, Pondicherry did not die with Martin. Many decades of French presence lay ahead of Martin's time, and I wondered what he might have thought, for instance, of the distinctive little restaurants now found on every street in the French quarter, some of which remain open fairly late at night. He might have approved of the brisk business and preservation of a lingering French flavour in small, hospitable cafes and bars with names like Rendezvous and Bar Qualithe. Instead of the ubiquitous idlis, dosais, and soggy pizzas, these establishments serve crêpes with honey, bouillabaisse, fillet mignon, and irresistible crème caramel, all laid out on gingham tablecloths spread over cane tables. For people driving in from Tamil Nadu, where there is partial prohibition, Pondicherry is associated strongly with alcohol, for here a meal can safely be washed down with a bottle of Indian wine, a couple of Bacardis or, for the faint of heart, a swig of Pondicherry Aqua Minerale. Beer can be drunk in glasses actually made of glass, rather than the ceramic mugs in which it is ordinarily disguised in the surrounding state. French wine—a commodity dearly prized among the Indian princes of the eighteenth century—is still a dream in a bottle, for although the day of royal demand is done, the object of its craving remains forbiddingly expensive. Be that as it may, there is nothing I enjoy more than a meal in Pondicherry's French quarter, for the staff are always friendly, the food invariably perfect, and the wine sure to take the shortest route to my head, causing a warm surge of good will towards my surroundings.

Perhaps it was such good will (albeit unaided by alcohol) that helped the town to stay afloat despite the trying times that followed Martin's death. The French had huge unpaid debts at Surat and matters in Europe were taking a bizarre turn, with the Compagnie des Indes now involved with grand schemes to improve the perilous state of French finances after the death of Louis IV. It was a Scottish financier named John Law[10] who influenced Philippe II, Duke of Orleans, into taking daring steps involving credit and paper currency that would have far-reaching consequences. Law's private bank became the chief tool in this scheme, which would eventually involve the colony of Louisiana,[11] the Compagnie d'Occident—the Mississippi Company—and the Compagnie des Indes. The Banque Generale became the royal bank in 1718, and Law merged it with the massive stock company, taking over a good fraction of the public debt and the administration of revenue. A tide of speculation rushed across France, with stock in this new company soaring to heights that could never expect a proportionate return from the colonies or from trade with Asia. This boom was followed by frenzied selling and the ruin of many investors. Although by 1720 Law's schemes had collapsed,[12] colonial enterprise was stimulated—and far-off Pondicherry benefitted by the appearance in 1721 of three ships, dispatched from France the previous year, laden with European merchandise, gold, and silver. The Compagnie des Indes had long abandoned commerce,[13] lacking the resources to take advantage of its privileges in the East, and the sight of these ships was a great relief. Wisely, the far-sighted officials in Pondicherry used the greater portion of the money that came in with the tide to pay off French debts. Although it meant that the company received a very poor return for a large outlay, this went a long way towards reestablishing the good credit of the French traders in India.[14]

It was on New Year's Eve one year that my boyfriend Rohit and I were walking down Rue Dumas on our way back to Le Club, a somewhat overpriced establishment at which we were staying for a few days. We had been far more impressed by the charms of the Villa Helena, another heritage guest house at which we had earlier stayed, with its beautiful courtyard, delicate cane and rattan furniture, and the old-world courtesy of its staff. As we were speaking of the charms of the latter, we passed a raucous bar that was heavily crowded with men, and outside which a great number of cycles, scooters and motorbikes were parked. It was not a normal Pondicherry sight; even the shadows of the night had fled such a noisy spot, and we hurried past in some dismay. When the west side invaded the east, it clearly did so with a vengeance, and without its wives. It was ironic, I thought, that this sort of thing was happening on a street named after Benoit Dumas, a governor-general who took office in 1735 and was known far and wide for his gentlemanly ways. These were put to the test in 1740, when the widow of Dost Ali Khan, nawab of the Carnatic, arrived with her children, dependents and jewels at Pondicherry's gates. To grant her refuge was to invite the wrath of the marauding Marathas, who, jealous of Muslim successes in the South, had marched into the Carnatic only recently and caused a great deal of turmoil. Dumas could not turn away a woman in distress, so after consulting his council, he admitted both her and the nawab's daughter, who was married to Chanda Sahib, a man who had risen to regional prominence. As expected, the Marathas—Raghuji Bhonsla, to be precise—wrote an angry and threatening letter to Dumas, going so far as to demand one of the women and to remind him of how they had overrun the town of Bassein after capturing it from the Portuguese. To this crude missive, Dumas made the following spirited reply:

> From them [the Mughals] we have received only favours. In virtue of this friendship, we have given shelter to the widow of the late Nawwab, Dost Ali Khan, with all her family. Ought we to have shut our gates and left them in the country? Men of honour are incapable of such cowardice . . .
>
> . . . You have written to me to make over to your horsemen this lady, and the riches she has brought here. You, who are a nobleman full of bravery and generosity, what would you think of me if I were capable of such baseness? The wife of Chanda Sahib is in Pondicherry under the protection of the King of France, my master, and all the French in India would rather die than deliver her to you . . .
>
> . . . Above all I place my confidence in Almighty God, before whom the most powerful armies are like the light straw which the wind blows away. I hope He will favour the justice of our cause. I have heard what has happened at Bassein, but that place was not defended by Frenchmen.[15]

Around the corner from Le Club, at the southern end of Goubert Avenue, stands the proud statue of Joseph François Dupleix, who took over from Dumas and, unlike the latter, plunged himself into aggressive schemes for French domination. With the War of Austrian Succession bringing England and France to blows in the West,[16] Dupleix masterminded a plan to overthrow Fort St. George, which was executed by the brilliant but not quite reliable naval commander La Bourdonnais.[17] The statesmanlike Dupleix, wanting to avoid the wrath of Anwaruddin, nawab of the Carnatic, wanted the captured fort to be handed over to the nawab rather than retained under French command. The fort would be lost to the French, but more importantly, it would also be lost to the English, and the friendship of the nawab would be preserved in the bargain. La Bourdonnais, who had been chafing for a while under Dupleix's authority, simply refused to acknowledge his requests or to see the good sense behind this plan; he continued mulishly to negotiate with the English for the payment of a large ransom for Fort St. George—of which, of course, a large part would be his personal bounty. The horrified Dupleix did all he could to persuade the arrogant commander to capitulate, and their correspondence took so long that La Bourdonnais stayed in Madras far longer than he had planned to—and the nort-heast monsoon set in with a cyclone that badly damaged the French fleet. Shaken by this dreadful turn of events, La Bourdonnais wrote to Pondicherry,

> My part is taken regarding Madras; I abandon it to you. I have signed the capitulation, it is for you to keep my word. I am so disgusted with this wretched Madras, that I would give an arm never to have put foot in it. It has cost us too much.[18]

When La Bourdonnais eventually returned to France, he was thrown into the Bastille for three years on charges of having disregarded the king's orders, entered into a secret understanding with the enemy, and diverted company funds for his own use. Although his name was eventually cleared—indeed, a street was named after him in Pondicherry—it was a sad end for a man who, had he been able to control his jealousy, sacrifice his personal motives, and work for the good of France, might with suitable reinforcements have even routed the English from Calcutta, destroyed their commerce, and established the French as masters of the Indian seas.

Looking up at the statue of Dupleix, and in its shadow the guest house of the Sri Aurobindo Ashram, I couldn't help thinking that Pondicherry had attracted some interesting people over the years. There was Dupleix himself, whose complicated schemes for getting rid of the English involved influence and interference in the local courts, intrigue of the deepest order, and outright warfare in a series of aggressions that came to be known as the Carnatic Wars. After he became master of Madras, he had to defend Pondicherry against the furious British, and just when he had succeeded in holding his ground and was planning further designs upon the enemy, all hostility was called to a close by the Treaty of Aix-la-Chapelle, which ended the war in Europe in 1748. The treaty called for mutual restoration of conquests in India, and thus Dupleix had to return the much-prized and jealously guarded Madras. Though peace had been called for, there was now a terrible, vindictive enmity between the English and the French in India. No longer were they mere traders, especially the French, for Dupleix's ambition grew increasingly violent with every passing day. Yet, as Malleson wrote,

> By the East India Companies in Paris and London this change was not even suspected. They fondly believed that the new treaty would enable their agents to recommence their mercantile operations. They hoped that the reaction after five years' hostilities would lead to a feeling of mutual confidence and trust. Vain dream! The peace that reigned in Europe, was it not then to extend to both nations in India? Alas! With ambition aroused, mutual jealousy excited, the temptation of increased dominion knocking at their doors, what had they to do with peace?[19]

By 1751 Dupleix had succeeded, with the help of the army under the command of Marquis de Bussy, in bringing all of the Carnatic and most of the Deccan under French control. His nemesis arrived in the form of the exceptional officer Robert Clive, under whose leadership the British began to regain their former position. The French government, now wishing to avoid further war, recalled Dupleix and his family in 1754, and with his departure went the last dreams of a French empire in India. Ironically, he was summoned to France at a time when, with reinforcements that had just arrived, he could finally have destroyed the English in India. Malleson, ever the admirer of this untiring Frenchman, was to write,

> When we think indeed how much he had accomplished—how he had built up the French power, how he had gained for it an unparalleled influence and an enormous extension of territory; and when we reflect that with half the two thousand men that Godeheu brought out with him, he could have crushed the English, already reduced to extremities at Trichinapalli—we cannot but marvel at the blindness, the infatuation, the madness, that recalled him. The primary cause was, no doubt, as we have stated, the degraded condition of the France of Louis XV. But there was yet, we believe, another reason, not entirely dependent upon the state of his country, for we have seen it act under other rulers than Louis XV, and under other Governments than France. To borrow the words of the French historian [Baron Barehou de Penhoen], 'Dupleix had against him that crime of genius, which so many men have expiated by misery, by exile, and by death.'[20]

All that is now left of Dupleix's grand ambition is the tiny French quarter in Pondicherry, including his proud statue on its waterfront. After his plans had come to naught, the French, despite a treaty with the English, continued their interference in local politics, eventually having to send the 'daring soldier' Count de Lally out to India to evict the English. Despite some initial success in tearing Fort St. David apart, the French soon lost the Hyderabad region and were faced with a siege of Pondicherry. In 1761, the town was razed to the ground by the British and lay in ruins for four years, during which the French completely lost their power in the South. Eventually the town was returned to France and rebuilt. It rose again like a phoenix from the ashes—to clash again with the English, repeatedly, but never again to dream of empire.

The Park guest house behind Dupleix's statue is a constant reminder of the other famous character Pondicherry nurtured, if not produced. Aurobindo, a Bengali freedom-fighter-turned-philosopher who believed in yoga and modern science, took up residence in Pondicherry, founded an ashram in 1926 and attracted a large following.[21] After his time, spiritual authority passed to one of his devotees, a French woman known as The Mother,[22] and their samadhi stands in the courtyard of the ashram. Many swear by the power of this tomb, saying that prayers made at the site will be answered, and describing 'vibes' that emanate from here to soothe the troubled mind. The ashram, however, inspires mixed feelings in the local people, for although it contributes generously to social causes, it also controls a large portion of Pondicherry's most valuable property. That the establishment is faintly supercilious is almost immediately evident; I have a greater affection for the people who live at Auroville,[23] a utopian township founded by The Mother on the East Coast Road. They, too, can be a little unfriendly to visitors, but their appealingly eco-friendly lifestyle and tasteful, high-quality produce—incense, lamps, pottery, clothes, shoes, organic foodstuffs—and the hard battle they fought with the ashram to retain control of Auroville after the death of The Mother— do much to foster respect. The conflict between the two factions is a strange reminder of that other great clash of personalities; it's as if there is something in the Pondicherry air that prevents great minds from working together. The strained relations between Dupleix and

La Bourdonnais in the 1740s all but cost France her empire, and in the 1970s the Aurovillians reached a state of near starvation as the ashram, which controlled the funds, began to withhold resources. The little territory seems to nurture a certain stubbornness; yet while Dupleix lost his dream, the Aurovillians triumphed in the end with the continual growth of their community and the ultimate completion of their astounding spherical, crystal-bearing Matri Mandir, which must rank as one of the most remarkable meditation chambers in the world.

Still, Pondicherry has a soul all its own, and neither the overbearing presence of the ashram nor the magnetic pull of Auroville can take that away. Its essence lies in the white and pastel facades that reflect the sun so brilliantly, in the profusely flowering trees in every courtyard, in the great rocks lined up so carefully by the bay, and in the pier that stretches an exaggerated distance into the sea. A part of its charm also lies in its people, from the French-speaking beggars who rush through Government Square to greet foreigners with 'M'sieur! M'sieur!' to the waiters who politely thank you for your 'teep' and the chef who, when asked where he learned to cook, draws himself up to full height and says, pityingly, 'Madame, I am a gourmand!'

And, of course, the French quarter has its famous flea market on Sunday evenings. Although this weekly event attracts a large, unmanageable crowd that swells the numbers on the waterfront to the point of spillover, it is an expression of the life within, of the very raison d'être of the town and the French quarter alike, for neither would exist but for the trade that brought them to life and bound them wrist to wrist more than three hundred years ago. They are still here, the foreigners, but this time as tourists, lined up to buy Indian cloth and craft; and the vendors, who come from far and wide, are all too happy to oblige.

Over this bustle and blare does Dupleix's statue preside, and I imagine that time has added a touch of the philosopher to that proud countenance. His grand schemes did not come to pass, but the place in which he had dreamed them still endures, and that, it seems, has added a hint of contentment to the otherwise strong-willed and restless face that now occupies itself in eternal contemplation of the bay.

Notes

1. G. B. Malleson, *The History of the French in India*, (1868; reprint, New Delhi: Gian, 1986), p. 1.
2. The French first based themselves at Surat, where the other European traders had already established themselves. Realizing the need for a place they could call their own, they tried to occupy the seaboard of Ceylon. Having tried and failed to take Point de Galle, and having taken Trincomallee but surrendered it to a Dutch fleet, the French finally sailed for San Thome on the east coast, which they took in a very short time in 1672, and established themselves as somewhat unwelcome neighbours of the English at Fort St. George.
3. One of the two kingdoms established after the fall of the Vijayanagar empire, the other being Golconda.
4. The Dutch allied with Golconda against the French, having convinced the king that the interlopers would not content themselves with a single port on the Coromandel, and that it would be in his interests to expel them. Thus, the forces of Abul Hasan attacked San Thome by land, while the Dutch bore on it by sea.
5. Malleson, p. 19-24.
6. The War of Grand Alliance was fought between 1688 and 1697 between Louis XIV of France and a league of European powers. It was triggered by Louis' invasion of the Palatinate (southern Germany) in the absence of Emperor Leopold I, who had gone on a campaign against the Turks, and encouraged by the promised support of James II of England. When William of Orange became William III of England, matters took a different turn and England entered the conflict on the side of the coalition.
7. Malleson, p. 30.
8. Ibid., pp. 33-35.
9. The French factory at Surat was established in 1668. In 1672, the French authority in the East was shifted from Madagascar to Surat, but the

establishment did not thrive. Trade was not as prosperous as that carried on by the Dutch and the English, and the location of the French factory there had no political advantage. The French settlements at Pondicherry and Chandernaggore became more important, and trade at Surat languished until at last it was abandoned at the beginning of the eighteenth century. The French agents left massive debts behind them, discrediting them completely in the eyes of the local merchants.

10. A young Scottish financier with a penchant for gambling, Law presented himself to the French regent within a month of the king's death, declaring that he could restore France to prosperity. He eventually died in Venice, where he had supported himself through gambling.

11. A North American colony at the mouth of the Mississippi, Louisiana was settled directly from France in the early eighteenth century.

12. For a detailed account of the episode, see Malleson, p. 43-56.

13. As early as 1682, the French East India Company was unable to buy enough goods to load its own vessels, and had sunk to the point of allowing private merchants to ship goods to India provided they used the Company's vessels and paid freight. In 1714, when its charter was renewed, it continued to rent its privileges out to others. Malleson, p. 40-41.

14. Malleson, p. 57.

15. Ibid., pp. 86-87.

16. The War of Austrian Succession broke out in Europe in 1740 when the Austrian archduchess Maria Theresa succeeded her father Charles VI, Holy Roman Emperor, as ruler of the Hapsburg territory. One of the contenders for the throne, Frederick the Great of Prussia, began hostilities with his attack on Silesia. The ensuing struggle was between France, Bavaria and Prussia on one side and England and Austria on the other. Naturally, it had repercussions in the colonies as well.

17. Bertrand François Mahe de La Bourdonnais—after whom Mahe on the west coast was named—was a sailor from St. Malo who joined the French East India Company and rose to become governor of the Isles of France and Bourbon, and a clever and ambitious naval commander.

18. Malleson, p. 178-179.

19. Ibid., p. 230.

20. Ibid., p. 428.

21. Aurobindo Ghosh would be remembered as a freedom-fighter even if his spiritual work had not brought him fame. Deeply involved in the politics

of his time, he presided over the 1907 session of the Indian National Congress, which saw a split between the Moderates and the Extremists. After a year in Alipore jail, Aurobindo began to move from politics towards spirituality, and from 1910 he devoted his life to a different sort of work at Pondicherry. He died in 1950.

22. Born Mira Alfassa, she first visited Pondicherry with her second husband, and eventually left him to join Aurobindo and take charge of the community that was growing around him. By the 1930s she had taken over the day-to-day running of the ashram, and when Aurobindo died, she took over as spiritual leader as well. She died in 1973.

23. Auroville was The Mother's vision of an international city. She inaugurated it with the words 'Auroville belongs to nobody in particular. Auroville belongs to humanity as a whole. But to live in Auroville one must be the willing servitor of the divine Consciousness.'

Tranquebar
Day of the Danes

Wednesday, 1ˢᵗ March, 1699—A General Letter from the Governor and Council of Tranquebar being translated was read; wherein they give an account of their being close besieged by the King of Tanjore's forces, consisting of 14,000 horse and foot, which daily increased; taking advantage of their Fort being weakly manned, by sparing so many of their garrison soldiers to their ships for their security against the Pirates; and therefore earnestly request us to assist them with men, arms, and ammunition, the charge whereof they promise thankfully to repay.

—From the Consultation book at Fort St. George

Like a deserted film set, Tranquebar flashed briefly on either side of the car as we drove through the town gate and across the sand right up to the Bay of Bengal, where the remains of a seaward fortification glistened redly in the low, calm waves of early summer.

'This is it?' asked Rohit, looking about with bewildered interest at the ruins that had drawn us all the way from Madras, an eight-hour drive along a road that had deteriorated to bone-shaking conditions in its last stretches.

I looked around, in the grip of the sheer possibilities of this abandoned town and fort, should anyone with half an imagination be permitted to restore them—fully, not piecemeal—to their original seventeenth-century state. We emerged from the car into the oppressive warmth of a March afternoon and, turning our backs on the ghost town, made our way to Dansborg Fort, a small but sturdy grey structure on the water's edge that looked as if it might at any moment disgorge a toy cannon and a hundred tin soldiers. The only signs of life in the area were a fisherman, who tried to sell us some blackish-green 'Danish' coins—which, Rohit later found with due amusement, were dated 1914—and a comatose gatekeeper who looked up in surprise from his desk as we entered the fort from its northern gate, the only one that appeared to be in use.

Dansborg was tiny—although large by Danish standards, apparently second only to Hamlet's Elsinore—and consequently a trifle claustrophobic. Standing in its central yard was a bit like standing at the bottom of a large concrete tank, with the small gateway looking for all the world like a plughole. The high grey walls loomed close on every side, and prompted me to quickly find an open staircase and climb to the top. From here I saw not only the deep blue bay, and the bright brick ruins shining through the water near the shore, but also, through a casement in the upper storey of the 'factory' that had been built along the east wall, a modest quantity of grain spread out to dry on the floor. Somebody, it appeared, other than the people who staffed the tiny fort museum, was putting the structure to use. A couple of crows sat on the ledge, debating whether or not to be scared away by the flapping bit of cotton hung in the window for that very purpose. I could not but feel sorry for the old fort, for it had been intended for glory, or at least for wealth; but the eastern seas had not been kind to the Danes, and their presence in India had ultimately been somewhat inconsequential compared with the more enduring designs of the others who sailed around the Cape.

The story of the Danish dalliance with India began in 1615, when two Dutch merchants proposed to Christian IV, king of the dual kingdom of Denmark–Norway, the founding of a Danish trading company along the lines of the British and Dutch East India companies. The king was extremely interested, for stories of the immense profits being raked in by voyages to the East were legion at the time. In 1616, Christian IV issued a charter giving the Danish East India Company a twelve-year monopoly on trade with Asia; but it was not until 1618 that enough capital had been raised to finance the venture, for Danish investors had not been as easily convinced as their sovereign of the company's likely success. Plans were initially made to trade with the Coromandel coast, but these were arrested by the arrival at the Danish court of a wily Dutchman called Boschouwer, who claimed to represent the emperor of Ceylon, on whose behalf he requested Danish protection from his enemies in return for trading benefits. The sails of the fledgling company were thus directed towards Ceylon, and the good ship *Oresund* was sent to reconnoitre under the command of a Roelant Crappé. She was followed by an 'expedition' of four Danish ships and a Dutch escort, their numbers being unexpectedly swelled by the capture of two French ships along the way.

When the expedition arrived in Ceylon in 1620, it was only to find that all had not gone according to script. When the *Oresund* had arrived earlier, Crappé had presented himself at the court of the raja of Kandy—presumably the closest personage to an 'emperor' that he could find—and entered into an agreement with him. He then began to make trouble for Portuguese ships. Just how ridiculous the scheme was became evident when the Portuguese, taking umbrage, retaliated by sinking the *Oresund* and taking Crappé with them to Nagapattinam, where a Portuguese trading post had been established within the territory of the nayak of Tanjore. Crappé was handed over to the nayak, and this is where the story of Tranquebar begins.

Ceylon being a disappointment, the Danish expedition proceeded to the Coromandel and negotiated a treaty with Tanjore, by which the

Danes were given fifteen villages and permission to build a fort twenty miles north of Nagapattinam at the little 'wave-town' of Tarangambadi, which came to be known as Tranquebar. They were allowed to maintain an army, administer justice and follow their own religion and custom, and in return the nayak demanded an annual tribute—which, in the years to come, would undo the little settlement .

Crappé, no longer a prisoner, was left in charge of Tranquebar, and by 1622 the Danes had begun trading, though the initial years were plagued by shipwrecks and a lack of funds. They had hoped to ship pepper home to Denmark, but soon found that it was more profitable simply to lease their ships to other European traders. Danish routes were established from Tranquebar to Tenasserim[1] and Macassar, and the Danes thus established themselves as part of the 'country' trade within Asia, forgoing their own trading in favour of carrying Dutch and Portuguese goods across the bay. More Danish factories were set up at Machilipatnam and other outposts further north, but the Danes were still beset by ill luck, and their profits seemed very small when seen, for instance, against the immense wealth generated by the British East India Company. By the end of the decade, left with barely a handful of ships and not enough money to pay tribute to the nayak, Crappé tried to hand over Tranquebar to the Dutch, who were unwilling to take it but agreed to help man the fort. Thus began a period of Dutch influence that culminated in Crappé returning to Denmark in 1636, leaving the colony in the care of a Dutchman called Barent Pessart, a free agent whom the Dutch had given permission to carry on private trade. This was to prove an expensive mistake.

Descending the narrow staircase and making my way around to the north-east corner of the fort, then up a ramp to the main seafront, I had a commanding view across the sand to the old street where the governor's bungalow, built in 1784, still stood, albeit in a state of utter neglect and disrepair. Plans had been made for a hotel chain to take it over and restore it, but these had come to naught; either the bungalow was too small, or the village judged too far from civilization for the scheme to have ripened. Suppressing a sigh, I went back to the yard, where Rohit was investigating an odd structure adjoining the west wall of the fort.

'This used to be the toilet!' he announced, his voice muffled as he poked his head around the wall. And then, somewhat less enthusiastically, 'I think someone's still using it.'

Laughing, we made our way up to the seafront where cannons still faced the sea, and entered the fort museum, a dank and poorly lit establishment where fragments from the Danish day were preserved. A shelf stacked with pamphlets stood in a corner and I looked through them hopefully. When my search yielded nothing more relevant than a history of the Vijayanagar empire and commentaries on distant archaeological sites, I asked the museum attendant whether he had any books on Tranquebar.

'Tranquebar?' he asked, bewildered.

'Yes, Tranquebar!' I said, a little tartly.

He shook his head slowly from side to side in the manner of a nanny refusing sweets to a podgy child. 'No,' said he, emphatically. '*Nothing* on Tranquebar.'

Perhaps one reason that nothing much ever came of Tranquebar was that its harbour was too shallow. Ships had to anchor several miles out at sea while goods and passengers were ferried to and fro in smaller boats, which frequently capsized.[2] Then, of course, there was the ever-looming debt to the nayak of Tanjore, and—to continue the story—the shambles that the Dutch agent Pessart made of the company accounts. Stockholders of the Danish East India Company wanted to dissolve it, but the king rejected this proposal, presumably still holding on to his belief that something would come of the Danish presence in Asian waters.

In 1639 two more ships sailed to India, one of which—the *Christianshavn*, which took three years to arrive—carried on board William Leyel, who had orders to take over Dansborg Fort. He was met with anything but a hospitable welcome; Pessart barred the gates and refused to let go command. Finally, when the fort was besieged with the help of the local people, Pessart was forced to open the gates. He fled forthwith, carrying with him the fort's books and money. Having gained control of Tranquebar, Leyel had a difficult task ahead, for he had not only to sort out a terrible financial mess, but also to cope with hostility from Golconda. To keep peace with powers much stronger than himself, the new commander was forced to call a halt to Danish privateering in the bay, and this led to an immediate loss of popularity among his own officers, who mutinied.

In 1650, after thirty years of struggle, the company was dissolved, and the Danish population on the Coromandel began to shrink until, five years later, there was only one Dane—Kongsbakke—left in Tranquebar.[3] By the mid-seventeenth century, the little port-factory was home to a new assortment of people, with Portuguese and Indo-Portuguese having been hired to man the fort. This replenished manpower came to good use when the nayak of Tanjore, in a fit of pique at not having received his due tribute, besieged the fort in the first of a series of attacks that the small colony managed to withstand. Kongsbakke re-established a connection with the mother country and at last, in 1669, a Danish vessel called the *Faero* arrived with a company of soldiers and an appointment for Kongsbakke as commander of the colony, ending Tranquebar's three-decade-long isolation from Denmark.

What kind of man had this Kongsbakke been, I wondered, he who had endured for fourteen years as the lone Dane in Tranquebar? Unlettered and ignorant in many ways, he had yet been one of the colony's more circumspect leaders. While as much of a privateer as some of his predecessors, he was wise enough to invest some of his gains back into repairing Dansborg, parts of which had been destroyed by the sea. He must have been an adventurer too, like those before him, for it is remarkable that a tiny, often insolvent mercantile establishment had played such havoc with ships belonging to Golconda and the Mughals. Ships had sailed uncontested across the bay until the privateering Danes entered the fray and managed with their tiny strength to stir up the waters considerably.

Looking out at the bay from the seafront of the factory, I found it difficult to picture any such headstrong activity being carried out on this placid blue water. Kongsbakke himself must have stared out at a similar surface on many occasions, but towards the end of his time at Tranquebar, his thoughts could not have reflected the mood of the calm summer sea. As it turned out, the Danes who arrived on the *Faero* had little respect for the unlettered commander, or for his marriage to a native woman. He was increasingly shut out of Danish affairs—by then a new Danish East India Company had been established with a forty-year charter—and died in a much-reduced position. An enduring monument to his time, however, is the city wall that he built around the colony when it was threatened by the nayak of Tanjore.

The second Danish company had a trifle more success than its predecessor, for a more concrete if somewhat strained peace was concluded with the nayak. New trade routes were drawn across the bay to Bantam and the Sunda islands, and Asian prosperity was enhanced by the end of the War of Grand Alliance in 1697, after which Christian V extended the company's charter for another four decades. It was not all smooth sailing, of course; the harbour was still not the friendliest, and Tanjore was yet a prickly neighbour. Europeans who had to travel through Tanjore territory had to pay excessive tolls, and there were sometimes raids across the border. The Danes still had to maintain an expensive army, controlled by the Danes and soldiered by Indians, though the nayaks of Tanjore had been defeated in 1674 by Ekoji, half-brother of the more famous Shivaji, and the Marathas then controlled the area. Socially, the colony was not an easy place to govern, as justice had to be dispensed by a complex and unwritten system that catered to Danish, Hindu and Muslim law while preserving European commercial interests.[4] Tranquebar did prosper somewhat in the late seventeenth century, but it did not have the strength to withstand prolonged misfortune, and when the Great Northern War began in

Europe,[5] the company suffered yet again. When peace was concluded in 1720, the king refused the company's appeal for help. This was the last blow; the company was dissolved.

The last few decades of Danish Company rule at Tranquebar, however, are interesting from a completely different point of view. As you walk along Tranquebar's main street, the Christian influence is tangible—churches stand out from the rest of the ramshackle structures on account of their relatively well-tended condition. Christianity had come to Tranquebar before the Danes colonized it— when they arrived there was already an Indian Catholic presence— but the overriding religious influence was to be that of the Protestants. For here in 1706 arrived the first Protestant missionary in India, the zealous Bartholomaeus Ziegenbalg—a man who spearheaded a movement that was to peacefully convert thousands of Indians and make immense contributions to society in the form of printing, education and literacy. There had been several Protestant ministers in India before the Lutheran Ziegenbalg, but they were not missionaries; they were simply sent by the European nations to minister to the needs of their countrymen. These men rarely had anything to do with the local population, hampered as they were by the language barrier, and they refrained from any sort of interference—chastised perhaps by the brutal record of the Portuguese Roman Catholics, who had blazed a fearful trail on the west coast. Ziegenbalg and his companion Heinrich Plutschau were actually commissioned by Frederik IV as royal missionaries, and sent to India for the express purpose of winning the Indians over to their faith. Here began another chapter in the history of Tranquebar, and a much more important one, in fact, than that of the Danes' minor mercantile enterprise.

When Ziegenbalg and Plutschau arrived in Tranquebar after sailing round the Cape on the *Princess Sophia Hedwig*, they were detained on the ship for three days on a diet of stale bread and water, as a punishment for Ziegenbalg's having remonstrated with the captain for harassing a woman on board. This episode must have given the missionaries some idea of the world they were about to enter, for the ways of the merchant were different from the ways of the missionary; indeed, the Danish East India Company had actually asked their governor, Hassius, to be discouraging towards the newcomers. Hassius was more than willing to comply, for he was alarmed at the thought of Protestant missionaries disrupting his good relations with the local Roman Catholics as well as upsetting the Danish chaplains, who, disagreeing with their Pietist theology,[6] might also have seen them as encroachers. Accordingly, he was most ungracious to the missionaries, offering no assistance of any kind, and confining them to the fort's guard room for a whole day before releasing them into the marketplace. All these hardships seem only to have sharpened their zeal—nothing daunted, they set about finding accommodation and learning the local languages. Plutschau began on Tamil while Ziegenbalg tackled Portuguese, and became so proficient that in just two months he was catechizing in the new tongue. Ziegenbalg's talent for languages had far-reaching consequences, for he then turned his attention to Tamil by the simple means of inviting a local schoolmaster to move his Tamil-medium school into the missionaries' house, in return for which he received free Tamil lessons. The two had long conversations in which each tried to convert the other, and, as Brijraj Singh observes amusingly in his book on the life of the great missionary, 'neither was successful in the venture but it did wonders for Ziegenbalg's Tamil.'[7]

The backstreets of Tranquebar are more orderly than those of the average Tamil Nadu village, but the contrast between the small dwellings there and the great bungalows of the Europeans is, as usual, marked. The humble, lived-in houses of the village still seem to cock a snook at the grand ruins on King and Queen Street. As we made our way down Goldsmith Street and Admiral Street, just wide enough for a vehicle to drive through, it appeared that not much had changed in three hundred years except the departure of the Europeans. Many of the structures had been standing in Ziegenbalg's day, and down these same narrow streets he must have marched in his enthusiasm to mingle with the local people; for the missionary was no racist, and this endeared him to the local Hindus though he strove to show them what he thought were the errors of their belief. He tended to side with the underdog, and this must have annoyed Hassius exceedingly, for one incident caused him to react strongly, almost irrationally. The missionary had taken up for an Indian woman who had cohabited with a Dane, and who upon the death of her 'husband' claimed that his property should come to her. So enraged was Hassius by Ziegenbalg's interference with the local social code that he threw him into a dungeon in November 1708, and there he languished until March the following year.[8] The incident did much to further his popularity with the locals, for they laboured under the Danish yoke and sided with Ziegenbalg simply because he too was out of favour with their masters.

Ziegenbalg's battle with Tranquebar's authorities does not seem to have abated with any speed. In 1711 he visited the British settlement in Madras, and his visit was recorded in the following entry in the Fort's Consultation book of 13 August 1711:

> The Danes Padre, Bortholomew Ziegenbalgh, requests leave to go for Europe on the first ship; and in consideration that he is the head of a Protestant Mission espoused by the Right Reverend the Lord Arch-Bishop of Canterbury, and the rest of our Episcopal Clergy, and that our Masters were pleased to send out their money freight free, we have presumed to grant him his passage without paying permission money.[9]

As Talboys Wheeler wrote, 'A few days afterwards, a member of the Danish council at Tranquebar arrived at Madras on his way to Bengal and asked that this permission might be rescinded, as a dispute between Ziegenbalgh and the Danish Commandant had been referred home to the King of Denmark. Accordingly, the passage was refused until the said missionary had obtained the consent of the Governor of Tranquebar.' Hassius later allowed

Plutschau to sail home, however, for he had served his term in India and there was little danger of his coming back. He returned to Europe on a British ship and quickly slipped into oblivion. There was no evidence that he did anything in Europe to help Ziegenbalg's efforts in India by raising funds or preaching in his support, or indeed that he kept in touch with Tranquebar at all.[10]

There yet stand two Protestant churches on King Street—the Zion church, originally built for the Danish population in 1702, and the slightly newer New Jerusalem Church, built in 1718 by Ziegenbalg to shelter his then-increased congregation. Construction of this church must have been quite an achievement for Ziegenbalg given the conditions under which he operated, yet it was not even his first. The original Jerusalem church had been built in 1707 from a few donations and half the annual salary of the two missionaries shortly after their arrival, and here Ziegenbalg had valiantly preached in Tamil. With a church in place, he had increased his missionary activities, though it must be said that he converted people cautiously, and only after a long period of instruction in Christian belief. His activities were not confined to Tranquebar; he held his discourses in the surrounding villages as well, occasionally going as far as the Dutch-held Nagapattinam.[11]

While Ziegenbalg's faith cannot be doubted, he was at heart a scholarly man, for he set out to learn almost as much about Hinduism as he taught about Christianity. His early reports on Hinduism, hampered much by a lack of understanding of any Indian language, were ludicrous, for they included a divine being called 'Isparetta', from whom came 'Kiwelenga', from whom in turn came 'Bramma, Wischtnum and Ispara'.[12] Although he never achieved a full comprehension of Hinduism, in time he became what Brijraj Singh calls 'a profound and sympathetic student of south Indian Hinduism', even going so far as to write prolifically on the subject. He felt that the Hindu religion and culture, and the Tamil language, should be shared with the rest of the academic world. Motivated by a strong sense of justice, he pointed out that the local people often led virtuous lives despite their heathen beliefs. However, his patron Francke saw this as undue sympathy with Hinduism, and refused to publish Ziegenbalg's *Genealogy of the South-Indian Gods*. The missionaries, he said, with cold logic, were sent to India to exterminate heathenism, 'not to spread the heathen nonsense all over Europe'.[13]

It was to both the erudition and the evangelism of Ziegenbalg that the South owed the renewal of a great process that had lain fallow since the Portuguese abandoned it at the end of the previous century— a process that was to stimulate and educate on a scale that seemed unimaginable in light of Tranquebar's tiny main street. It was, of course, printing that Ziegenbalg revived when, in 1712, he set up a mission press that began with Portuguese and German works and moved with astounding rapidity to the production of Tamil works the very next year. Among the first works to be published at this time were a 'Letter to the Hindus' written in 1711, a four-page tract called *The Abomination of Paganism*, and translations of Luther's catechism and Ziegenbalg's *A Ordem a Salvacão* (The Method of Salvation). The most important Tamil publication was Ziegenbalg's translation of the New Testament; he also wrote an anglophone Tamil grammar called *Grammatica Damulica* a few years later.[14] From these early beginnings in Tranquebar, printing was continued only fifty years later in the British settlement further up the coast, when a press was set up to handle both government and diocesan printing, with equipment that the British general Sir Eyre Coote looted from Pondicherry in 1761.[15] Printing had now come to the South to stay.

Thanks to this very real connection with the local people—an understanding and propagation of their language—Ziegenbalg led a remarkably integrated life in Tranquebar. He did not get along with the Danish authorities, to be sure, but he managed to marry and settle down in the community, and he became much beloved even to those who did not convert—and many did not. For Ziegenbalg was of an early order of missionaries, an order that came out before Robert Clive was even born. As Brijraj Singh writes,

> [I]n two important ways he was very different from the British missionaries who followed in the wake of Britain's conquest of India. First, he was not a racist. Second, he wanted India to be Christianized but not Westernized. Indeed, he was keen that people did not become *déraciné* when they converted; for this purpose he insisted on teaching Indian classics and Indian music in his schools . . .

Yet Ziegenbalg was not opposed to colonialism, and indeed was impatient with the British reluctance to colonize. He saw the establishment of British political power as the only vehicle strong enough to tow Protestantism along with it and spread the faith across the Subcontinent.[16]

While Dansborg is dilapidated and the Danish town limits are now partially eaten away by the sea, the Christian buildings in Tranquebar flourish still, for they remain living structures, used regularly by local Christians. It is a strange juxtaposition—the once grand but now ramshackle colonial buildings that sprang from the daydreams of a Danish monarch four centuries ago stand forlornly by the sea, as if awaiting their destruction, while the modest church establishments have endured in a way that the mercantile structures have not. If only Ziegenbalg could see this day, I thought, when, although the fort was all but in ruins and no one seemed to care whether Tranquebar existed or not, the church lived on.

Casting aside this fanciful thought, I turned around to take a last look at Tranquebar as we drove out of its town gate—one of the few structures that has been restored by the ASI—and reflected that the powers-that-be need not have bothered. With its boldly whitewashed arch and the pale-yellow ghost town behind it, the gate looked more like a film set than ever, contributing its bit to the surreal, somnolent vision that is Tranquebar. As we drove away, the last thing we saw was a large herd of slick, swishy-tailed black buffaloes disappearing four abreast through the gate and proceeding ponderously down King Street as if they owned it. Which, coming to think of it, they did.

Notes

1. Tenasserim was a territory (with a coastal city by the same name) that once belonged to the ancient kingdom of Pegu. A centre of the Asian spice trade, it was known to the Europeans for its brazil, a dye-wood that yielded an excellent vermilion. In 1506, Leonardo Ca' Masser described it as 'the first mart of spices in India', yielding pepper, cinnamon, galanga and two varieties of camphor. *Hobson-Jobson, The Anglo-Indian Dictionary*, p. 914.
2. Brijraj Singh, *The First Protestant Missionary to India: Bartholomaeus Ziegenbalg (1683-1719)* (New Delhi: Oxford University Press, 1999), p. 41.
3. Ibid.
4. Ibid., pp. 41-43.
5. In 1700, Sweden's fleet of thirty-nine ships controlled the Baltic and cut off Russia's sea route to European ports. Fought over twenty years in the early eighteenth century, the Great Northern War was really the culmination of an animosity between Russia and Sweden that had existed since the time of the Vikings, reaching its peak during the reign of Peter the Great. Into the fray were drawn a number of other nations including Denmark, who came to the aid of Russia with her naval force.
6. Pietism was a movement that had its origin in late-seventeenth-century Germany. A hundred years into the Protestant Reformation, some of those who had grown disillusioned with the fractured Christian church organized a new movement that was intended to be spiritually-minded, as opposed to the intellectualized faith in vogue at the time. Pietism had no new theology; it was simply a step towards achieving what the Reformation had not quite achieved. It advocated a more participatory church, a life of devotion to Bible study and prayer, and the importance of right living. With all this emphasis on propriety, it is not surprising that Hassius, head

of an isolated company of weather-beaten mercantile souls, looked with scant patience upon Ziegenbalg's righteous ambitions.

7. Singh, pp. 15-18.
8. Ibid., pp. 25-26.
9. Quoted in J. Talboys Wheeler, *Madras in the Olden Time: A History of the Presidency from the First Foundation of Fort St. George to the Occupation of Madras by the French (1639-1748)* (1861; reprint, New Delhi: Asian Educational Services, 1993), p. 316.
10. Singh, p. 31.
11. Ibid., p. 26-27.
12. Ibid., pp. 20-21.
13. Quoted in ibid., p. 78.
14. Ibid., pp. 31-32, 36.
15. S. Muthiah, *Madras Rediscovered* (Chennai: East West Books, 1999), p. 241.
16. Singh, p. 157.

Hampi
City of Victory

The whole of [the old city] is dotted with little, barren, rocky hills and immediately north of it the wide and rapid Tungabhadra hurries along a boulder-strewn channel down rapids and through narrow gorges . . . The alternate burning days and chilly nights . . . have seamed and split in every direction the huge masses of solid rock . . . and the earthquakes of remote ages and the slower processes of denudation have torn from their flanks the enormous boulders which were thus formed and have piled these up round about their sides in the most fantastic confusion or flung them headlong into the valleys below. In places, cyclopean masses stand delicately poised one upon another at the most hazardous angles, in others they form impassable barriers, while those which have yet to fall often stand boldly out from the hills . . . or range themselves in castellations and embattlements which but for their vastness would seem to be the work of man rather than of nature.
—A.H. Longhurst, *Hampi Ruins*

Dawn broke hesitantly as I stood on the roof of an ancient temple that had been built on the summit of a hill in honour of Virabhadra, a form

The Temple Trail

of Shiva. This remote place of worship was a point of strength and power in a surreal landscape, a small, determined superstructure on an island that had survived the twisting of seismic currents to rise high above an ocean of rock, with boulders lifting themselves around it in motionless waves of arrested obeisance. The sun, hidden behind a massive bank of clouds, sent out a whimsical light, illuminating only such features and objects as caught its fancy and adding to the magic of the scene: in the valleys there were flashes of silver where the Tungabhadra wound its way over the plateau, and hints of green from the awakening trees and creepers. On the hillocks and boulder swells, patches of gold, white and rust danced and changed places mischievously, and inky dots metamorphosed into birds and took flight across the banana plantations. Between all this would momentarily appear the outline of a stone temple or rest house, or the fleeting geometry of an erstwhile intersection of streets. A rash wind rushed through the natural corridors that separated the rocks, bending tall stalks of grass almost to the ground and battering hysterically against the impervious stones.

The efforts of the wind were amusing, for this was no ordinary concatenation of earth and rock: this was the ancient capital of an empire that had held the South in a protective embrace for 250 years, despite frequent inroads from the North. This was an archaeological graveyard of astounding proportions, where the immense ruins of rock-cut buildings lay strewn about an inhospitable terrain, creating a bizarre superimposition of strength on strength and stillness on stillness. This was Hampi, a city that had seen the best of times and the worst of times: the magnificent ascent of a visionary dynasty, a long period of prosperity and renown under various rulers, and then a cataclysmic fall, when all that had been built over two centuries was torched in a bloody six-month invasion that seemed to leave nothing in its wake but rubble and ash.

Despite this vengeful and murderous destruction, many of the rock structures of that time still remain—or are in the process of being unearthed—as an epitaph to a great Hindu empire that was vanquished only when all of its enemies attacked it at the same time.

The odd thing about Hampi—or Vijayanagar, to use the name of the ancient city—is that the ruins do not exude any of the bitterness and grief of the generation that was axed, or of the impossible pride that so incensed the marauders that nothing would satisfy them but to annihilate every reminder of it. Ironically, the ruins emanate a feeling of peace, a philosophical repose, the slow-breathing, eternal sleep of a city that did its duty to the South, indeed brought it greater glory and gain than it had ever known before. Curiously, there is also the distinct—and distinctly erroneous—impression of a city that was shut down and abandoned rather than destroyed, an illusion doubtless left by the many centuries that separate the ruins of the present from the blood and gore of the past. Wrote Robert Sewell, meticulous historian of what he called the 'forgotten' empire,

> With fire and sword, with crowbars and axes, they carried on day after day their work of destruction. Never perhaps in the history of the world has such havoc been wrought, and wrought so suddenly, on so splendid a city; teeming with a wealthy and industrious population in the full plenitude of prosperity one day, and on the next seized, pillaged and reduced to ruins, among scenes of savage massacre and horrors beggaring description.[1]

Looking at the serene remains below me—an excavated street lined with the skeletal pillars of once-busy shops, and a half-destroyed temple complex—I could only reflect that the great city must have been destined to fall by a single violent blow, then left to wild beasts. In this manner, it was spared a gradual fade into unimportance and oblivion.

The empire that had come to such a catastrophic end was born in the shaky decades of the early fourteenth century, out of the tumult and anarchy following the invasion of Malik Kafur, the great Delhi general who led the forces of Allauddin Khilji into the Deccan in 1310. Though still under Hindu rule, the South was severely rattled by the inexorable approach of the banner of Islam. Sewell writes evocatively of this period:

> [T]he period at which our history opens, about the year 1330, found the whole of Northern India down to the Vindhya mountains firmly under Moslem rule, while the followers of that faith had overrun the Dakhan and were threatening the south with the same fate . . . With the accession of Muhammad Tughlaq of Delhi things became worse still. Marvellous stories of his extraordinary proceedings circulated amongst the inhabitants of the Peninsula, and there seemed to be no bound to his intolerance, ambition and ferocity . . . Everything, therefore, seemed to be leading up to but one inevitable end—the ruin and devastation of the Hindu provinces, the annihilation of their old royal houses, the destruction of their religion, their temples, their cities. All that the dwellers in the south held most dear seemed tottering to its fall.[2]

Out of the crying need for a kingdom powerful enough to dam the flow of conquest and subjugation from the North rose the tremendous Vijayanagar empire, which took root in the tiny fortified town of Anegundi (the ruins of which can still be seen across the river from Hampi) and grew into an all-powerful, immensely wealthy state that extended from coast to coast and from present-day northern Karnataka to the very tip of the peninsula.

Before we can even begin to unravel the tangle of archaeological sites that is Hampi, to distinguish between its scores of ruined structures, and to picture them as they were in their heyday, we must find a quiet bit of shade and acquaint ourselves with the empire's intricate history. The precise origin of the confident founder of the Vijayanagar dynasty is lost in legend, but Sewell finds this the most reasonable account:

two brothers, Hukka and Bukka, sons of Sangama, were minister and treasurer in the service of the raja of Anegundi when Mohammed bin Tughlaq invaded the principality in pursuit of—of all people—his nephew. The powerful sultan defeated the local raja and left a deputy in charge, but this gentleman was so unpopular that Tughlaq restored the principality to the Hindus, raising Hukka to be king and Bukka to be minister.[3]

Before dawn, during the cool grey-skied drive to Hampi, the guide who accompanied me had pointed out two massive stones near an entrance to the city of Vijayanagar, and called them, in tones of marked affection, 'Hukka' and 'Bukka'. He explained that the local people still call the stones by these names almost seven centuries after the empire's founding. This seemed fitting to me, for under Hukka, the extent of the territory widened considerably even as the empire was in its infancy, and under Bukka, who followed his brother as king, it grew to include all of the South and to repulse the dangerous threat from the neighbouring Bahmani state.

'Suddenly,' wrote Sewell, '. . . there was a check to this wave of foreign invasion—a stop—a halt—then a solid wall of opposition; and for 250 years Southern India was saved.'[3] The Sangama dynasty ruled the immense Vijayanagar empire for well over a century, after which the Tuluva dynasty came to the throne in 1505. By the time the empire fell in 1565, the 'city of victory' had held sway over the South in every possible way and left permanent evidence of a prosperous and cultured era, not least in the magnificent architecture of Hampi and of sites as far afield as Vellore and Srirangam.

Krishna Deva Raya, the most powerful of the Vijayanagar kings, who ascended the throne in 1509 and to whom much of the ancient city's glorious architecture is attributed, belonged to the Tuluva dynasty. Such was his success, and so intense the pride that followed it, that after a victorious battle with the sultan of Bijapur he received entreaties from the other Deccan powers to return the conquered city of Raichur to the vanquished. To this he replied, according to Fernão Nuniz, a mid-sixteenth-century traveller to Vijayanagar:

> As regards the Ydallcão [Ismail Adil Shah of Bijapur], what I have done to him and taken from him he has richly deserved; as regards returning it to him that does not seem to me reasonable, nor am I going to do it; and as for your further statement that ye will all turn against me in aid of him if I do not do as ye ask, I pray you do not take the trouble to come hither, for I will myself go to seek ye if ye dare to await me in your lands . . .[4]

Krishna Deva Raya's glory was not, however, destined to be carried down the generations. Less than fifty years after he had dispatched these arrogant words, the capital from which he ruled was brought to its knees and beheaded in 1565 by the combined forces of several Deccan Muslim states. It seems sad that the successors of such a proud ruler were so craven as to desert their own capital after being defeated by a league of five during the battle of Talikota,[5] abandoning the undefended city to the mercy of their approaching foes. After the destruction of the capital, the empire declined rapidly; its kings ruled from Penukonda[6] and then took refuge in Chandragiri, a small fortress near Tirupati. In the mid-seventeenth century, it was the raja of Chandragiri who granted a small piece of land on the Coromandel coast to a group of British traders; the resulting fortified settlement became the foundation of the modern city of Madras and, though even the British didn't know it at the time, for British domination of the Subcontinent and sizeable parts of the rest of the world. Thus, unwittingly, did the embers of one empire spark the kindling of another, almost as if an exhausted runner had passed a torch to another with the energy of youth but not even a nascent understanding of the distance he was destined to run.

Squatting on the roof of the little temple for fear that the monsoon wind would blow me right off the highest hill in the area, I found it difficult to imagine Vijayanagar as a city of half a million, its streets so crowded with people and animals that they were difficult to pass. Domingos Paes,[7] an early-sixteenth-century traveller who had climbed to the top of a hill here—perhaps the very same one that I had—was inspired to describe the scene thus, five hundred years ago:

> The size of this city I do not write here, because it cannot all be seen from any one spot, but I climbed a hill whence I could see a great part of it; I could not see it all because it lies between several ranges of hills. What I saw from thence seemed to me as large as Rome, and very beautiful to the sight; there are many groves of trees within it, in the gardens of the houses, and many conduits of water which flow into the midst of it, and in places there are lakes (tamques); and the king has close to his palace a palm-grove and other rich-bearing fruit-trees . . . The people in this city are countless in number, so much that I do not wish to write it down for fear it should be thought fabulous; but I declare that no troops, horse or foot, could break their way through any street or lane, so great are the numbers of people and elephants.[8]

Today a few villagers and cattle wander desultorily among the ruins, eking out an existence during the long, hot summer and the violent rains that follow, waiting expectantly for the 'season' when foreigners descend upon the sleepy little village of Hampi and breathe money and marijuana into its otherwise stagnant economy. As the sunlight grew stronger that morning on Matanga Hill, the bleakness of the terrain became increasingly apparent, and the stories of local thugs and muggers more credible. On the way up the hill I had seen an eerie cave where a thief was said to have lived a few months earlier, making an easy living by stealing from unsuspecting tourists at knifepoint, until he had gone too far and murdered someone, and was finally arrested.

'He's finished, now, that fellow,' the district tahsildar said with considerable satisfaction when I asked him about the incident. 'He used to steal expensive cameras from foreigners, especially women who went up there alone, and sell them in the bazaar without knowing their value. But he was shot in the leg when they caught him.' It was easy to picture the thief watching from his rocky lair as explorers made their way up to the hilltop temple to catch the sunset or even stay overnight to bring in the dawn. Later, when he made his assault, screams of protest would have been lost in the wind, as it hurled the feeble sounds against the thousands of rock surfaces on and around the hill and echoed them emptily through the caves and hollows.

Although the great city has lain bleak and barren for most of the last five centuries, pockets of the old capital have sprung to life once more, some of them in the suburbs that Krishna Deva Raya added and liked so much as to actually inhabit himself. The crowded modern town of Hospet grew on the site of one such suburb, though not much remains of any ancient construction. I had halted in Hospet the previous night, at a guest house built on a hill overlooking a large dam and the great lake formed by the stopping of the Tungabhadra. The dam is perhaps Hospet's best-known attraction: it was built in the 1950s, and present-day townspeople take the air in the gardens laid out near the river. In the old days, travellers from Goa and the west coast approached Vijayanagar this way, and this is one tradition that has survived: Western travellers who holiday in Goa often find time to travel by the busload to Hampi, by way of Hospet, in search of history and tranquillity. What the travellers of old saw, of course, before reaching the suburb itself, was the outer circle of the complex fortification of the larger capital area. Reported Abdur Razzâk, Persian ambassador to Calicut and Vijayanagar in the mid-fifteenth century (his very title indicating the importance of south India on the world map of the time): 'The city of Bidjanagar is such that the pupil of the eye has never seen a place like it, and the ear of intelligence has never been informed that there existed anything to equal it in the world. It is built in such a manner that seven citadels and the same number of walls enclose each other.'[9]

After passing through the first gate into the capital territory, travellers must then have reached present-day Hospet through the entrance in the second fortified wall, and so on through four more walls before reaching the seventh and innermost—the remains of which are still in reasonably good shape—that protected the citadel or royal enclosure south of the river. The present road from Hospet to Hampi and Kamalapuram passes through Anantasayanagudi, a village named for its temple of the reclining Vishnu, and the antiquity of the route is evident from the old shrines and buildings along the way. Referring to this road, Paes observed,

> [F]rom [the city of 'Bisnaga'] to the new city goes a street as wide as a place of tourney, with both sides lined throughout with rows of houses and shops where they sell everything; and all along this road are many trees that the king commanded to be planted, so as to afford shade to those who pass along. On this road he commanded to be erected a very beautiful temple of stone, and there are other pagodas that the captains and great lords caused to be erected.[10]

The most interesting present-day pocket of habitation is the village of Hampi itself, just south of the Tungabhadra, where life has been sustained down the centuries thanks to the temple of Virupaksha, an incarnation of Shiva and patron deity of the Vijayanagar kings. Even after the capital fell, the kings continued to patronize this temple; a copper-plate inscription dated 1576 refers to a grant made by Shriranga II in the 'presence of Virupaksha of Pampakshetra'.[11] People have evidently worshipped here ever since, for a local chief built its northern tower around the eighteenth century. From the top of Matanga, the temple dominates the view to the west, a large and intricate cream structure rising conspicuously out of the surrounding stone and earth. It looks oddly new and incongruous, but of course its putative modernity is only the result of a fresh coat of whitewash. At its heart, beneath the layers added during the empire, is an original site of worship that dates back as far as the twelfth century.[12]

Pampa, a local goddess, is said to have wedded Virupaksha, and so the old structure is often called the Pampapati temple.[13] Hampi gets its name from this original goddess, for the tendency in the contemporary Kannada language is to change the 'P' sound in old Kannada into an 'H'.

When Paes visited Vijayanagar, he wrote of a temple that he somewhat laboriously called 'Aōperadianar', almost certainly the temple of Virupaksha, and was evidently much taken with its lavish illumination:

> All the outer side of the gate of the temple up to the roof is covered with copper and gilded, and on each side of the roof on the top are certain great animals that look like tigers, all gilt. As soon as you enter this idol-shrine, you perceive from pillar to pillar on which it is supported many little holes in which stand oil lamps, which burn, so they tell me, every night, and they will be in number two thousand five hundred or three thousand lights.[14]

The copper and gilt have disappeared, yet worship continues enthusiastically, judging by the number of people pressed sweating into its sanctum on a weekday morning. I entered and joined them, for there seems to be no restriction today on non-Hindus entering the sanctum; Paes, on the other hand, had to bribe the Brahmin doorkeepers to get in.

It is easy to while away an hour or so in this crowded but easy-going temple; nobody bothers you while you explore its stone corridors, fiddle with its ancient bells, drums and wind instruments, and admire the inverted shadow image of the tower cast upon an inner wall, or the curious three-headed Nandi at the entrance. The entrance itself is a curiosity, for the gateway to the temple is supported by an old metal beam that clearly bears the inscription 'Made in England'. A British Collector, F.W. Robertson, repaired the northern tower in 1837, at which time the colonial administration was in charge of temples. As I stood near the eccentric figure of the Nandi, completely blackened by the ghee with which it had long been anointed, a real bull sauntered in—an emaciated, dull-brown specimen with drooping horns, inclined to make up for its lack of impressiveness with sheer attitude—and strode haughtily past its stone brethren to take a quick tour round the temple in search of victuals. Finding little more than a withered banana skin, it marched off the way it had come, pretending it had not really been hungry after all. Quite distracted by this animal, I failed to notice another one, an adolescent monkey that was sitting on a lamp-post near the inner tower of the temple and making all sorts of gestures and sounds to attract my attention. When I finally looked up at him, he promptly clasped the top of the lamp in both hands and stood on his head, kicking his legs in the air as his companions, comfortably nestled in the diminishing niches on the tower, screamed in wild encouragement. I was reminded that the nearby hills were, according to Hindu belief, the actual location of Kishkintha, the monkey kingdom of the Ramayana.

At one end, the Virupaksha temple opens out into Hampi Bazaar, a wide street along which temple chariots are ceremonially drawn. This street has met with considerable controversy in recent years, for here, among the stones and pillars of an earlier day, has grown a haphazard marketplace full of careless and ignorant constructions. It is admittedly marvellous that the street has survived down the centuries while the rest of the city is half-sunk beneath the sand—a bizarre living bridge across five centuries, perhaps continuing chiefly due to the unbroken ritual of the annual temple chariot festival. However, the weight of its history has now caused it to collapse upon itself, and to draw the censure of archaeologists and conservationists the world over. Many of the original stone structures remain; some have been used as the foundation for newer buildings, while others have had their stones dragged away to other locations. Although what one now sees is a strange juxtaposition of the old and new, it is still easy to identify with Paes, who was probably referring to Hampi Bazaar when he wrote,

> In this pagoda, opposite to its principal gate which is to the east, there is a very beautiful street of very beautiful houses with balconies and arcades, in which are sheltered the pilgrims that come to it, and there are also houses for the lodging of the upper classes; the king has a palace in the same street, in which he resides when he visits this pagoda.[15]

Soon, the last generation of inhabitants will face displacement and reconstruction of their establishments in a different location, for this is the only way to preserve the structures that have already been mutilated and even destroyed to make way for new shops and buildings. For the moment, however, Hampi Bazaar is still the main street, as it were, of the ruins, for here you can procure anything from silver jewellery to a French-speaking guide, and even stay the night—like the pilgrims of old—in supremely inexpensive rooms. It is this area that plays host to long-staying foreign backpackers, who arrive every winter after the river has fallen to its normal level and the rocks and boulders are no longer slippery and treacherous.

'Madam, you have to see it to believe it,' remarked the tahsildar. '*Five thousand* people a year!' And then, lowering his voice: 'Everything that you see abroad, you can see here also. What can I say, it is like a mini England.' I nodded sympathetically, though I had only the vaguest idea what he meant.

Down the ages, Vijayanagar has always attracted visitors and traders from around the world. Paes wrote of a Moorish quarter within the city; evidently a Muslim community was welcome to live here and participate in commerce and military affairs despite the king being at loggerheads with the surrounding Muslim states. Indeed, Paes observed 'men belonging to every nation and people', and attributed this to Vijayanagar's thriving trade and plentiful gems, particularly diamonds.[16]

Close to Hampi Bazaar are a number of structures that form eccentric interjections on the Vijayanagar trail, the most delightful of which are the Sasivekalu Ganesha and Kadalekalu Ganesha, great monolithic sculptures of the elephant god. Quite apart from the quality of sculpture, which gives the figures a soothingly benign and rounded appearance, there is an endearing humour to their names, for *sasivekalu* means mustard seed and *kadalekalu* means gram. The idea of these massive sculptures having such modest origins must raise a chuckle among the villagers from time to time.

'It is a joke, you see,' my guide kindly explained when I had stopped grinning.

A short walk from the rotund Ganeshas is the largest and most startling monolith: a figure of Narasimha, an incarnation of Vishnu who takes on the man-lion form. He is seated on the serpent Adisesha, who raises his hood protectively over the god from the rear. Although terribly mutilated, the sculpture was apparently restored to the fullest extent possible, and now glares disturbingly from bulbous eyes at the fields and foliage around it. It was here, beneath the savage countenance of the broken Narasimha, that I had the most vivid impression of the destruction that had been wrought on this city; for his wounds have a freshness about them, and the whole monolith exudes a sense of anger that is altogether unusual here.

'Beautiful, no?' asked the guide. This time I realized he was not joking, and was reminded of A.H. Longhurst's observation that horror and even grotesqueness of representation do not prevent an Indian god from winning intense love and devotion.[17] I murmured my agreement, and edged away from the god's stony glare.

A little way back down the path is the area's third odd site: a temple that catches the sunlight through its roof, keeping its brown linga bathed in a beautiful white light. Like the temple of Virupaksha, this is a functional place of worship, complete with a priest who keeps watch over the massive polished stone and greets visitors with a shy smile. The linga stands in a pool of water, and although a modern author attributes this to recent irrigation of the area, Longhurst wrote during the colonial era that its base was 'permanently under water'.[18] In any case the water adds a dreamy touch, making the temple a pleasant place to while away the hottest part of the day, and perhaps recover from the violent effects of Narasimha.

South of the Virupaksha temple are the relatively small Hazara Rama temple, which gets its name from the endless Ramayana scenes sculpted on its walls, and the remains of imperial buildings in what must have been the city's original citadel. At the present-day entrance to the citadel lie, in ironic horizontal welcome, two halves of a massive stone door complete with bolts and sockets—a strangely intact memorial of what is to follow. Here, in a bleak and dusty plain free of the usual rocks and boulders, are a number of raised masonry platforms: the remains of the great buildings that must have once graced the citadel. The stone door could have belonged to any of them, and was found lying under 'debris and bushes' during the colonial period. The first and most evocative structure is called the Dasara Dibba, a throne platform used by the king during the annual nine-day Dasara festivities. Paes calls this structure the 'House of Victory', noting that it was built by Krishna Deva Raya after he returned triumphant from a conflict with the king of 'Orya' (Orissa). Running around the base of the platform are carved stone panels, a moving reminder of the glorious times in which they were crafted. Etched out of schist, the base of the triumphant building must once have glowed as if it were sculpted from emeralds. Even today, after several centuries of being worn by wind and rain, and the upper part of the building having disappeared completely, the panels preserve a certain royal dignity and brilliance of execution that are simply rivetting.

Walking on top of the Dasara Dibba, now bare, I could not help thinking of Ozymandias, king of kings, for there was something very arrogant about Krishna Deva Raya and his treatment of his Muslim neighbours. Here, on the tremendous flattened foundation of his House of Victory, came the inevitable end and equalizing, for even he who demanded that a sultan should kiss his foot to recover lost territory had come to dust, and his kingdom had later fallen like a skittle at the most unexpected moment. It was sobering to contemplate how the mighty king had reviewed his armies, according to our faithful observer:

> [T]he king passed along gazing at his soldiers, who gave great shouts and cries and struck their shields; the horses neighed, the elephants screamed, so that it seemed as if the city would be overturned, the hills and valleys and all the ground trembled with the discharges of arms and musquets; and to see the bombs and fire-missiles over the plains; this was indeed wonderful. Truly it seemed as if the whole world were collected there.[19]

Very close to the throne platform, and in a considerably better state of repair, is one of the most incredibly intact sights from the age of empire, uncovered only in the 1980s. Chiselled from sharp-edged schist, the royal bath is a series of beautifully designed steps leading into a progressively smaller area to which water was conveyed by a stone aqueduct. In an early photograph, this aqueduct is shown leading to the bare ground;[20] only recently did excavations reveal its connection to the buried bath. I climbed down the almost modern-looking steps to the bottom and looked up at the sharp geometric patterns all around. Suddenly they seemed to crowd in upon me, with their wicked green-black knife-edges, as if daring me to remain.

Clambering out in a hurry, I half wished the stone aqueduct still carried water, for its liquid ripples and reflections would have eased the visual impact of so many straight lines and right angles. I sat on the top step and looked up at the aqueduct, marvelling at the pains that had been taken to bring water to this dry and dusty ground.

The Vijayanagar kings were famous for their irrigation works—travellers to the city often commented on its water supply and the greenness and fertility of its fields and orchards. The Tungabhadra, being lower than the city, could not supply water directly, so the city's plentiful receptacles originally depended on the monsoon. It was Krishna Deva Raya's dam and channel at Korragal, and other feats of ancient irrigation such as the Basavanna channel, that account for pockets of Vijayanagar still appearing cultivated five centuries later, appearing confusingly green in an otherwise arid landscape. It is sad that one of the largest irrigation projects undertaken here—a lake, possibly intended to supply water to the suburbs as well as the fields—came to naught. Both Paes and Nuniz describe its construction, and Sewell estimates its location at the north-western mouth of the valley, entering the Sandur hills south-west of Hospet.[21] That the lake, though used after construction to irrigate paddies and gardens, was ill-fated and destined to run dry is not altogether surprising; while it was being built, Krishna Deva Raya, on the advice of his 'wise men and sorcerers', sought to appease the gods by, of all things, beheading all his prisoners 'who deserved death'.

Unlike Hampi Bazaar, which still throbs with life, a number of Vijayanagar's markets have simply been buried by time. Abdur Razzâk remembers seeing countless crowds of people between the third fortification and the walls of the citadel itself, and speaks thus of the markets in this 'agreeable locality':

> By the King's palace are four bazaars, placed opposite each other. On the north is the portico of the palace of the rai. Above each bazaar is a lofty arcade with a magnificent gallery,

but the audience-hall of the King's palace is elevated above all the rest. The bazaars are extremely long and broad.[22]

Who were the people, I wondered, who frequented the bazaars? Razzâk spoke of the roses that were sold throughout, remarking that people apparently could not live without roses; they were as necessary as food. Varthema, an Italian traveller who came to India at the time of the Portuguese, wrote that the common people went about 'quite naked, with the exception of a piece of cloth about their middle', but the king wore 'a cap of gold brocade two spans long', and his very horse was 'worth more than some of our cities on account of the ornaments which it wears'.[23] Paes, who had a great eye for detail, observed that the majority of people 'go about the country barefooted', and when they wore shoes, these had 'pointed ends, in the ancient manner' or were 'nothing but soles' with straps, 'made like those which of old the Romans were wont to wear, as you will find on figures in some papers or antiquities which come from Italy'.[24] Barbosa, a cousin of Magellan, observed that Hampi's streets were 'constantly filled with an innumerable crowd of all nations and creeds', that the city had an 'infinite trade', and that the governors and councillors of the land came to see the king 'in very rich litters on men's shoulders'.[25] And Nuniz recorded, in some shock, that 'these people have such devotion to cows that they kiss them every day, some they say even on the rump—a thing I do not assert for their honour—and with the droppings of these cows they absolve themselves from their sins as if with holy water.'[26]

The women of Vijayanagar have also been described in enchanting detail, for evidently they were a colourful and attractive lot: the women 'of the temple', who were reputedly of loose character but enjoyed a high status; the wives of Brahmins, whom Paes found beautiful, retiring, indeed some of the fairest in the land; the richly adorned queens and courtesans of the king, and their numerous attendants; and the palace women, who included dancers, bearers, wrestlers, astrologers and soothsayers, accountants, writers and musicians. There is not much mention of the common women, except for the fact that they took part in city festivities with great enthusiasm; travellers seemed to have been more impressed with the king's glamorous establishment. In search of an epitaph to this era of near-captivity— for the queens never left their boudoir—I wandered along to what is now called the zenana enclosure, possibly the site of the royal women's quarters (though some say the area simply contained the king's public offices). It is tempting to believe that this was the zenana, for its high, solid walls and watchtowers seem to have protected something precious and vulnerable. The watchtowers were actually designed to accommodate a number of people besides the guards; with their many windows, they could have served as viewing galleries from which women could watch unhindered the proceedings of the outside world. The zenana enclosure contains a miraculously intact building of the Indo-Saracenic style, a pretty, airy structure now called the Lotus Mahal even though we do not know how it was used. Perhaps the Muslim invaders left it standing because of its Islamic look, particularly its arches and pillars: there is no other reason why they should have spared only this building, the nearby elephant stables and the queen's bath (another beautiful little building somewhat despoiled by a layer of pink paint and some etchings of dubious antiquity), which wear a similar hybrid look.

On the veranda of the Lotus Mahal sat a withered old woman, a sweeper who had laid her broom down and was catching forty winks in the heat of the day. I marvelled that the old building still served as a place of rest, its cool pavilions soothing tired limbs not of royalty, but of a humble woman of the village. Whether or not these buildings are what they seem to be, travellers' descriptions of royal ladies are fascinating. Nuniz, for instance, tells us that Achyuta Raya, Krishna Deva Raya's half-brother and successor, had five hundred wives, 'and as many less or more as he wants, with whom he sleeps; and all of these burn themselves at his death. When he journeys to any place he takes twenty-five or thirty of his most favourite wives, who go with him, each one in her palanqueen with poles.'[27]

I thought of these women as birds in a gilded cage, for whatever the luxury of their lifestyle, they were destined to meet a hideous death by fire. Sati was part and parcel of the Vijayanagar lifestyle; more than one traveller describes or at least mentions the dreadful ritual, and a number of *sati kals*—stone memorials to widows who immolated themselves on their husband's funeral pyres—are pathetic reminders of the custom. The sati kals of Vijayanagar, visible on the road to Hampi and elsewhere, bear sculptures of female figures with one arm raised, bent at the elbow, a symbol of the sacrifice performed.

It was difficult to leave the sleeping zenana behind, with its impossibly high walls, its romantic towers, and its few remaining trees and ponds. The windows of the towers were dark and brooding; they seemed to still protect the forms of unseen spectators, and to look at them was to suppress a shiver. Tearing myself away, I made my way back across the capital to the northernmost point of the ruins on the banks of the Tungabhadra. I was eager to see the Vitthala temple, far and away the most striking building in the capital, built by Krishna Deva Raya and almost completely desecrated by the invaders. The temple is heavily guarded today as an important archaeological site, so uniformed guards watch suspiciously as you enter and stare in disbelief at the beautiful structures within. The first sculpture is a large stone chariot, tastefully carved and in reasonably good condition. Behind it stands the lower storey of what must have once ranked among the most beautiful buildings in the world, with its rich sculpture and impossibly lovely backdrop of hills and boulders. Even in its ruinous condition, with all its cracks and imperfections and asymmetry, the Vitthala is magnificent: the building exudes such power and vitality that the very countryside around it is energized by its presence. That the splendid temple was ever actually used is doubtful, for it was not completed or consecrated, and its construction, begun in 1513, was probably abandoned when the city fell in 1565. However, as Longhurst wrote of its large hall, 'in spite of the fact that the roof over this magnificent hall was never completed and that many of its beautiful pillars have been grievously damaged by the destroyers of the city, it is still the finest building of its kind in Southern India, and to quote Fergusson, "shows the extreme limit in florid magnificence to which the style advanced".'[28] To stand in this hall and look out on low hills, boulder swells, and an excavated street and stone corridor is to feel the passionate heartbeat of the ancient city, and to sense something of the vigour and intensity of its builder-kings.

The most curious thing about the temple is its series of hollow musical pillars. These are not mentioned by historians, perhaps because they seem too kitschy; yet my abiding image of Vitthala is that of a slender young girl standing with her ear to a granite pillar, looking out at the boulders and ruins beyond. Her face was absolutely transfixed, her soul transported to another era by the musical notes she was hearing as someone tapped a spot in the rock.

From the splendid temple, the best place to retreat, your ears ringing with the gentle granite music, is to the river itself. Not far from here is the point where you can catch a coracle across the water to the ruins at Anegundi. The coracles of Vijayanagar are an age-old tradition: these perfectly round country boats built on bamboo frames were in use when Paes came to the capital in the early sixteenth century. He described people crossing to 'Senagumdym', the old capital of the kingdom in

> boats which are round like baskets; inside they are made of cane, and outside covered with leather; they are able to carry fifteen or twenty persons, and even horses and oxen can cross in them if necessary . . . men row them with a sort of paddle, and the boats are always turning round, as they cannot go straight like others; in all the kingdom where there are streams there are no other boats but these.[29]

It is simply incredible that the same sort of boat is still afloat, albeit with a few changes; the bottoms are covered with plastic sheeting instead of leather, and the heavy loads carried are not horses or oxen but motorbikes, parked neatly three abreast. Hailing a coracle from the opposite bank, I was rowed up the Tungabhadra, the banks covered with a silken bloom the very shade of mustard fields in winter. Great walls of rock rose all around, casting gloomy reflections in the river and evoking images of ancient Vijayanagar, crowding in one upon the other as I trailed my hand in the water: ancient crossings such as this, rose-strewn festivals and prodigious feasts, richly dressed dancing girls, fierce wrestlers, their bodies slick with oil, companies of armoured men and horses, congregations of elephants so great that they appeared to Razzâk like 'the waves of the sea', and around all these things the great fortifications of the capital. Suddenly, I thought of something else the district tahsildar had said:

'The foreigners, they come here and have full moon parties on the Anegundi side . . .'

It was strange, I reflected, that people travelled from so far to stir up the ashes of a charred and disfigured capital, then abandoned them for the older, even more silent citadel across the river.

Notes

1. Robert Sewell, *A Forgotten Empire: Vijayanagar* (1878; reprint, New Delhi: Asian Educational Services, 2001), p. 208.
2. Ibid, p. 5.
3. Ibid., p. 5.
4. *The Vijayanagar Empire: Chronicles of Paes and Nuniz* (1900; reprint, New Delhi: Asian Educational Services, 2003), p. 349.

5. This battle was fought in January 1565 between the overconfident Rama Raya of Vijayanagar and the five Muslim states of the Deccan. Rama Raya was killed, and the Hindus took flight. Talikota was due north of the capital, twenty-five miles north of the Krishna river in the Muslim territory of Bijapur.
6. A town a little to the north of Bangalore, in present-day Andhra Pradesh.
7. Author of a narrative that was sent from India to Portugal around AD 1537. Paes' narrative, along with that of Fernão Nuniz, was sent by an unidentified person, probably from Goa, to another unidentified person in Portugal, probably the historian Barros. The sender of the two descriptions wrote in an accompanying letter that Paes had visited 'Bisnaga' (Vijayanagar) at the time of 'Crisnarão' (Krishna Deva Raya).
8. Paes and Nuniz, pp. 256-257.
9. Quoted in Sewell, p. 88.
10. Paes and Nuniz, p. 253. Sewell, commenting on Paes' description, says that the stone temple is probably the temple of Anantasayana.
11. Anila Verghese, *Hampi* (New Delhi: Oxford University Press, 2002), p. 17.
12. Verghese, p. 40.
13. Anila Verghese writes that 'This local folk goddess came to be "Sanskritized" in the pre-Vijayanagara period by being wedded to Virupaksha, a form of Shiva. Marriage with Shiva or one of his incarnations was an almost universal method in south India by which local goddesses were absorbed into the Brahminical pantheon.' Verghese, pp. 6-7.
14. Paes and Nuniz, p. 261.
15. Paes and Nuniz, p. 260.
16. Ibid., p. 253.
17. A.H. Longhurst, *Hampi Ruins* (1917; reprint, New Delhi: Asian Educational Services, 1981), p. 36.
18. Longhurst, p. 95.
19. Paes and Nuniz, pp. 278-79.
20. Longhurst, p. 52.
21. Sewell, p. 162.
22. Quoted in ibid., p. 90.
23. Quoted in ibid., p. 118.
24. Paes and Nuniz, p. 252.
25. Sewell, pp. 129-30.

26. Paes and Nuniz, p. 391.
27. Ibid., p. 370.
28. Longhurst, pp. 125-26.
29. Paes and Nuniz, p. 259.

Mamallapuram
Masons and Moonrakers

And on the sandy shore, beside the verge
Of ocean, here and there, a rock-hewn fane
Resisted in its strength the surf and surge
That on their deep foundations beat in vain.
In solitude the Ancient Temples stood,
Once resonant with instrument and song
And solemn dance of festive multitude;
Now as the weary ages pass along,
Hearing no voice save the ocean flood,
Which roars for ever on the restless shores;
Or visiting their solitary caves,
The lonely sound of winds, that moan around
Accordant to the melancholy waves.

—Robert Southey, 'The City of Bali'

A peculiar form of life flourishes between the cracks and crevices of the ancient rock-cut temples that stand by the bay at Mamallapuram, an extraordinary village about thirty-five miles south of Fort St. George.

A motley lot inhabits this tiny place, from modern-day stonecutters, their students, and a small, eccentric population of European budget travellers to the local fishing community and those among them who have changed their livelihood to serve the heaving swell of tourists. The great rocks, bearing their 1300-year-old carvings with a still and heavy patience, brood distantly over an unlikely combination of porridge-eating foreigners and dark-skinned, sinewy crab hunters, impervious to the continuum of life. It is as if they look deliberately away, preferring not to take in their immediate environs. Yet they too form part of the twenty-first-century scene: age-old sites of worship, abandoned for unknown reasons by an earlier race, amidst little shacks and lean-tos housing a multitude of restaurants and trinket shops.

The five rathas of Mamallapuram are a set of monolithic temples excavated from wind-blown mounds of sand about two hundred years ago by the British. They now stand, unfortunately, in a grim wire-fence enclosure not unlike a school playground. Though the monoliths appear to be Shaivite, and bear symbols of the Hindu deities Indra and Durga, the style of building is traditionally associated with Buddhist architecture. The monoliths are popularly named after the Pandavas and their common wife, Draupadi, to none of whom they bear any actual connection. The square rathas resemble Buddhist viharas or monasteries, and the oblong ones, once used as assembly halls or porticoes, were probably prototypes for the Dravidian gopurams of a later day. While examining whether these were meant to be a standard pattern for the guidance of temple builders, Percy Brown, former secretary and curator at the Victoria Memorial in Calcutta, found the rathas

> solitary, unmeaning, and clearly never used, as none of their interiors are finished; sphinx-like for centuries these monoliths have stood sentinel over mere emptiness, the most enigmatic architectural phenomena in all India, truly a "riddle of the sands". Each a lithic cryptogram as yet undeciphered, there is little

doubt that the key when found will disclose much of the story of early temple architecture in Southern India'.[1]

Fergusson, an early authority on the temples of the Subcontinent, dated the rathas of Mamallapuram to between AD 650 and 700, stating that in the absence of any fresh evidence, this period might 'be safely relied upon as very nearly that at which the granite rocks at Mahavallipur were carved into the wondrous forms which still excite our admiration there'.[2] Although the village is often called Mahabalipuram—linking it with the demon Mahabali, who was overpowered by Vishnu in his dwarf incarnation—ancient Chola inscriptions refer to it as 'Mamallapuram', which remains the official name of the village. The name 'Mamalla' is probably a corruption of Mahamalla, a surname of the Pallava king Narasimha Varman I. Because King Narasimha was mentioned in 'the earliest inscriptions on the Rathas', Fergusson deduces that the village was called Mamallapuram after Narasimha Varman I, and that the earliest of the rathas were cut from the rock at his behest. The rest of them were also executed by the Pallavas, but possibly at a later date.

Standing a little away from the other rathas—which appear to have been carved out of the same large rock—is the Sahadeva ratha, named after one of the younger Pandava brothers. Between this distinctly Buddhist piece of ancient architecture and the rest of its family are the stone elephant and lion that so delight visiting children, and a little way towards the sea is a stone Nandi. The first and northernmost in the row of chariot-temples to the south of the Sahadeva ratha is that of Draupadi, a small rock-cut *pansala,* or cell, once used as a priest's dwelling. The entrance to this cell is flanked by two sculpted female doorkeepers with Buddhist headdress, and inside are sculptures of a female goddess and the figure of a man grasping his hair in one hand and cutting it off with his sword, possibly as an offering. Draupadi's ratha, the most complete and perfect of the monoliths, looks a little like a hut with a thatched roof; and indeed it is possible that this temple was a replica of a portable shrine used by a village community, for its base is supported by animals whose attitudes suggest they are bearing a heavy burden. They might conceivably have been dragging the shrine in procession.

Of the other rathas, Arjuna's is a small copy of Dharmaraja's, a large structure with four storeys and two parapets. This ratha, built in the style of a Buddhist vihara, contains images of Brahma, Vishnu and Shiva, and inscriptions (little more than a string of epithets) that some say refer to a Pallava king.

While Dharmaraja's ratha is the best illustration of the metamorphosis from Buddhist monastery to Hindu shrine, the monolith I have always found the most intriguing is the cracked and imperfect Bhima's ratha with its beautiful barrel roof, not unlike a wagon top. There is something very human about this ratha, which was clearly crafted by ambitious but not adequately skilled people—the roof developed a large crack, possibly because it was too heavy for the structure. However, the west-facing Pallava-style pillars, each held up at the base by a horned lion, are a photographer's delight as they catch the rays of the dying sun. At this hour the peace in the ratha's large portico is palpable, despite the excited children milling around it and screaming with pleasure as they swing from the pillars to the whitehot sand below. Looking up at it, with my nose covered to keep out the rising swirls of dust, I felt more uplifted by its elemental contours than I would later feel in the presence of any of the great southern gopurams that succeeded it, with the sole exception of the Brihadisvara temple at Thanjavur. Bhima's ratha preserves an incredibly moving air of forgotten peace and sanctity.

In colonial times, visitors often took a night boat from Madras down the nineteenth-century Buckingham Canal, or travelled by rail to 'Chingleput' and then by jutka for eighteen miles to the place they called the 'seven pagodas'.[3] There was also an old road from Madras to Mamallapuram, but one had to board a ferry to cross the canal. Along one of these three routes, or perhaps all of them, travelled the scholar

J. W. Coombes, whose 1914 book on the village is still entirely readable—for between his historical and religious information on the carvings runs a thread of undeniable fancy. Who, asked Coombes, would be able to 'weave with tinsel the beautiful-bordered romance' of the village? In unconscious reply, he wove a bit of it himself:

> The temple so close to the sea that the waves foam and dash against its doorway, and the presence of large quantities of stone which partially appeared buried in the water, indicate that in the days when the Mahabarata was written, buildings existed which have become destroyed and overwhelmed by the ocean's encroachment. But whether caused by tides or by earthquake, whether the action was gradual or sudden, whether Chandra and Surya conspired together to overthrow the city, matters not to the visitor. He reads in the solitary temple standing on the shore the last page of the story anterior to the events that followed and are interpreted by the monumental records situated inland. Even here, though the outward form of the pagodas is complete, the ultimate design has not been accomplished, but seems to have been defeated by some convulsion in nature or in human society.[4]

In Coombes' time, this old—though by no means oldest—village temple must have been rather more romantic, situated as it was at the very water's edge. In its present location, a manicured and anachronistic lawn around the shrine only strengthens the essence of its loneliness and incongruity. Built around the ninth century, the shore temple was the first Pallava building—that still stands—to be actually 'constructed' out of dressed stone, in contrast to the rock-cut architecture found in the rest of the village. It is in many ways an unconventionally designed South Indian temple, with the vimana, or tower, over the actual shrine being the principal structure and the gopuram, or gateway, being relatively insignificant.

In his eloquent chapter on Pallava architecture, Percy Brown wrote:

> As proof of its excellent workmanship, for over a thousand years the 'shore' temple has endured on this exposed spur of rock, buffeted for half the year by the monsoon rollers . . . Yet even with the careless activity of the sea on one side, and the insidious menace of the drifting sands on the other, its twin towers are still erect and its shrines remain intact, immutable it stands, a silent record of a great but forgotten people.[5]

The shrine, with its heraldic lions projecting from every angle, faces eastward so as to be illuminated at dawn by the rising sun. It also served as a beacon by night, doubtless bearing a lamp to guide vessels in to port. Coombes urged visitors to visit the temple after dark:

> About the time of the full moon, when solitude reigns and the moon with its sparkling radiance lights up the waters of the sea, and the sound of the roaring waves is heard as they cast their foam within a few fathoms off the sacred mound. The deity of the waters seems to revel then in delight, while the mild effulgence of the silvery moon filtering through the open door of the edifice bewitches the human senses into lingering ecstacy. The sea bubbles with pleasure at the sight of his offspring Chandra, who, being born at the churning of the ocean, supplies the note of triumph that lifts the scene above the commonplace at the touch of the enchantress's wand.[6]

Barricades now prevent one from approaching the temple after sunset, and a large breakwater keeps the waves away from its age-old door. Much as I appreciate the efforts of the authorities to preserve the structure, I also harbour a perverse sympathy for the ancient shrine, for the overwhelming feeling at the site is that of an achingly lonely old age. The last of its set, the shrine seems to gaze beyond the breakwater sadly, as if waiting to join the others of its day where they lie at the bottom of the sea.

The Mamallapuram of the present thrives on a system of narrow parallel streets running close to the shore temple. Stone carvers make replicas of temple images, and rows upon rows of stone elephants, Nandis and Ganeshas; European women cycle briskly past them in brilliantly coloured, tightly wrapped cotton sarongs, sometimes carrying a beggar child behind them for a ride. The foreign visitors who stay for a long time are determined to live each day at the lowest possible cost, so it is something more than their contribution to the economy that endears them to the villagers. As I watch them over the years, I realize that it is a certain facility of theirs to ignore the great divides of India—the caste system, the heavy line that separates rich from poor and clean from dirty—that ensures they belong to the backstreet life of the village to an extent that Indian tourists rarely do. Thanks to years of symbiotic living, it is not unusual to hear recorded jazz playing softly in eating shacks owned by locals, or to see a child of mixed descent seated at a table gravely eating oatmeal for breakfast while his Tamil father haggles with fishermen over the day's catch. Over everything, especially at night, there hangs a cloud of cigarette smoke, fumes from the strong Indian rum being liberally consumed, and the sickly-sweet smell of marijuana. The temples are all but forgotten as 'Moonraker', 'Le Rose Jardin' and, more mysteriously, 'Tina Blue View' swell with guests speaking a bewildering mixture of Continental languages and bickering genteelly over the relative merits of garlic prawns and buttered calamari.

It is only in the morning, then, when a fierce sun beats down on the little village, that an interest in the rock-cut structures is revived, and people begin to trickle down the main street to the rathas and the other sights. A few steps to the east of the rathas is the Bay of Bengal, deep-blue in the heat of summer and dull grey during the rains. There are always craft on the water: giant commercial and passenger vessels bound for Madras harbour lined up on the horizon, and fishing boats with small blue sails that venture out almost every day, even during the monsoon. Though I have looked out on the bay in its every mood, it is hard to imagine, sitting on a fallen coconut trunk as its edge, that the tiny village of today was once an important port to which ships sailed from Europe and the Far East. Coombes explains:

> The coins of Rome, China, and other distant lands, found till recently in the debris, give us good reason to believe that when the Ephesians were worshipping in the ancient temple erected to the great Goddess Diana, the people of Tarsis and of Phoenicia and of the isles thereof resorted to the Coromandel Coast for barter. Moreover, Chinese and other coins often washed ashore in storms evidence the supposition that this was one of the centres of Eastern trade, a port frequented by foreign ships, of which some must have been wrecked and sunk in the vicinity. The discovery of large deposits of ancient bricks form sufficient ground for the belief that here there was an ancient city built some two centuries before the Christian Era, having commercial relations with foreign countries. Buddhist remains point to the attraction this same city must have had even for the peoples of this land.

Before the Pallavas were subjugated in the tenth century by the Cholas, and the great temples of the latter eclipsed everything that had been designed before them, Mamallapuram had thus been a seaport and the second capital of the Pallavas; and here, on the giant rocks by the sea, they had left, between the fifth and eighth centuries, indelible impressions of their rule. Brown, in a passage that captures the far-reaching influence of this early architectural achievement, says of the Pallavas' port:

> The drifting sands have covered up and obliterated most of its land marks, while the warring elements of wind and tide have

altered the contours of the coastline, so that its ancient appearance can only be imagined. But in its art connections alone this port had more than ordinary significance. For there is little doubt that from Mamallapuram, in the middle of the first millennium, many deep-laden argosies set forth, first with merchandise and then with emigrants, eventually to carry the light of Indian culture over the Indian Ocean into the various countries of Hither Asia. Amidst the opalescent colouring of Java's volcanic ranges, and on the lush green plains of old Cambodia, in the course of time there grew up important schools of art and architecture derived from an Indian source. That the origin of these developments is to be found in the Brahminical productions of the Pallavas and before them in the stupas and monasteries erected by the Buddhists under the rule of the Andhras, is fairly clear. It is possible to identify in the Khmer sculptures of Angkor Thom and Angkor Vat, and in the endless bas-reliefs on the stupa-temple at Borobudur, the influence of the marble carved panels at Amaravati, while the architecture that this plastic art embellishes owes some of its character to the rock-cut monoliths of Mamallapuram.[7]

A short walk from the five rathas rises the hill that must have first attracted royal attention as the bedrock from which many structures could be carved. In its rocky sides are ten mandapas, or excavated pillared halls that, together with the monolithic rathas, were built during the early phase of Pallava architecture. They were most likely halls of display for the sculpted mythological scenes within. Architecturally, solid pillars were their chief feature: Pallava pillars that had reached their full maturity in the mandapas of Mamallapuram. Although the simple block brackets of earlier Pallava architecture are still seen, a number of pillars are particularly graceful, representing the coming of age of the heraldic lion so much used by the Pallavas. In one of these mandapas, the Mahishasuramardini—my favourite of the ten—the lion is almost natural, not the grotesque horned figure seen in the others. This mandapa also contains, on its right wall, one of the loveliest of all Mamallapuram reliefs: the goddess Durga overpowering the buffalo-headed demon Mahishasura. This eight-armed Durga is fearsome yet lithe and beautiful, and the powerful, thick-set demon and his helpers, unable to withstand her onslaught, lean away from the goddess and her retinue of attendants, creating a lifelike tension. K.A. Nilakanta Sastri aptly described this scene as the most outstanding creation of Mamallapuram art, calling it 'the most powerful expression in stone of the victory of divine nature over evil'.[8]

Opposite Durga, and in marked contrast, is a sculpted scene showing Vishnu's cosmic sleep, which epitomizes his role as preserver of the universe. The great god lies in a yogic trance on his lotus, the coils of his thousand-headed serpent pillowing his head. Brown, with his love of comparison, observed:

> These figure subjects at Mamallapuram are endowed with that same passionate spirit which pulsates in the Christian art of Europe of the corresponding period, but with even a finer feeling for form and more experienced craftsmanship. There is a notable sense of restraint and refined simplicity specially in the bas-reliefs of single figures, yet even more pronounced in several of the larger dramas, as for instance in the Vishnu panel of the Mahishasura mandapa.[9]

More might be said of restraint and refined simplicity, for these are the characteristics of today's village as well. Though a part of Mamallapuram caters brashly to tourists and day-trippers, it is for the most part a poor yet cheerful place, where people accept the vicissitudes of life with greater equanimity than I have seen elsewhere in Tamil Nadu. Into this simple way of life, so dependent on the moods of the sea, enter the long-term European visitors, with a will. They do not, of course, fish for a living, but they spend their mornings and evenings in the sea like the fisherfolk, and their afternoons in the cool of their rooms, rented for a ridiculously low price from villagers who give out a portion of their homes. At night, after the dinner restaurants close and the faint-hearted retire to their rooms again, only a few establishments stay open: places where one can dance to strange, wailing music with people so much under the influence that they barely remember their own names. Mamallapuram is a place where many come to forget; yet when you spend enough time here, you begin to realize that these are interesting people who have not just come for the free beach and cheap stay, but have formed their own quiet, tolerant community. Well I remember a night when a singer of my acquaintance took up residence on a side street and began to carol at the top of his voice at one o'clock in the morning, drawing not the slightest censure from his neighbours. After a while, when he had sung himself to heaven and back and grown bored with this old-fashioned mode of entertainment, he went to a window overlooking the street and began to shake his fist at groups of stragglers returning reluctantly from a party in the village.

'Go back, you *stupid whites*! We don't *want* you!' he yelled, enjoying himself hugely. I clutched my cushion in alarm, and looked out cautiously through another window.

The stupid whites, however, were only mildly amused by this abuse, and a couple of them waved affectionately at the singer, who having forgotten his sudden rage, was now stretching his arms out to them in a maudlin gesture of universal brotherhood. The town, as far as he was concerned, could *now* pull down its shutters and retire for the night.

The little village had, of course, been a port and a marketplace for centuries, and must have grown accustomed to all kinds of people coming home to it. Watching over the shutters of these small homes and establishments, at the very top of the rocky hill, stands the temple of Olakkanesvaraswami, which once served as a lighthouse. The story goes that coins were collected from each shop in the village until they made up an *olakku,* or quarter measure, which was given to the god of this temple. It was on this hill with the old lighthouse-temple that traces were found of a citadel, within which were palaces and mansions—a far cry from the poor village of the present. This is not surprising, for, given its location near the mouth of the Palar river, Mamallapuram must have been very important to the Pallavas, who ruled forty miles upstream at Kanchipuram. The buildings on the hill must have been raised on masonry basements with wooden frameworks and brick and plaster walls, now long eroded by the elements. Nothing remains of all this former glory; so much of Mamallapuram is left to the imagination.

Another prominent feature of the Pallavas' second capital was its elaborate system of tanks and canals fed by the Palar, a water system that connected many of the temples and that led archaeologists to believe that a system of water worship might have prevailed at that time. Some of the temples were designed with cisterns and conduits, and the great bas-relief on the east side of the hill—apparently the largest of its kind in the world—had a cleft down which water could have been made to flow.

Brown violently objected to the common name for this bas-relief, Arjuna's Penance, claiming it was a misnomer. 'This rock-cut drama,' he wrote, 'is an allegorical representation of the holy river Ganges issuing from its source in the distant Himalayas, the water, fed from a receptacle above, cascading down a natural cleft in the rock in the centre of this magnificent picture in relief.'[10] Whatever the scene was meant to depict—the origin of the holy river or the dramatic penance performed by Arjuna in order to obtain the celestial weapons guarded by Indra—there is no doubt that the bas-relief is marvellous, as Sastri says, a 'classical poem in stone'.[11]

By night, the relief is spectacular, as it is thoughtfully illuminated. By day, unfortunately, it loses some of its magnificence and dons quotidian clothes, for it has to cope not only with the exhaust fumes of vehicles passing through the village, but also with the eccentric attentions of a family of goats who leap in fickle fashion from the shoulder of one god to the foot of another. I have watched them ascend the hill by means of these divine footholds and disappear over the top, one by one, and one day I decided to follow them. The path from the northern side of the hill leads straight to the flat rock above the bas-relief, and there, to my horror, were several generations of goat droppings, which had, over the decades, actually changed the colour of the rock. To one side of this odoriferous spot I found a reasonably clean rocky perch, occupied only by a pair of frightened and half-witted kids deserted by their wayward parents. I decided to explore a little further before returning to join the little animals at this vantage point.

A short walk to the north led me past the Ganesha temple, an intact and almost complete monolith originally dedicated to Shiva. This is a good place to watch the sun go down over the paddy fields, for the ancient veranda grants a marvellous view of the countryside on the leeward side of the rock. I sat there a while, enjoying the feeling of being sheltered by such an ancient structure, and laid my hand on one of the Pallava lions supporting a nearby pillar. The beast continued, of course, to glare malevolently at the world, and I eventually left it to its dark leonine thoughts, hoping to walk up to Krishna's butterball and back to the top of the bas-relief before dark.

The butterball is not, naturally, made of butter, but rather is a giant boulder balanced precariously on the edge of the hill. Village children darted about nearby, and when they saw me approaching, they affected to hold the boulder up (it was at least ten times their height) and begged me to take a photograph. As I hadn't a camera, they asked for a pen instead and I willingly parted with an old ballpoint, warning them that there wasn't much ink left. It wasn't really the pen they wanted, though, for they hung around, a wild, happy little bunch, addressing the odd remark to me in broken English and laughing uproariously at my attempts to speak Tamil. Pretending to be hurt, I set off back to the top of Arjuna's Penance in a make-believe huff, leaving behind me, grinning from ear to ear, the heart and soul of Mamallapuram, these children who play among the ruins and entertain themselves with the eccentricities of those who visit their village.

The little goats were curled up head to tail, exactly as I had left them. After patting their smelly heads for a while to assure them I meant no harm, I sat down on the ledge and looked down over the village, which was preparing for the Mamallapuram dance festival, an annual event at which Bharatanatyam, Kathakali and Kuchipudi are performed on a roughly constructed stage in front of Arjuna's Penance. Every now and then someone would test the loudspeaker system with a series of ear-splitting hellos, or a dancer would walk nervously past a microphone, ankle bells jangling loudly, and the kids would start nervously and rearrange themselves, each trying to get closest to the rock face. Groups of un-self-conscious Europeans trickled in wearing their usual sarongs and paper-thin pyjamas, delighted at the prospect of some ridiculously inexpensive 'culture'. At the bottom of the hill, past the stage, was the road that led to the bus stand and out of Mamallapuram. I would soon follow it back to Madras, where the temples of a later day took some of their architectural cues from the elemental structures below me.

After Mamallapuram, an era of great temple-building began: these structures appeared everywhere, some hewn from rock and others assembled from fashioned stone. Brown suspected that this epoch was characterized by religious concentration and intensity of purpose, 'corresponding in some respects to that wave of passionate building which swept over much of Europe in the Middle Ages, and of which it has been said that it was as if the whole population had, to a man, been apprenticed to the stonemason'. Just as Europe had been covered by a 'white robe of churches' in the eleventh century, he continued, 'so too in India every hamlet had its cluster of shrines, and in every town the tall spires rose of temples singly and in groups, as proved by the remains observable all over the country to the present day.'[12]

The sun, having set behind me, provided just enough light to keep the ghosts away, and at this early approximation of the witching hour I closed my eyes and blotted out the street scene below. The loudspeakers, now thoroughly tested, had fallen silent. I heard a pair of breathless voices speaking excitedly in Russian just behind me; but these too stopped in mid-conversation and faded away, their owners disappointed, for they must have been hoping for the seat I occupied. In the heavy silence that followed, I thought of the unfinished rathas and wondered what on earth could have halted their building. Historians have found no evidence of any cataclysmic event that caused the people to flee the port and the workmen to abandon their tools; it is more likely that the patronage of rock-cut architecture ended with the death of Narasimha Varman in AD 674. Under his successor, Rajasimha, a new, more modern movement must have begun, and no more effort was put into the excavated mandapas or the monoliths hewn from large rocks. Construction with dressed stone, perhaps, became the way of the future, and the old rock method grew obsolete and uninteresting. Yet to me, Mamallapuram was a village of rathas and mandapas, for in these lay its early character, and its effort to copy into rock the types of sacred buildings in the land at that time. This, I thought, was executed under the patronage of a true visionary. For all his might, Mahamalla must have had an artist's soul.

I opened my eyes with a start—the repeated metallic sound of a stonecutter's axe was drifting up from the village, just as it must have done thirteen centuries before. The air around me grew heavy with my imaginings, for in my head I heard the ringing of a hundred axes, and knew it was time to leave.

Notes

1. Percy Brown, *Indian Architecture (Buddhist and Hindu Periods)* (Bombay: D.B. Taraporevala & Sons, 1956, p. 79).
2. Quoted in J.W. Coombes, *The Seven Pagodas* (1914; reprint, New Delhi: Asian Educational Services, 1999), pp. 60-61.
3. The Buckingham Canal is a part of one of India's longest canal systems. In 1876-78 a terrible famine occurred in south India, and the governor, the Duke of Buckingham and Chandos, began a construction project as relief work: the building of an eight-kilometre canal connecting the Adyar and Cooum rivers. This was later extended to other existing canals, linking Markanam in the South with Kakinada in the North. In time, the entire system came to be known as the Buckingham Canal. (See S. Muthiah, *Madras Rediscovered*, Chennai: East West Books, 1999, pp. 142-43).
4. Coombes, pp. 18-19.
5. Brown, p. 81.
6. Coombes, pp. 56-57.
7. Brown, p. 78.
8. K.A. Nilakanta Sastri, *A History of South India from Prehistoric Times to the Fall of Vijayanagar* (1955; 4th ed., New Delhi: Oxford University Press, 1990), p. 414.
9. Brown, p. 80.
10. Ibid., p. 78.
11. Sastri, p. 415.
12. Brown, p. 62.

Thanjavur
In the Womb of the South

The unsettled state of the Tamil country, brought about by the conflicts between the various dynasties such as the Pallavas, Cholas, Pandyas, Chalukyas, and Rastrakutas, all striving for supremacy, precluded any great cultural advance or any notable enterprises being undertaken during the last centuries of the first millennium. Out of this struggle for power the Cholas finally emerged triumphant, and proceeded in the course of time to become paramount in southern India.
—Percy Brown, *Indian Architecture (Buddhist and Hindu)*

It was May. To the uninitiated, that is a simple and unallegorical statement, but to anybody who has spent more than a year in India, the very word causes a painful constriction of the throat. One might refer to March and April without raising a boil, or even carelessly allude to June in the company of children; May, however, exists defiantly by itself in a sort of lonely and timeless limbo, weathering, as it were, the intense dislike of generations. It was that unspeakable time of the year again, and the South was raw and blistering under a naked and relentless sun. Instead of sensibly confining my body and belongings to the air-conditioned capsule of my room, I was at the start of the unthinkable for this time of the year—a journey to Tanjore, Trichy and Madurai, three temple towns in southern Tamil Nadu. I hasten to explain that it was more than just my native eccentricity that led me towards the deep South, an area that was, if anything, even more heat-ravaged and inhospitable than steaming Madras; it was a writing assignment that compelled me to book a flight to Trichy, from where I was to begin my travels in the oven-like womb of the South.

Having emerged from Trichy's small and uninspiring airport into the dizzying afternoon sun, and done battle with half a dozen unwashed and belligerent drivers, I found myself being bumpily borne to Tanjore in an ancient ruin of a taxi. This mutinous vehicle broke down a little way down the road, refusing—quite reasonably, in retrospect—to move another inch until its fuel tank was replenished. Waiting for the driver to fetch a can of petrol, I shifted about uncomfortably, opening a door and watching the heat haze shimmer on the tar. The grimy towelling beneath, having gallantly absorbed perspiration from numerous sources over the summer, had evidently reached a point of saturation and was now exuding a richly perfumed dampness all its own. As I tried to peel it gingerly off the seat, my bottle of water rolled away from beside me and fell out of the car, emptying its precious contents on to the roadside. I watched this little filler act in silence, stricken, as I often am, by the impertinence of inanimate objects. At length—and I use the word in a markedly elastic sense—the driver returned, enervated by the delay and, no doubt, by the wholesome fun of catching up with his cronies at the petrol bunk. We started off again, this time with Tamil film music blaring from a vintage tape recorder and hot air pouring through the windows in a furious blast, and swerved violently past buses and bullock carts in an attempt to retain ownership of the narrow road. By the time we arrived in Tanjore, or Thanjavur, to give the town its rightful name, I was quite ready to relinquish my tough-traveller image and give in to heatstroke and a headache.

It was immediately apparent, even if my guidebook had not mentioned it fifty times in the first paragraph, that Thanjavur, the capital of the later Cholas, was a town of rare nobility. There was an air of culture and antiquity about its streets that made me quite forget my petulance at the heat and humidity. It dawned on me that we had actually arrived in this town of which I had been reading for the last month, and I began to feel a nebulous sense of anticipation. Colleges and libraries stood alongside historic buildings and newly built or renovated hotels. The usual grime and scruffiness that seem inseparable from small-town India were markedly diminished here; this was a place that had retained its dignity and managed to remain distant and separate from the whole.

'*Periya koil*,' announced the driver suddenly. 'Big temple.'

I was, of course, looking out of the wrong window, and when I turned, it was one of those moments that branded itself into my memory so sharply that I reeled from the shock of its intrusion. The great thousand-year-old Brihadisvara temple—the object of my visit—rose to my left like a mountain, its very proportions stunning me and its rust-gold rock carvings, which had been left unpainted, giving off a wrenchingly evocative glow in the late afternoon sun. The driver slowed down questioningly, and it was very tempting to stop, but there were tourists and worshippers thronging to enter and a veritable fair outside, with beggars and fortune-tellers, flower carts and badly parked minibuses. I collected my thoughts enough to reckon that dawn would be a better time to visit, and decided to reach the temple early enough the next morning to claim it for myself and do justice to its every crevice.

I had known that I would be impressed by the generosity of vision that had prompted a Chola monarch to have such a large temple built in an age when every stone was lifted by human effort or animal strength. Nothing, however, had led me to anticipate a sight one quarter as powerful or arresting as the Brihadisvara temple, of which Percy Brown had written,

> It must have been a profoundly spiritual impulse which moved this ruler [Rajaraja Chola] to commemorate the material achievements of his line in the great Siva (Brihadesvara) temple at Tanjore erected about the year 1000. Apparently the largest, highest and most ambitious production of its kind hitherto undertaken by Indian builders, it is a landmark in the evolution of the building art in southern India. In size alone, regardless of its superb architectural treatment, its proportions are considerable, as the main structure is 180 feet long, above which rises a massive pyramidical tower 190 feet high, and from these dimensions some idea of the magnitude of the work and the courage and skill required to complete it may be realized.[1]

All that I had read about the temple until then had created a sort of bleached historical skeleton in my imagination: but when I saw the temple in the flesh, so to speak, every word instantly took on meaning.

I had expected, in my ignorance, to encounter a lonely, withdrawn structure like the shore temple at Mahabalipuram, so old that it had turned inward upon itself, shutting out the clamour and confusion of a world it no longer understood. The temple in Thanjavur, though only a few centuries younger—it was completed in 1009—suffered no such shrunken disease, nor melancholy collapse; it retained every bit of its magnificent spirit and physique, and did not stoop to brood over glories past. The Cholas who built it faded after a five-hundred-year reign, disappearing by the fourteenth century. After a blank period in the Thanjavur annals came a brief Nayak rule, starting circa 1500, that lasted a little over a century before the Marathas took over. They were followed by Britannia's fine-meshed colonial net, a swathe of which was cast in this direction in 1779. The temple soldiered on regardless, surviving the vicissitudes of time with virility far greater than that of the generations which passed it by. It was a living, breathing giant of an edifice, standing tall over the hot, fertile Cauvery delta with a soul unchastened by its great age, proudly conscious of its sole duty to its creators: to remain eternally larger than life.

Rajaraja Chola, the king who had ordered the building of this triumphant piece of architecture, ruled Thanjavur about 150 years after his ancestor Vijayalaya—possibly a Pallava feudatory—had taken over the town from the Muttarayar who ruled it, and made it his capital. Sometime in the mid-9th century, Vijayalaya founded a temple in Thanjavur to the goddess Nishumbhasudini, otherwise known as Durga. After these first—albeit small—steps towards the re-establishment of Chola power in the South, the most important occurrence was the wresting of the Pallava kingdom from Aparajita during the reign of Aditya I, the son of Vijayalaya. Now in overlordship of a territory that extended all the way up to that of the Rashtrakutas, the Cholas under Parantaka also took over the neighbouring kingdom of the Pandyas, with their capital at Madura. For the next thirty years, however, after the end of Parantaka's reign, the Chola kingdom began to face a serious threat from the Rashtrakutas and eventually shrank to a tiny state. The real establishment of Chola power is therefore attributed to Arumolivarman, who crowned himself Rajaraja Chola in 985 and for the next three decades took Chola imperialism forward on a splendid scale.[2]

In his effort to establish a Chola supremacy south of the Tungabhadra—which would last uninterrupted for two hundred years—Rajaraja began by stamping out the Pandyas and their friends, the Kerala kings. In an expedition to Ceylon, he conquered the northern part of the kingdom, destroying Anuradhapura and establishing a Chola province with its capital at Polonnaruva. After extending the empire through parts of modern Mysore, he turned his attention to the threat of the western Chalukyas under Satyasraya, who had invaded Vengi, an eastern Chalukya kingdom in the affairs of which Rajaraja was accustomed to interfere. Satyasraya was properly chastised and only with great trouble freed his country from the Cholas, who retired south of the Tungabhadra replete with the spoils of victory.[3]

Towards the end of Rajaraja's reign, the Thanjavur temple was completed, and it was a fitting architectural climax to all that he had achieved. Even as the great tower loomed freshly hewn over the Cauvery delta, Rajendra Chola, the son of Rajaraja, continued the work of imperialism, and 'raised the Chola empire to the position of being the most extensive and most respected Hindu state of his time'.[4] He completed the conquest of Ceylon that had been started by his father, and fought an exciting campaign in the North which took his army as far towards the Himalaya as the valley of the Ganga, returning thereafter to the immodestly named Gangaikondasolapuram[5]—a new Chola capital that was being developed in present-day Tiruchchirapalli district. Between Rajaraja and Rajendra, the whole of south India was unified into a single powerful kingdom with control over the seas, and this happened at a time when the North had been fractured and fragmented into a number of states that were perpetually at war with each other and weakened by repeated Islamic inroads.

By the early eleventh century, the Cholas were in command of an empire that stretched from coast to coast and included Ceylon, the Maldives and Srivijaya, a maritime state that comprised the Malayan peninsula and parts of present-day Indonesia. The boundaries of that great empire have long been erased, as have the sails of its enterprising navy been laid to rest—but in the temple of Rajarajesvara, later to be called Brihadisvara, survive a mental energy and spiritual conviction that remain unsurpassed in the South, though they left their mark on the land and the popular consciousness for centuries to come. The temple, as I understood it, was not merely a heavy-domed reminder of the supremacy of the Cholas, or even the grand pinnacle of an age of religious revivalism. It was a majestic tribute to a time of prosperity and imperial achievement, stability, agricultural success and effective administration. For the two great Cholas had not merely been imperialists; they had implemented a highly organized system of central control of the administration and encouraged the self-governance of village assemblies as no power had done before them.[6] If the superbness of Rajarajesvara's temple could so impress me in the twenty-first century, I could not imagine the psychological effect it must have had on people ten centuries earlier. Aptly did Sastri say that the superb Shiva temple of Tanjore was a fitting memorial to the material achievements of the time of Rajaraja. 'The largest and the tallest of all Indian temples,' he wrote, 'it is a masterpiece constituting the high-water mark of South Indian architecture . . . The whole temple from the heavily moulded parts of its high basement to its finial is a magnificent example of solidity combined with proportion and grace of form.'[7] We drove away slowly, but I hung out of the window and craned my neck to look at the temple as long as I could, unable to resist its incredible magnetism, and bold rejection of all that was limited and mediocre in its time—or indeed in any time.

The town thereafter was a perfect warren of narrow streets, and we passed what appeared to be the same coffee house three times. I began to wonder if the driver was cleverly taking advantage of my temple stupor to disorient me before bearing me off to some unknown den of vice. In my paranoia, I was about to ask him where the dickens he thought he was going when we emerged on the other side of the small, crowded town centre. The car turned into a quiet lane by a river that I knew was the Vennar, a branch of the Cauvery, though it looked weary and wisp-like in these parts, and was in fact unrecognizable as the mother river I knew so well. Presently we reached a red-and-white riverside hotel, my anxiety vanished as if it had never been, and I bid the driver goodbye with genuine gratitude. I carried my bag across to a room on the first floor and found that it looked out on the river, a pathetic web of brown and silver rivulets in the dry season. Much of the riverbed was exposed and sandy, while I was used to seeing it full and lively on the plateau. Perhaps after the grandeur of Brihadisvara I had expected everything, including the landscape, to spit flames.

Sitting on my veranda later in the evening, trying unsuccessfully to be taken by the parched summer sights, I was treated to one of the most stirring natural displays I have ever seen. I had unwittingly arrived in Thanjavur on the same day as the rains, of which there had been no sign whatever all afternoon. The clouds began to roll up on the horizon at the behest of booming thunder, masking the sun and sending out a surreal mauve light. The very air was tense and electric, and it was as if the stage was being set for something thoroughly out of the ordinary. Sure enough, a gigantic cumulo-nimbus appeared, bursting with energy and ardour, and elbowed out the lesser clouds to dominate the sky with extravagance. It settled over the river and lined itself with dramatic shades of pink, purple and orange, emphasizing its intent with blinding forks of lightning. The whole thing was like an exotic courtship display, with the massive cloud fully conscious that the ground below was straining to receive, sending up that distinctive moist-earth smell that forms a mute and incredibly sensuous appeal for rain. The wind shook the trees in gusts and they swayed obligingly, tossing their branches this way and that, for all the world like a row of nymphs lined up to tempt a disdainful warlord. It went on for an hour, this obvious coquetry, this damp, dark, bodice-ripping foreplay, until at last the tumescent cloud was master no longer and great heavy drops of rain began to fall.

In no time the water came down in opaque sheets, and the weak, dehydrated stream grew torrential in the space of an hour. My table and chair were drenched as the rain drummed in with the wind, and the room filled with insects and lizards seeking refuge. Defying their prudent example, I opened a stout umbrella and made my way down to the bank, determined to watch the water as it greedily devoured the once-dry islands of sand on the riverbed. It was an intensely satisfying feeling, standing there in the pouring rain and knowing that the river would flow swollen and strong through its delta for the next few months, until the heat of the next summer reduced it to a stream again. I then felt I understood something of the spirit of Thanjavur and its temple—for everything on this evening of first rain spoke of hardship followed by revival. What I had witnessed was an established event, for two hundred years earlier, the traveller Francis Buchanan had observed,

> All over the coast of the *Coromandel*, it is common in May, June, and July, to have occasional showers, and at some period of that time to have even three or four days heavy rain, which somewhat cools the air, and enables the cultivation for dry grains to take place. The weather now [at Kanchi in July 1801], although hot, is cloudy, with strong winds from the west. Such weather usually prevails about this time for eight or ten days; and at *Tanjore* is known to precede the rising of the *Cavery*, which is at its highest when the periodical rains prevail in *Mysore*. These clouds seem to be an extension of those which before and during the violence of the monsoon collect over the western *Ghats*. When these have poured down, and have occasioned the swelling of the river, the rains even in *Karnata* abate, and the weather clears in the countries below the eastern *Ghats*, until October, when the easterly monsoon brings on the proper rainy season of the sea-coast.[8]

Soaked to the skin, and conscious of a few horrified waiters observing my progress, I slipped and slithered back to the hotel, splashing barefoot through puddles and slush and trying to keep hold of my umbrella. One of the waiters ran up to relieve me of it, and administered a few well-chosen words of advice on the subject of promenading in the rain.

'Madam,' he said, his voice lowered, 'better you not proceeding.'

I thanked him for his help, and assured him with a sheepish smile that I would not under any circumstances be proceeding, as I was tired and sleepy and on my way to bed. I climbed the stairs to my room feeling a bit like a school-girl who, having been caught red-handed in some piece of girlish mischief, had been let off just this once with a kindly warning.

Indoors, I showered to get rid of the mud, watching the grains of sand collect near the drain and pushing them towards it thoughtfully with my toes, wrinkled like prunes after my adventures in the rain. The water was cool and soothing and I stood there for a very long time, enjoying the spotless bathroom and thinking vacant thoughts. When I came out, the room was warm even after the storm, and I eyed my mosquito net with disdain, knowing it would block the breeze and stifle me through the night. That, however, was a relatively minor consideration. First, the bed had to be rid of the few score rainflies that were now treating it like home and sending out generous invitations to their kin. Being fond of these pretty, short-lived things, I gathered them up carefully in the counterpane and shook them whirring and protesting out of the window. As I got into bed and drew up the covers, I discovered one persistent insect rather coyly trying to share my nightclothes with me, and had to get out of bed in an attempt to dissuade it from such youthful foolishness. Then the electricity went, and the room was so dark I could not see my fingers when I held them up. Having lit a candle with much fumbling and some unprintable profanity, I picked up a wad of photocopies wrested from a Madras library and returned to the once-bright world of the Cholas.

What had possessed this dynasty, I wondered, to build such marvels as the temples at Tanjore and nearby Gangaikondasolapuram, where the capital later stood? It was all in the timing, perhaps. The Cholas came to supreme power after the South had suffered several centuries of conflict between various royal lines. In a century-and-a-half of Chola rule, much had been conquered and consolidated, and the architecture of the time reflects this achievement. In the early days, over the ninth and tenth centuries, the Cholas undertook local rather than imperial constructions, and some of their first stone temples still survive in and around Pudukottai: the temple of Sundaresvara at Tirukattalai, that of Vijayalaya-Cholesvara at Nartamalai, and the 'triple' temple of Muvarkoil in Kodumbelur, with its two surviving sanctuaries. Of these temples, the lucid Brown was led to observe,

> All these small structures are very complete in their formation
> and display a freshness and spirit in marked contrast to the last

productions of the declining style of the Pallavas. So much so that they appear to either herald a new movement, or to denote some stimulation received from another and more virile source.[9]

The virile source is uncertain, but Brown speculates that it might have been a throwback to the time of the Chalukyas, an unearthing of an even earlier style that had reigned before the Pallavas commenced their temple building.

These tentative yet perfectly finished ventures do not, however, constitute the best example of pre-Brihadisvara Chola temple building: this is undoubtedly the temple of Koranganatha at Srinivasanalur near Tiruchchirapalli. It is clear that the Cholas were in a period of architectural transition, for this temple—which, by legend, was defiled by a monkey and therefore not consecrated—does not boast gigantic proportions. It is deliberately simple and uncomplicated in design, with far less of the detail that occupies the surface of the earlier Pallava temples. As Brown cleverly noted, the builders appreciated the value of plain spaces, and a sense of the character and correct location of the architectural features required for embellishment. Sculpturally, too, there is a difference from the Pallava style, with the human figure receiving a far more voluptuous treatment, a treatment that in fact makes the work look more like statuary than relief. It is as if the Cholas were testing their ground before unleashing their full potential at Thanjavur less than a century later. Brown, who occasionally interjected romantic spirit into his otherwise stout and factual essays, conjectured that during this brief intervening period, 'the Chola dynasty had been made aware of its vast power, and had had its character revealed to itself.'[10] On this altogether satisfying note, I laid aside the now dog-eared bundle of papers, for it was impossible to read any more by the flickering light.

A deep sleep followed, and it seemed as if no time had passed at all when the beeping of my alarm woke me. It was still pitch dark, and I wondered where on earth I was. All I could hear was the hypnotic dripping of water from the trees. Slowly it all returned to me—there was a temple to visit and a very long day ahead. Fighting the urge to close my eyes again, I struggled out of bed and got my act together in a slit-eyed, somnambulistic way. In a corner, blown there by the ceiling fan, lay a pile of tiny, gauze-like wings, all that was left of the previous night's rainfly invasion. With some regret, I left the peaceful cocoon of my room, bag on one arm and an untidy sheaf of notes from Brown and his brethren under the other. Outside, another dilapidated car stood under a palm tree, waiting to take me to the temple. The driver had lit an incense stick and was performing an elaborate set of devotions to mark the beginning of another period of wakefulness and productivity. I felt mildly ashamed of my own perfunctory devotions, which had consisted of squinting through the window at the dark trees outside, and wondering if it was technically possible to fall asleep while brushing my teeth. The only thing that roused me to spiritual heights at the start of a new day was appreciation of the sun—and then only if it filtered itself gently through the curtain lace and woke me like a lover. All this furious activity before dawn was a little rough on the nerves.

Presently, however, a faint light became apparent from behind the clouds, and I forgot to be bleary and disgruntled. The first signs of the new day were painted vigorously in the sky as we hurried along the deserted, rain-washed roads. When we pulled up to the temple, I stood by the entrance and watched transfixed as the dawn slowly picked an outline of the crumbling brick ramparts that surround it. I had noticed them earlier, but they were more visible now that there were no vehicles parked here. The ramparts are old, but nowhere near as old as the temple itself, and must have been thought a necessary precaution in their time; it was the Nayaks, a branch of the sixteenth-century Vijayanagar empire, who had erected them for safety. I could not, however, imagine even the most irrepressible of enemies daring to attack this mammoth temple, which was as much a reminder of sheer human will as it was an architectural manifestation of the spiritual and divine. Yet it had been used as a military stronghold even as late as 1777, when the French—with deplorable audacity—had occupied a portion of the temple and converted it into an arsenal. Looking upwards beyond the defences of the complex, it seemed as if an invisible restoration artist was at work, with busy brush strokes that brought the structures before me to wakefulness again. The enormous temple tower, which had dominated the townscape for an entire millennium, was bathed in honey-brown, and its individual storeys began to stand out in increasingly sharp relief. Carefully, the work of a thousand ancient sculptors was revealed, with a series of quick, deliberate butter-coloured strokes that teased every last detail out of the rock. The sun appeared, low over the horizon, and the whole complex turned cream and ochre, like a masterfully executed watercolour.

It was not difficult to imagine away the present day and picture the ancient scene of temple construction, to momentarily share the great pains that many must have borne for the sake of this tremendous achievement. I repressed a shiver, for it was truly a humbling thought. Not only had a king with an extraordinary spiritual impulse commemorated the material achievements of his line, but hundreds of sculptors and labourers had also been a part of this effort—and such an effort as theirs had not until then been conceived in the history of the South. The gate of the temple was open, and I read a notice outside that said that it was a World Heritage site. This explained the relatively good job of preservation that had evidently been done, if one were to overlook the stray banana peel or pile of rubbish. I removed my sandals and, leaving them in the car, walked through the great doorway, feeling for a moment as if I were entering a fort rather than a holy place. Inside, pillared corridors lined the walls of a massive temple yard, empty, completely deserted. There was no sign of life whatsoever and I felt, even more strongly, that I was wandering in time. There was simply no connection to reality, no contemporary feature anywhere in sight. Shaking myself, I began to look around and take note of the numerous structures looming ahead. In the centre of the great enclosure were a Nandi pavilion, a pillared portico, and a large assembly hall.

The most striking of these elements is of course the grand two-hundred-foot tower over the vimana, or inner shrine, with its massive, unnervingly simple design. At its base, two storeys support the tower; above these rise horizontal tiers of diminishing size, intersected by individual vertical shrines, each containing a figure that is central to it. Although at first sight the tower is perfect and symmetrical, a closer look reveals irregularities and asymmetries that give the structure a distinct personality. Each of the figure-niches is a work of art in itself, one not necessarily bearing relation to the other—and yet as a whole the tower remains rivetting. It appears to be the work of an eccentric master-architect, a man who was bent on finding rules and then breaking them as he fancied. Perched atop all this method and madness is the great stone cupola, said to weigh eighty tonnes and to have been moved to the top of the tower by means of an earthen ramp that began six kilometres to the north-east in the village of Sarapallam. The immense dignity of this structure is due in no small part to its breathtaking simplicity—square vertical base, tall body and graceful, crowning dome—yet also to the wealth of sculpture that adorns the shrines set into its diminishing tiers.

I walked along the margin, trying to ignore the overpowering presence of the temple in the centre and devoting my preliminary attentions to the Chola frescoes along the perimeter, restored from beneath the paintings of the latter-day Nayaks. It was quite futile, for halfway round the courtyard I could resist the pull of the centre no longer and went towards it, quickening my pace considerably. I took a deep breath and entered the massive structure in the direction of what I presumed was the garba griha, or sanctum. At first I could not see very well, but the feel of the place staggered me even before my eyes adjusted to the dim light. Incense billowed profusely from a fire while a lone priest chanted monotonously in Sanskrit, and the massive cave-like interior with its enormous lingam contained an atmosphere of sanctity that seemed to go back much further than the eleventh century. The priest ignored me and I stood to one side, accepting his tacit dismissal with the distinct feeling of having stumbled upon an ancient secret, hidden from the public eye by the ramparts and carved rock outside. Yet this was no clandestine sect at work—the Cholas who had built this temple to Shiva had done much for the revival of their religion. Among other contributions, Tamil hymns of the previous era had been organized into canonical books;[11] and, of course, the dancing Lord Nataraja was crafted time and again in glorious bronze.

The inscriptions found on walls and pillars all over the temple are invaluable records of the economy of such a large religious establishment. It was recorded for posterity that Rajaraja had donated more than 41,500 *kalanjus* of gold, about five hundred pounds (each kalunju being about seventy grains). He also gave the temple large quantities of jewels, silver and fertile land throughout his territories, even as far as Ceylon. Devadasis from all over the empire were put to service at Thanjavur, each given a house and a piece of land. Also in service at the temple were more than two hundred male dance masters, musicians, percussionists, goldsmiths and accountants, who received allotments similar to those given to the devadasis; and a fifty-strong choir was employed on daily wages to recite the *Tirupaddiyam* litany to musical accompaniment. The king was not the only person who made endowments to the temple—in Rajaraja's time, his sister Kundavai also gave generously to the temple both gold and utensils; others such as queens, groups of soldiers, and officials also made contributions that were faithfully and precisely recorded on the temple walls and pillars. All these gifts were used not only for the upkeep of the temple—including the purchase of such products as camphor, cardamom, and flowers—and its large force of attendants but also as lending material to village assemblies who borrowed from it at an interest rate of twelve per cent![12]

Outside again, I gazed up at the great tower and slipped back in time once more: here had the Great Trigonometrical Survey of India attempted to do its job by raising to the top of the structure that wonderful contrivance known as the Great Theodolite. The survey, under William Lambton, had set out in the early nineteenth century to map India by applying the principles of trigonometry rather than actually measuring every inch of the territory. As Lambton worked his survey through the South, he began to ask the local Brahmins for permission to use the temples he passed, as they afforded convenient heights for his operation. Scaffolds were built atop the temples and the theodolite—which weighed half a ton—was laboriously pulled up. Unfortunately, a rope snapped and the theodolite plummeted to the ground, crashing against the tower in its descent. John Keay, virtual biographer of Lambton and storyteller of the survey, explains that Lambton mentioned nothing at all in his records about possible damage to the temple; he was too stricken by the damage to his theodolite.[13] I couldn't help thinking that the old Chola spirits must have had something to do with this mishap—a band of intruders attempting to hoist a mysterious foreign body on their beloved tower must to them have been audacity unmatched.

By the time I left the great temple yard, my head swimming with the impressions of the last few hours, people had started to enter: tourists, villagers, and townsfolk. I could hear a guide proudly point out that one of the carvings in this ancient temple, executed long before the rise of Western colonial ambition, was that of a European in a hat. This was actually true: I had been told to look out for it, and had sought and found it for myself, and if indeed the figure was intended to be European, I was quite taken with the possibilities. So, evidently, was the guide. Behind me, I could hear him telling his group of open-mouthed Russians that in those days the seers were very powerful and could look accurately into the future. Just imagine, he said, in the manner of one who delivers important information and stands back for applause, the pundits *even knew* that the British were going to come to India. Ah, nodded the visitors, politely, understanding one word in ten. Resisting a tremendous urge to giggle, and wondering if the prophecy could have had anything to do with Lambton's visit, I made my way back to the waiting car, reflecting that I might have done myself a grave disservice by minding my own business, and missing this marvellous conflation of the sublime and the ridiculous.

Note

1. Percy Brown, *Indian Architecture (Buddhist and Hindu Periods)* (Bombay: D.B. Taraporevala & Sons, 1956, p. 85).
2. K.A. Nilakanta Sastri, *A History of South India from Prehistoric Times to the Fall of Vijayanagar* (1955; 4th ed., New Delhi: Oxford University Press, 1990), pp. 158-60, 163.
3. Ibid., p. 164-65.
4. Ibid., p. 165.
5. Rajendra Chola built a magnificent temple at Gangaikondasolapuram in AD 1030. Although the temple now stands by a small village, it was once surrounded by a town, and the elaborateness of its construction shows that Rajendra tried to outdo the temple of Rajarajesvara at Thanjavur. Each is beautiful in its own way, the Thanjavur temple with its powerful straight lines and its successor with its gentler curves. Of the two vimanas, Brown says, 'Each is the final and absolute vision of its creator made manifest through the medium of structural form, the one symbolising conscious might, the other sub-conscious grace. But both dictated by that "divinity which has seized the soul"' (p. 86).
6. Sastri, p. 186.
7. Ibid., pp. 422-23.
8. Buchanan, *A Journey from Madras through the Countries of Mysore, Canara, and Malabar* (1807; reprint, New Delhi: Asian Educational Services, 1999), p. 466.

9. Brown, p. 84.
10. Ibid., p. 84-85.
11. Sastri, p. 387.
12. Ibid., pp. 294-95.
13. John Keay, *India Discovered* (London: HarperCollins, 1981), pp. 185-86.

Kodaikanal

Epilogue
Woodsmoke and Roses

With all the changes, the essence of Kodai remains the same—an essence compounded of the scent of roses and eucalyptus, the sound of cicadas and running water in the Sholas, woodsmoke rising from the cottage chimneys, sunset on the glassy lake, Perumal calling up the mist from the valleys, squadrons of cloud ships launched from the western hills, the roar of rain on zinc roofs while eucalyptus trees bend before monsoon winds that threaten to blow the whole settlement off its lofty shelf. These things can never change.
—Charlotte Chandler Wyckoff, *Kodaikanal 1845-1945*

It was late, and unusually cold. I had very little business being out alone on the ridge, treading stiff-kneed down a path that spilled steeply over the hill like an errant length of brown wool. The first of the town lights were beginning to flicker across the lake, causing me to pause and consider the long road home, but the call of the narrow unlit path was irresistible, and I continued my crab-like descent. Behind me the stately blue gums swayed and creaked to themselves, impervious to the fickle mist that rolled and rose between them, darkening the path and adding dampness to the chill. Pulling my beret tighter over my ears, I passed overgrown hedges of Devil's Trumpet and now-wilted Morning Glory, and solemn stone cottages almost completely hidden from sight by the shroud of dusk that lingered over the mountains.

The air grew husky with a desperate tenderness; and the path crowded with memories that stole out of wooden gates to meet and wander once more in the gloaming. I shivered momentarily, and, as always on such a solitary yet oddly companionable walk, it occurred to me that I would return to Kodaikanal time and again, for as long as I was able. Though other mountain towns beckoned occasionally, I had not befriended the bends in their lanes nor the dew on their windowpanes in quite the same way as I had this precious settlement in the upper Palanis. It was a remarkably endearing place, its very openness leaving it susceptible to misuse by visitors, but its charms enduring despite the great invasions in the summer. I knew I would not surrender my peculiar bond with it as long as there were little-used paths that led down the mountain and as long as the woodland air made one's breathing deep and pleasurable, one's very existence a heightened and more sensitive state.

The town and its environs overwhelmed me, and I was blind to all shortcomings: Kodai had caught me young and filled my head with its whimsy and romance. Mine was no original love; it was simply a dot on a long, fond continuum, for families have come here to escape the hot weather from as early as the 1840s. It was then that foreign missionaries in the deep South had first thought of building a retreat in these hills, an offshoot of the Western Ghats, where the delicate could be sent to escape the heat and cholera of the Vaigai plain. From tiny and inaccessible beginnings—a couple of cottages built on the edge of a great *kanal,* or forest—the little settlement became a place of comfort and delight, where the seeds of idyll were idly sown all summer long. People began to return every year and some settled here permanently, unwilling to break the cool embrace of the mountain air. With these first settlers I bore the deepest empathy, for on every visit I find it almost impossible to turn my back to the woods, and return to lower altitudes with a dull ache in my soul.

The twilight spirits that seemed to mingle between the cottages were eerie enough to make me quicken my step, but my heart did not beat faster when I passed an old and disused cemetery with queer gargoyles and cenotaphs looming dark over the fence. With its pleasant and peaceful history, Kodai is a town of benign ghosts. The Palanis had given sanctuary to village folk fleeing the oppressively taxed seventeenth- and eighteenth-century kingdoms of the plains. They had also been home to aboriginal tribespeople—some of whom still survive in far-flung villages—and before that, well beyond the reach of recorded history, to an unknown megalithic race who had left little trace of their existence except mysterious dolmen circles and burial urns. No one is certain why these early folk lived at such an altitude; only the Palanis hold such secrets, and they have grown bent and ridged with the weight of their ancient knowledge. It is these deep furrows and wrinkles that Christian missionaries began to explore in the nineteenth century, children of a new age and gospel.

As the deep-purple light thickened further and the path curved upwards to join the Berijam road, I saw a figure approaching. I stiffened instinctively, but it was only an elderly lady from the American school walking her dog back home. As she nodded and smiled, our exchange of pleasantries holding us but a moment, I thought it surprising that it had been the Americans rather than the British who had forged the modern connection between the Palanis and the plains. Although a Lieutenant Ward had been dispatched by the East India Company to survey these hills in 1821, he had not mentioned the basin that lay at the southern end of the upper range. The discovery of the spot that would develop into Kodaikanal was left to the Reverends Taylor and Muzzy of the American Mission at Madura, who explored the top of the range in 1845 and declared it suitable for a sanatorium. Family after family followed these early explorers up a tortuous bridle path each year, braving the dense shola forest with what they, being

Americans, liked to think of as a certain pioneering spirit. Those who could ride came up on mountain pack ponies, with Indian coolies carrying the women and children in makeshift palanquins. They used the now overgrown and forgotten—but still visible—route called 'Coolie Ghat', travelling over the Adukkam pass and then the rim of the basin. The coolies sang all the way up from Kistnamma Naik's Tope to Shembaganur and beyond, to climb at a uniform pace and keep wild beasts off the path.

The mission folk clung possessively to their find and came to love it with great intensity, for the cool greenery and the pleasant streams and waterfalls offered a contrast with the plain so sharp that none could fail to be moved by it. In 1945, a hundred years after the settlement had been founded, Charlotte Wyckoff, a daughter of one of the earliest families, was led to write that Kodai was a 'bit of home' to them all.[1] To the Scots, she said, 'it is a reminder of mountains and lochs and glens; to the English, of trim box hedges and rolling downs; the Australian owns the tall blue gums that bend in the monsoon winds, the Scandinavian chooses the steep hillside where the pines grow; and the American sees the Blue Ridge, the Sierras or the Adirondacks in every turn of the trail.' And all these nationalities left their mark on this town by the kanal, for even today there is an American school and a great many lanes, streams and pools named after those outsiders who first created or stumbled on them.

The path had led me through a fair amount of tree-covered property still belonging to the American residential school, which was established fifty years after the first settlers arrived. For close to a century, it was the founding Americans who dominated Kodai society, having bought large tracts of land from the colonial government. The sons of empire did not appear to resent the American monopoly, for they had chosen Ootacamund in the Nilgiris as their own, and that hill station eventually grew into a sort of southern Simla. The government was benevolent towards the Kodaikanal settlement in its infancy, and seemed on occasion to actively encourage its development. A collector,

Sir Vere Levinge—after whom one of the prettiest streams in the area is named—helped to bring an American missionary's dream to fruition by granting a contract for the swampy Kodai basin to be turned into a lake. In this low-lying area, a stream was dammed and a starfish-shaped lake created. In 1867, Dr Fairbank, a naturalist of the American Mahratta Mission in the Bombay Presidency undertook a walking trip over the Palanis and stopped, naturally enough, to admire the picturesque new addition. He noted that at Christmas, 'ice grew in stalks like crystal mushrooms just underneath the surface of the ground in a cold, wet place near the lake'—and added, a trifle unscientifically, that the settlers made ice cream with this ice and ate it with strawberries. It was here that children were permitted to row such sturdy craft as *The Lily* and *The Duck* without undue risk to their small persons, and soon enough the pretty, irregular lake became part of the settlement's identity.

Coming up along the steeply banked main road, I caught glimpses of the silver-black lake between the trees. Even in the deep dusk, the hedges and wildflowers between the road and the water below were luxuriant and soothing, especially when compared with the dismal shrubs and thorns, ragged palms and struggling paddies of the districts below. The rarefied air and delicate surroundings must have somewhat softened the Quaker-like sternness of the early missionaries, for there could be no greater testament to the delicacy of the Kodai foliage than that made by a staunch Christian matron, and faithfully reported by Charlotte Wyckoff:

> One Puritan among the mothers who at first refused to let her daughters wear ribbons or frills because they were 'worldly' was heard to murmur, as she studied the ruffled edges of a fern, 'If God took the trouble to make anything as pretty as that, perhaps he won't care if we wear frills too!'

In a little under half a century, the nineteenth-century mammas had relented a little further: the 'gay nineties' began, and the settlement developed an enviable six-month-long season commencing each year in March. After the missionaries left at the end of May came the time for pursuits more frivolous than the usual riding, fishing and rambling: the hills echoed with the sounds of dancing, theatre, and lavish 'at homes' such as those given by the raja of Pudukottai. For yes, the Indians too had begun to discover Kodai, and the prominent among them to contribute generously to its social life. This was the day of the butler, the snow-white tablecloth and the caterer—Tapp's Dairy, Bakery and Tea Room—with carriages: bullock carts with curtains and seats, known, rather unfortunately, as 'Tapp's bandies'. A giddy era, it lasted a few more decades before social and political change drifted down to the southern hills and buried the greater part of a distinctly colonial culture.

The bells of a nearby church chimed a delicate seven o'clock as I sat down on a culvert to catch my breath and absorb the last peace of the dying evening. The missionaries still have a presence here, and Kodai's churches, some extremely pretty and overlooking marvellous views, bear sturdy witness to the town's Christian roots. The first two settler communities, the American Congregationalists and the British Anglicans, came together as early as 1858 to build a common church, an enterprising institution with a roof, it must be recorded, crafted entirely of Huntley and Palmer biscuit tins. In the light of this original construction, one can only wonder at two things—the din in the establishment when it rained, which it must have done frequently, and the fact that there appears to be no record of injury when the building collapsed in the subsequent monsoon. Undeterred by this dismal—and no doubt cacophonous—demise, the devout took a new subscription and another church was erected in 1860 near the original two mission houses in the lower shola. It was simply called Church under the Hill, and was shared by all denominations and languages until more churches were built in the century to follow.

From where I sat on that mossy stone ledge, the lichen growing thick around my feet, I could see a cobbled walkway that led between two compound walls towards a precipitous path called Priests Walk. One September morning, as I had made my way there with my old friend Israel, I found that the Roman Catholics too had done their bit to influence the settlement. Israel, who with his beehive beard and simple mountain ways had come to represent all that was good about Kodai in a single body, had pointed out, as was his manner, several points of interest that morning: some milk-white mushrooms that had come up in the night, a Malabar whistling thrush, and a church in the distance. Distracted by the heady view down to the plains and the danger of free-falling all the way there if I missed my footing, I had not paid much attention then. Later, while reading Wyckoff, I realized that this was La Salette, a Catholic shrine on the edge of Mount Nebo, the steep hill into which Priests Walk and other pretty paths had been cut. Of the spectacular view from this shrine, a Father C. Leigh had written in 1933:

> As you look, veils of mist suddenly rise up from the valleys, and the plains and hills fade from sight; then, as suddenly, the veils rend and you get glimpses of dark forests and of ponds glistening in bright sunshine. (At other times again) you look down from your high vantage ground upon a sea of dazzling white clouds, above whose heaving billows the peaks of the lower ridges jut out like islands.

Often had I seen this very view, and to find it described so well and so long ago left me with a definite lump in my throat.

For it is hard to share a view with one who has not seen it, or to describe the joys of rambling along trails that wind through pine and wattle forest and into the native shola, to those who have not been there. Sometimes the only creatures I come by on long walks are the giant squirrels that stare at me from lofty perches atop the trees, and the dainty green lizards that allow themselves to be picked up and placed on my palm. How much more companionable it must have been in the early days, when parties of young people rode out to explore the area, naming their findings Dolphin's Nose, Devil's Kitchen and Neptune's Pool. These and dozens of other discoveries became popular with their adventurous set, and then with their children and grandchildren. I felt a certain compassion for a Major Douglas Hamilton, who so grew to love Berijam—another still, whispering lake in the Palanis—that he wanted to move the entire Kodai settlement there. The inaccessibility of this site from the plains made the plan impractical, but it was as small consolation named Fort Hamilton, even in the conspicuous absence of a fort. Says Charlotte Wyckoff, 'Think what sport it must have been to find and name waterfalls, and to come upon Pillar Rocks unexpectedly and explore its caves.' What sport indeed, for even today there are well-hidden places along unused trails that can make you catch your breath and grow giddy with the pleasure of discovery.

Israel, whose little cottage stood on the hill opposite Mount Nebo, had often accompanied me on my exploratory walks, giving me breakfast thereafter with his English wife June and their three beautiful children. It was he who had first taught me about the shola, the ways of the forest and the simplicity of life in the hills, for he had neither running water nor electricity in his home, and walked a gruelling distance to the town and back each day. I had spent innumerable evenings eating freshly baked apple crumble and drinking hot lemon at Manna, his small restaurant on the Bear Shola road, where one went for 'slow' food and the pleasure of watching the dough rise and the kettle bubble. Invariably we would end such evenings with brandy and hot water, and Israel would walk me home swinging a candle torch from one hand. This was a cut-away tin with a taper burning in it, and well I remember a night when we did not need its light—a night when Israel pronounced, in his usual decisive way, that we should watch meteorites.

'There's a meteorite shower on tonight, I say!' he said excitedly, in the tone anyone else would use to announce a new film being released on Friday. So we found ourselves, at two o'clock in the morning, walking around the lake until we reached a suitably dark patch. There we laid ourselves down—plumb in the middle of the road, to the extreme mystification of some drunken passers-by—and stared up at the brilliant night sky, my teeth chattering with the cold. The meteorites passed languidly overhead, so close and so slow that it seemed as if someone was setting tennis balls on fire and flinging them in low arcs across the lake.

'Look at that!' breathed Israel every single time, his joy undiminished.

Israel's interest in astronomy was something many people in the settlement shared, owing to the great observatory that was a landmark in the town. I could not see the observatory from where I now sat by the edge of the road, and it was too far to walk there even supposing they would let me in at this hour; so I contented myself with staring at the stars as they came out in the sky like freshly polished crystal. A few years before 1900, a meteorite weighing thirty-five pounds had been dug up in a Kodai compound and eventually moved to a museum in Calcutta. This event caused a stir in scientific circles, to the extent that Madras's century-old Meteorological and Solar Observatory was eventually shifted to Kodai.

The stars shone dimmer the year Israel left Kodai, just as suddenly as he had come twenty-odd years before. The creepers grew strong around Manna, and wild dogs played in what used to be the yard around his cottage. I thought that Kodai would never be the same— but there I was mistaken, for Israel's legacy was not one that could easily be lost. The trails beckoned just as tantalizingly, and after much questioning at the local bakeries, I managed to track down someone else from the Manna days. My friend Vijay knew as much about the area as Israel had, and in fact worked as a guide for those who wanted to see more than just the town and the lake. My calves were still aching from the strain of a recent expedition with him, and I massaged them a little gingerly. The pain made me reluctant to get a move on home, even though night had fallen and I knew that my mother's twin sister, who lived in one of the old school cottages down the lane, would expect me home before long. The thought of my Aunt Aruna's warm wood fire and the meal of rice, ghee and beef that I was sure to receive was attractive, but I sat a while longer, for this was my last evening in Kodai. The icy breeze played with the strands of hair on my neck, and I tucked the ends back into my beret and thought about the previous day's climb.

Together, Vijay and I had schemed to climb Perumal 'Peak', the high, oddly shaped point on a neighbouring ridge that was often mistaken for a mountain. For years I had wanted to climb to its tiny bald summit but had lacked the courage to go alone, so this time a plan was hatched, albeit a shaky one. The road to Perumal was closed, the monsoon made the whole endeavour a bit of a risk, and I could see that Vijay was uneasier than he liked to say. Was I sure, he asked me several times, that I didn't want to try something more approachable? The weather was at best unpredictable, and if we were to get caught in an afternoon storm it would be very difficult to come down again. Looking at the distant, cloud-swathed summit towering blackly over the range, I had blanched, and almost given in to the prospect of a short, ladylike ramble among the pines. Something made me persevere, however, and I insisted that we take our chances and turn back if the weather grew rough. I had badly wanted to climb Perumal, if only to see if its old stone trail still existed.

The trail had been put in during Kodai's age of exploration, when it became every youngster's ambition to climb the peak and return triumphant. The culprits behind this popular adventure were a bold pair: the Reverends Horsley and Chandler, who decided to climb Perumal in 1874. On their return they wrote,

> There was no path past Silver Cascade and down the valley of the Parappar. We left Kodai at 6:30 a.m., on ponies, and rode

over the great ridge of Shembaganur, then led our ponies down
the cattle paths to Neutral Saddle, where we tied them and
made the four mile climb on foot.

Having no ponies to ride, Vijay and I made our way down to
Shembaganur by bus, and then to the tiny village of Perumalmalai.
Finding, as we had expected, that the road was closed, we took a
detour and began climbing a well-constructed but seldom-used jeep
track built by the forest department. There was, of course, no sight of
the peak, as we were at the bottom of the ridge; still, it was a pleasant
enough hike past clumps of thorny blue raspberry and razor-sharp
lemon-grass. After a couple of miles this gently winding track came to
an end, but not before we had passed massive spoor in the soft, soggy
monsoon earth, and a bunch of village woodcutters had warned us
not to go any further because of the number of kaadumaatu, or bison,
up ahead. I tried not to look as nervous as I felt, and it was now Vijay's
turn to bolster my enthusiasm. Come on, he said in comradely fashion,
we can always give up and come back if we see too many of them. I
swallowed and tried not to think of the implications of 'too many'
such animals in this wild and desolate territory.

We climbed higher and found ourselves on Neutral Saddle, the
ridge mentioned by the young priests in their account. It was a high
and beautiful ridge with views of the valleys on either side, and derived
its lovely name from the fact that it separated the ranges of the lower
and upper Palanis. Presently we came to a dense thicket of tree ferns.
There were bison close by, we knew from the patches of freshly
flattened grass, but none to be seen. This was the most arduous stretch
of the climb, for when we did come upon the stone trail—as solid as
if it had been built yesterday, and with a milestone intact—we found it
too overgrown and thorny to be of any use. Disappointed, I followed
my friend along narrow paths through the ferns that he said were
bison trails. Up and up we went, the summit now tantalizingly within
sight, every inch of the four miles from Neutral Saddle to the top

extracting its chest-wracking due.

At last the trail came out of the thicket onto the flat grassy table of the summit, about which our predecessors had written: 'We found a spring of clear water near the top and took cups of it to the cairn of stones on the summit.' I searched in vain for the spring, but easily found the pile of stones and settled down near it in delight, watching the shifting views and picking out the path of the ghat road through the hills below. There were wild-boar diggings all around, but no animals anywhere in sight. Beside me a leopard-skinned butterfly alighted on a rock, and above me an eagle soared, annoyed to have been disturbed. Across the deep valley I could see Kodai, its highest point sticking out of a wad of cloud; and beautiful though it was, it did seem like a terribly long way back. The mist was beginning to grow thick and it was now past noon, so we did not linger, and instead began the difficult descent. Vijay began to look worried as we approached the now misty and treacherous thicket in which there had been clear signs of bison on our way up, and we stopped, wondering what to do next.

It might be possible to try the stone trail, he suggested doubtfully, and I agreed with enthusiasm, for that had, after all, been the object of my climb. It was hard going but worth the effort, for we came out upon view after view as the trail wound down the ridge. It seemed as if it had been designed as much for the scenes below as for the journey up, yet few people seemed to have used this path between the old days and the present. The thorns and stems grew thicker and less penetrable, and just as we had finished crossing a fallen tree trunk and had entered a place where the bushes were higher than our heads, we heard the snuffling, stamping sound of bison from only a few feet away. We backed off a bit, and crouched nervously beneath the ferns. The great chocolate-and-white animals, however, were more wary of us than we were of them, for we heard their hooves drumming down the hill and looked at each other in silent relief. *That was a big one*, mouthed my friend, wiping his forehead, and had I heard the little one bolt first?

Gulping, I nodded. I had not, of course, discerned any difference between the footfalls, but he was of the hills and knew these sounds. I followed him wordlessly, chastened at my own lack of knowledge and admiring his confidence in such a situation. Had the animals decided to chase us, as irate males sometimes did, there would have been little chance of escape.

It took us almost four hours to reach the bottom again, during which time we lost our way, fought an impossible number of stubborn bushes and were tripped and scratched at every step. I remember thinking about three-quarters of the way down, as I bushwhacked exhaustedly, my face streaming with perspiration, that if I had wanted an adventure, this was certainly it. As we climbed down the last section of the path and met the ghat road again just below Perumalmalai, we were the subject of some comment among a group of passing villagers.

'Who are these two people, grandfather?' asked a little boy sitting on the shoulders of a dour-faced old man and looking at us with unconcealed interest.

'Some foreigners who climbed the mountain,' replied the old man.

'But why did they climb the mountain if they are not carrying anything back from there?' persisted the child, coldly logical.

The old man paused for thought. 'Must be mad.'

Hobbling to the bus stop on blistered and rapidly swelling feet, praying for speedy deliverance, I was somewhat inclined to agree.

Perumal lay far across the lake and valley from where I now sat in the dark, and would not be seen through the trees until daybreak, but I could sense its presence, tall and forbidding, and shuddered. How much wilder it might have been, I thought, had we camped the night on that wind-blown summit with none for company but the boar and the roosting bird of prey. My aunt's cottage seemed more welcoming than ever, and I had already stayed out as late as possible in the lonely evening, so I put aside my thoughts, picked up my knapsack and got off my comfortable perch. It was not much of a walk to the cottage, and a few minutes later, slim coils of grey-blue woodsmoke came into view, rising from weather-beaten stone chimneys. I stood a while on the grassy verge by the old garage, looking at the smoke writhing upwards to join the mist, and my heart grew heavy at the thought of leaving on the morrow.

Indoors, in the lamp-lit cocoon of the cottage, I shrugged off a growing depression and attempted to console myself by reading a little about the journey down to the plain in days gone by. The ghat road followed the contours of the range, winding gradually down from Kodai to Vattalagundu, through Shembaganur, with its large Catholic presence, and the impenetrable Tiger Shola, now notably devoid of tigers. A Colonel Law had been sent in the 1870s to 'trace a bridle-path to the plains of a gradient of not more than one in nineteen, the same to be widened later for wheeled traffic'. When first built, it was just wide enough for carts and carriages between Kodaikanal and Tiger Shola, and petered out to a trace after that. The project had been started partly to provide labour during the great famine of that decade, and after Law left in 1878, the path remained unsuitable for wheeled traffic for the next thirty years. It was only in 1914 that Law's Ghat—so named to this day—was finally opened to motor traffic, and at that time cars could be brought up to Kodai only on the condition that they were not actually used in the settlement. I thought with some regret that this had been an eminently sensible rule.

Setting aside my book, I peeled off various layers of clothing and sat down by the fire to thaw. It was well past dinner time, and my family had been overtaken by a pleasant inertia. The good aunt dozed comfortably in a rocking chair, her feet stretched out by the blaze. Beside her sat one of her teenaged sons, exhausted by the exertions of the school day into an uncharacteristic silence. My mother, who was up on a long visit, ate a blueberry muffin meditatively and contemplated the crumbs on her blue jerkin with deep interest. In the next room my grandmother lay on her bed, lost in her thoughts, and bundled in enough woollen garments to have kept a small army snug in Russia.

This hearth was a remarkable one, I thought, for those who gathered round it always added to its brightness and warmth. Leaving the cottage was as difficult as leaving the town and the woods, for over the years, all these had grown synonymous in my affections.

With my spirits ebbing, I could not help thinking of the many times I had left this place, always knowing I would return but utterly disconsolate as I made my farewells. The journey down would invariably be a lonely one, and only when I reached the little station at the foot of the hills did I ever remove my jacket and cap, acknowledging grudgingly that I was back on the plain and could not possibly wear them any longer. The very thought of descending to the lower districts was repulsive, and I suppressed a deep sigh.

Aren't any of you eating dinner?' enquired my aunt gently, almost as if she had read my thoughts and deemed it wise to intervene.

'I'll get the rice,' I offered, and got up gratefully, stooping to remove splinters of firewood from my socks. As I moved away from the fire, I felt the cold instantly. The long, white kitchen was out at the back, and from it I could see the steep wall of rhododendrons that grew behind the cottage, keeping it safe from passersby and ensuring that the dogs did not run out at night. They raised their heads from where they slept in the little backyard and I heard the soft thumping of tails being wagged sleepily against the flagstones. In half a minute a long and lugubrious face made its appearance at the window, and I leaned out and patted the larger and more obstreperous of my aunt's dogs. He looked at me with liquid eyes, scratching pathetically at the windowsill in the hope of being allowed indoors for a brisk roll on the living-room carpet. I grinned despite myself and shooed him away, stopping at the window to stare out into the night. The silhouettes of trees and bushes were very sharp, for a yellow moon hung low over the pines, interrupting the blackness magically. The picture thus framed looked like an illustration from a book of bedtime stories, I thought, going back to the hearth with a warm dish in hand and my spirits much restored.

Note

1. All references and quotations in this chapter are from Charlotte Chandler Wyckoff's *Kodaikanal 1845-1945* (Nagercoil: London Mission Press, 1945), which is sadly no longer available except in a few libraries.

Thanks

Shobhana Verghese, for bringing home books that I asked for, and more.
Michael Watsa, for criticism of the sort that made me write entire chapters all over again.
Kamala Watsa, who encouraged my earliest efforts to write, mostly, I now realize, to keep me out of mischief.
Margaret Singh, for having taught me poetry when I was too young to know that it was different from prose.
Sidney and Phyllis Watsa, whose love of reading was a more valuable inheritance than anything I could have asked for.
Sylvia Upot, for preserving copies of my first attempts at journalism.
Hugh Warren, my best friend until I was eight.
Vatsala Watsa, for help and advice at critical moments, particularly with regard to Hampi.
Mrinalini and Nayantara Watsa, whose faith in my writing has made me feel like a charlatan more than once.
Aruna Rajkumar, whose home in Kodaikanal is a place of comfort and rest, and woodsmoke and roses.
Alex Adamson, thanks to whom I once put in an hour of writing every day without even knowing it.
Rahul Matthan, who knows my writing style almost as well as I do.
Mr. S. Muthiah, who let me proofcheck his manuscripts.
Bubla Basu, old teacher and friend, whom I learnt the art of laughter

so loud that it could be heard across the hall.

Mrs Radhakrishnan, Mrs Kar and Miss Chatterjee, erstwhile staff of La Martinière, Calcutta.

Daniel Baretto, chief librarian of the Vidhana Soudha Library, Bangalore.

Last, but by no means least, Christine Cipriani, my editor, without whom the book might still have been written—but five years hence.